Families in
Transition

Families in Transition

– An Annotated Bibliography –

Judith
DeBoard
Sadler

Archon Books
1988

Printed in the United States of America

Library of Congress Cataloging-in-Publication Data

Sadler, Judith DeBoard, 1938–
Families in transition : an annotated bibliography / Judith
DeBoard Sadler.
Bibliography: p.
Includes indexes.
ISBN 0-208-02180-9 (alk. paper)
1. Family—United States—Bibliography. 2. Single-parent family—
United States—Bibliography. 3. Stepfamilies—United States—
Bibliography. 4. Unmarried couples—United States—Bibliography.
I. Title.
Z5118.F2S23   1988   016.3068'5—dc19   87-37347

Set in Palatino by Coghill
Composition Co., Richmond, Virginia
Designed by Patricia Larsen Barratt

The paper used in this publication meets the minimum
requirements of American National Standard for Information
Sciences—Permanence of Paper for Printed Library Materials,
♾ ANSI Z39.48-1984.00

Dedicated to the members of my family:

my husband, Larry E. Sadler
the memory of my first husband,
Kenneth G. Donnalley, Sr.
the memory of my father, James R. DeBoard
my mother, Charlotte N. Jarvis
my stepfather, J. B. Jarvis
my stepmother, Hazel L. DeBoard
my stepson, Kenneth G. Donnalley, Jr.
my stepdaughter, Lora Dale Sadler
my son, Jason K. Donnalley

Contents

Introduction

This bibliography is intended to encourage the exchange of information between various groups and individuals who are interested in changing family structures. It is meant as a resource for family professionals from different disciplines as well as for those who are themselves in nontraditional families. By covering in one work various interrelated topics, a wide array of information is made available to more people. For example, information about adoption may be sought by professionals, foster parents, stepparents, or never-married singles, and may be found under headings for stepfamilies, adoptive and foster families, surrogate parentage, and singles.

While individuals in Western society have found various ways to meet material needs, no one has yet devised a more successful alternative form for providing emotional security than the family. The family, whether traditional or nontraditional, provides our needs for acceptance and love, the preparation of children for adulthood, and a framework that gives meaning and happiness to our lives.

Despite the increase in new and changing family structures more people than ever are still choosing to marry, and the majority of them want to have children. The desire to marry and raise a family remains almost universal in the United States today. About 95 percent of our population aged forty and over have married at least once. "A good family life" is rated by Americans as the top social value.

The term "family" in this country has traditionally been understood to refer to the nuclear family consisting of a father, mother, and children living in the same household who are related by blood, marriage, or adoption. Yet despite an increase of seventeen million in the number of families in the United States between 1970 and 1981, the number of married couples with their own children aged eighteen and under actually declined during the same period.

There are a number of social and economic forces that have fostered changes in the structure of families. The single biggest contributor to this change during the last two decades has been the staggering rise in the divorce rate. Between 1965 and 1979, the divorce rate increased by 115 percent. According to the National Center for Health Statistics (NCHS) the average marriage in the United States now lasts 9.4 years, and the NCHS is projecting that 50 percent of couples married since 1970 will eventually divorce. Even though the Census Bureau reports a leveling off of the divorce rate during the 1980s because of older first-time brides and grooms and a change in social attitudes toward maintaining marriages, this new stability does not mean a return to the family arrangements of the past because the rate of divorce remains high: divorce will continue to affect one-half of today's marriages.

Over one million children per year are now involved in divorce. One out of every five children lives in a single-parent family and one out of every four families is headed by a single parent. Of the 23 percent of all children who live in single-parent homes, 90 percent of these households are headed by mothers.

According to the census estimates, approximately 75 percent of divorced women and 83 percent of divorced men remarry. These remarriages also have a 50 percent survival rate. Sixty percent of these marriages involve an adult with custody of one or more children, which means that about a half million adults become stepparents each year in the United States. Between one-sixth and one-third of all children in the United States have at least one stepparent. Current projections indicate that by 1990 the number of stepfamilies and single-parent households will be greater than the number of traditional families. No longer is the nuclear family predominant in this country. As a result the American family is in a state of transition.

In addition to traditional families and their problems, there are now single-parent families, stepfamilies, dual earner families, and commuter families. The challenges families confront include latchkey kids, day care, custody, child support, displaced homemakers, teenage pregnancy—which is on the rise and points to another high-risk group for contacting AIDS—parental kidnapping, surrogate parentage, and homosexual parents to name a few.

The materials in this annotated bibliography were written for people facing such challenges, families themselves and the ever increasing number of people interested in these changing family lifestyles: relatives and friends, educators, counselors, librarians, psychologists, sociologists, ministers, day care personnel, social workers, lawyers, court officials, mediators, youth workers, and medical professionals.

This bibliography consists primarily of books and articles published in the 1980s and later 1970s. Approximately 65 percent of the materials were published in the 1980s, 26 percent in the later 1970's, and 9 percent prior to 1975. The latter were included because they are often cited as references or listed in bibliographies. Books for adults consist of 47 percent of the works, books for children and young people make up about 14 percent, articles consist of 33 percent, and audiovisuals 6 percent of the items listed. The bibliography includes basic introductory works, professional works, psychological and sociological studies, handbooks, guidebooks, case studies, personal narratives, and popular works. It is supplemented by a list of associations and organizations. Indexes to subjects, authors, and titles are also included.

This work has been organized into sixteen chapters, most of which are divided into two sections, books and articles. Chapter 14 is divided into fiction and nonfiction, Chapter 15 consists of films, audiocassettes, and videocassettes with all three forms arranged alphabetically by title in one listing. Other chapters are arranged alphabetically by author's name, and some cases by title.

Chapter 1 lists general materials about love, marriage and the family, alternative family styles, family mediation, unmarried couples, communal living, commuter families, military families, and families of the incarcerated. Works which combine various topics, such as *The Complete Legal Guide to Marriage, Divorce, Custody, and Living Together*, which includes the subjects of marriage, divorce, custody, child snatching, adoption, and child support, are also listed in this general chapter.

Chapter 2 covers single parents/single-parent families, and chapter 3 stepfamilies.

Chapter 4 includes materials about adoption and/or foster care of older children, children with special needs, interracial and transcultural adoption, and a new form of adoption, advocated by many professionals and adoptees themselves, called "open adoption."

Chapter 5 lists works dealing with how divorce and remarriage affect the family, new ways of reaching agreement through divorce mediation rather than litigation, comparison of remarriages with first marriages, and changes in divorce laws.

Chapter 6 presents information about new laws that help in the collection of unpaid child support as well as the changing outcomes of child custody cases being determined more often now by what custody arrangements serve the best interest of the child. Materials are also listed about joint or shared custody.

Chapter 7 addresses the growing problem of parental kidnapping when the parent who is not awarded custody takes matters into his/ her own hands by stealing the child/children away from the custodial parent. This chapter covers the laws to combat this practice, their effectiveness; personal experiences; the prevention of parental kidnapping; and the recovery of kidnapped children.

Chapter 8 on children of divorce tells how divorce affects children, and how parents, schools, and others can help children deal with it.

Chapter 9 which offers materials about fathers is included to balance the attention paid to mothers in chapters 2 and 6. There is a growing awareness and interest in fathers and their importance in child rearing today. Fathers are playing a larger role in the care and development of their children than ever before, regardless of the family structure.

Chapter 10 concerns working parents and latchkey children. Along with the rising rate of divorce and dual income families there are an estimated seven million children between the ages of five and thirteen who care for themselves before and/or after school until their parents return home. This is the fastest-growing special interest group in the schools. Materials cover the effects of self-care, how the schools and local communities can help, what children who sometimes care for themselves, should know and projects and programs developed for latchkey children.

Chapter 11 on teenage pregnancy and parenthood describes another topic that is of increasing concern and lists materials about the consequences and effects of teenage pregnancy/parenthood on girls' education; future marriage stability; income potential; and the costs of all this to society. Some of the items listed give the young unwed father's point of view. This chapter describes some programs which are helping teenage parents remain in school and graduate.

Chapter 12 presents materials about families that include homosexual members and how they handle such issues as telling children and other family members about their homosexuality. It offers personal insights of homosexuals and their desire to have children, either with a mate, a friend, or through adoption.

Chapter 13 on miscellaneous works includes various topics which are related in some way to the changing family styles and are listed alphabetically by author. These subjects include displaced homemakers; grandparents and their rights; househusbands; singles; surrogate parentage; widow/widowers; and living-together contracts.

Chapter 14 includes both fiction and nonfiction books for children. Various topics covered in the previous chapters are listed in both sections, which are arranged alphabetically by author.

Films, audiocassettes and videocassettes are listed alphabetically by title in Chapter 15 and represent various topics covered in previous chapters.

Chapter 16 lists only bibliographic citations of books which were located too late or published too recently to be annotated or indexed.

References

The American Family and the State. Edited by Joseph R. Peden and Fred R. Glahe. San Francisco: Pacific Research Institute for Public Policy, 1986.

Berman, Eleanor. *The New-Fashioned Parent.* Englewood Cliffs, NJ: Prentice-Hall, 1980.

Collins, Glenn. "All-American Stepfamilies Becoming More Typical." *News and Observer* (Raleigh, NC), 30 October 1983.

Mattis, Mary. *Sex and the Single Parent.* New York: Holt, 1986. "Playing Both Mother and Father." *Newsweek* 106:42 (15 July 1986).

Schmid, Randolph E. "Divorce Rate May Be Stabilizing." *Daily Reflector* (Greenville, NC), 9 April 1987.

Acknowledgments

I would like to express my gratitude to the many people who helped me to complete this work. I would like to thank my professional colleagues in the Department of Library and Information Studies at East Carolina University who gave their support and encouragement, especially the chairperson, Emily S. Boyce, and Dr. Veronica S. Pantelidis. I wish to acknowledge the department's graduate assistants who helped me at various stages of my work: Jane Cunningham, Amanda McDaniel, Lynn Taylor, and Nancy Williams. I am appreciative of the invaluable assistance and support of the Joyner Library staff of the University and most especially of its director, Dr. Ruth Katz; the circulation department's interlibrary loan librarian, Pat Guyette; and the reference department's Marilyn Stephenson. To my family, who gave of their time and patience, I offer my deepest appreciation and thanks.

1
General Works

A. Books

1 Bach, George, and Peter Wyden. *The Intimate Enemy*. New York: Morrow, 1969. 405 pp.

The Institute of Group Psychotherapy conducts sessions for couples who need to learn how to "level" with each other in order to have a genuine relationship. The authors describe techniques including marathon group sessions over long weekends, and explain how couples can argue and fight in a fair manner.

2 Berger, Bennett M. *The Survival of a Counterculture: Ideological Work and Everyday Life Among Rural Communards*. Berkeley: University of California Press, 1981. 264 pp.

Looks into the ways communards maintain, modify, use, and otherwise live with their convictions. In analyzing the ideological work done by rural communards, the author asks three specific questions: How do they rear their children in the isolation a commune provides? What are the effects of technology on their goal of selfsufficiency in living? What circumstances affect their intimate relationships?

3 Berman, Eleanor. *The New-Fashioned Parent: How to Make Your Family Style Work*. Englewood Cliffs, NJ: Prentice-Hall, 1980. 138 pp.

Provides guidelines for traditional families, stepfamilies, and single-parent families.

4 Bernard, Jessie Shirley. *The Future of Marriage*. New Haven, CT: Yale University Press, 1982. 383 pp.

Explores the future of marriage and recommends many changes, including an upgrading of the status of women, shared roles, alternative living arrangements, and other options.

5 Blumstein, Philip, and Pepper Schwartz. *American Couples: Money, Work, Sex.* New York: Morrow, 1983. 656 pp.

Overview of the ways in which contemporary couples deal with the issues of money, work, and sex. The authors used twelve thousand volunteer couples in large urban centers who responded to media announcements and answered questionnaires left in public places. Studies cohabiting and gay couples as well as married ones.

6 Bohannan, Paul J. *All the Happy Families: Exploring the Varieties of Family Life.* New York: McGraw-Hill, 1985. 262 pp.

Looks at contemporary marriage and divorce. The title is misleading since more than half of the book is devoted to divorcing and unhappy families. Deals with one-parent families, postdivorce families, and stepfamilies.

7 Broderick, Carlfred. *Couples: How to Confront Problems and Maintain Loving Relationships.* New York: Simon & Schuster, 1979. 224 pp.

Based on Dr. Broderick's experiences as a marriage counselor, this book offers advice for married couples. Includes adaptations of the Masters and Johnson exercises for sexual dysfunction and recommendations for maintaining sufficient emotional space, and communicating in an unambiguous and noncompetitive way. Exercises at the end of the chapters help to put advice into practice.

8 Carter, Hugh, and Paul Glick. *Marriage and Divorce: A Social and Economic Study.* Rev. ed. Cambridge: Harvard University Press, 1976. 508 pp.

A study which presents systematic documentation of important trends and variations in demographic aspects of marital behavior in the United States during recent decades. It explores such factors as variations in relation to separated and divorced persons, widowers and widows, marital status and health, family composition and living arrangements, etc. A final chapter highlights the extensive recent changes of life-style in relation to marriage, divorce, and remarriage.

9 *Contemporary Families and Alternative Lifestyles: Handbook on Research and Theory.* Edited by Eleanor D. Macklin and Roger H. Rubin. Beverly Hills: Sage Publications, 1983. 416 pp.

This handbook represents an effort to document and synthesize research on the wide range of contemporary family forms, including single-parent families, reconstructed families, gay male and lesbian relationships, dual-earner families, and the more traditional breadwinner/housewife/children families.

10 Coulson, Robert. *Fighting Fair: Family Mediation Will Work for You.* New York: Free Press, 1983. 196 pp.

Written for people who want to settle family disputes without going to court as well as for people who might want to become, or use, professional mediators. Some topics addressed are the types of family problems that can be mediated, teaching mediation in the schools, divorce mediation, children and custody, how to act as a family mediator, and family disputes and the law.

11 Eisler, Riane Tennenhaus. *Dissolution: No-Fault Divorce, Marriage, and the Future of Women.* New York: McGraw-Hill, 1977. 279 pp.

An analysis of family laws and of the social values and realities they reflect. Also discussed are the changes of the traditional American family itself, and the rapidly changing status of women.

12 *Exploring Intimate Life Styles.* Edited by Bernard I. Murstein. New York: Springer, 1978. 302 pp.

Consists of papers dealing with the variant forms of life-styles. Assesses the strengths and weaknesses of each variant form in order to estimate its function in present-day society and its viability for the future. Includes sections such as open marriage, communes, group marriage, singlehood, and homosexuality.

13 *Family Law Handbook.* Edited by S. Joel Kolko. Washington, DC: Bureau of National Affairs, 1985. 272 pp.

Emphasizes the changes in family law and the increasing involvement of the federal government with the passage of three bills in 1984: the Domestic Relations Tax Reform Act, the Child Support Enforcement amendments, and the Retirement Equity Act. Other examples of the federal government's involvement in family issues are given. The text of these laws, and others, are presented with comments and court interpretations.

14 Fleming, Jennifer Baker, and Carolyn Kott Washburne. *For Better, For Worse: A Feminist Handbook on Marriage and Other Options.* New York: Scribner, 1977. 406 pp.

Written to answer questions about how to prevent marital problems. Information includes the legal and economic aspects of marriage, motherhood, alternate life-styles, lesbianism, violence in marriage, and dealing with change.

15 Fromm, Erich. *The Art of Loving.* New York: Harper & Row, 1974. 112 pp.

This is one of the all-time great books on the subject of loving. A combination of psychology and philosophy, it will have new meanings for readers at different times in their lives.

16 Gerstel, Naomi, and Harriet Gross. *Commuter Marriage: A Study of Work and Family.* New York: Guilford Press, 1984. 228 pp.

Examines commuter marriages of couples who, because of dual careers, live apart at least three nights a week. In-depth interviews were conducted separately with 121 commuters, including both spouses of 50 couples, 16 wives only, and 5 husbands only. Some chapters cover the decision to commute, the positive results of separate living arrangements, difficulty of maintaining relationships outside the marriages, and a comparison of merchant marine and commuter families.

17 Hauser, Thomas. *The Family Legal Companion.* New York: McGraw-Hill, 1985. 227 pp.

Hauser, a lawyer, bases this book on the column he writes for *McCalls*. The information is presented in a question-and-answer format and is organized into sections such as jobs, landlords, marriage and divorce, consumer rights, and children. Not intended to be a how-to guide, but rather designed to explain the law as it applies to everyday life.

18 Howard, Jane. *Families.* New York: Simon & Schuster, 1978. 282 pp.

Looks at alternative family styles including nuclear, gay, and stepfamilies. The author uses a direct-interview format. Interview subjects are from a variety of economic and cultural backgrounds.

19 *In Support of Families.* Edited by Michael W. Yogman and T. Berry Brazelton. Cambridge: Harvard University Press, 1986. 293 pp.

Contains fifteen essays compiled by two Harvard-affiliated pediatricians who survey and interpret recent studies on the family. Examines child development, stress and coping, new parenting roles, work and child care, the special stress of divorce, teenage pregnancy, and social policy.

20   Kelso, Lloyd T. *North Carolina Divorce, Alimony, and Child Custody*. Norcross, GA: Harrison, 1983. 318 pp.

A handbook for lawyers and judges which incorporates statutes and court decisions of the North Carolina law relating to annulment, separation, divorce, alimony, child custody, and support.

21   Kimball, Gayle. *The 50-50 Marriage*. Boston: Beacon Press, 1983. 256 pp.

Kimball interviewed 150 couples who share money making, home and child care, and decision making, in order to study the mechancis and success of what she calls "equal marriages." The author analyzes the slowly changing family scene and looks at how American attitudes and institutions fall behind western Europe in the kind of support that encourages full participation in work and family life for both sexes.

22   Lake, Steven R. *Hearts and Dollars: How to Beat the High Cost of Falling In and Out of Love*. Chicago: Chicago Review Press, 1983. 174 pp.

Recommends that couples contemplating marriage consult not one but two attorneys to draw up a prenuptial agreement. If one partner balks at this idea, Lake reminds readers that it is less expensive to break up before the marriage than after. Most of his advice requires the services of a lawyer. The author states that this is not a do-it-yourself book, but a don't-do-it yourself book. Includes sections on paternity and other aspects of unwed parenthood, grandparents' rights, and the costs of remarriage.

23   Levitan, Sar A., and Richard S. Belous. *What's Happening to the American Family?* Baltimore: Johns Hopkins University Press, 1981. 206 pp.

An overview of the contemporary family which treats such experiences as divorce, working women, single parents, female-headed families, and poverty families. Uses census data and considers predictions for the future.

24   Lieberman, Susan Abel. *Let's Celebrate: Creating New Family Traditions*. New York: Perigee Books, 1984. 156 pp.

Offers ways to avoid the hassles of traditional holidays by being creative and molding "new traditions" to shape your family's lifestyle and needs.

25 Masnick, George, and Mary Jo Bane. *The Nation's Families: 1960–1990*. Boston: Auburn House, 1980. 175 pp.

This work is a part of the Outlook Report Series, and the authors are associated with the Joint Center for Urban Studies at MIT and Harvard. Statistics and data on marital status, household composition, family living arrangements, and patterns of women's labor force participation are analyzed. Future trends and changes in life-styles linked to family composition and work are also covered.

26 Melville, Keith. *Communes in the Counter Culture: Origins, Theories, Styles of Life*. New York: Morrow Quill Paperbacks, 1972. 256 pp.

Traces the commune's origins in history and puts it into intellectual, social, and political perspective by including the revolt against suburbia and the search for alternative realities.

27 *The Military Family: Dynamics and Treatment*. Edited by Florence W. Kaslow and Richard I. Ridenour. New York: Guilford Press, 1984. 316 pp.

Written primarily for professional therapists working with military families. Discusses the particular training and supervision of these mental health professionals and examines the disruptive moves, special problems of military children, legal issues in military families, divorce and child custody, and coping with long separations.

28 *Nontraditional Families: Parenting and Child Development*. Edited by Michael E. Lamb. Hillsdale, NJ: L. Erlbaum, 1982. 364 pp.

Reviews the effects of nontraditional family styles on parental behavior and child development in the United States, Sweden, Israel, and Australia.

29 *North Carolina Family Law Practice Handbook*. Rev. ed. Walter W. Baker et al. Winston-Salem, NC: Wake Forest University School of Law, 1984. 606 pp. Supersedes: *Family Law Handbook, North Carolina, 1980* and its 1982 Supplement.

Treats all major areas of family law practice, points out problem areas, provides a quick overview with key references and forms. Although detailed at times, it is not intended to be an exhaustive treatise and directs readers to other sources when necessary. Some topics covered are: marriage, prenuptial agreements, divorce, child custody and support, separation agreements and consent decrees, enforcement and modification of agreements and orders, setting legal fees, equitable distribution, and guardianships.

30 O'Donnell, William J., and David A. Jones. *The Law of Marriage and Marital Alternatives*. Lexington, MA: Lexington Books, 1982. 252 pp.

Each topic is considered by tracing legal codes from past to present, surveying the current social situation, and considering where changes seem necessary and likely to be forthcoming. Topics include various issues in conventional marriage, parent-child relationships, divorce, no-fault divorce, common-law marriage, marital rape, child custody, premarital contracts, and artificial reproduction.

31 Ruben, Harvey L. *Supermarriage: Overcoming the Predictable Crises of Married Life*. New York: Bantam Books, 1986. 261 pp.

Defines the three stages of marriage—the early, middle, and mature years. Identifies the crises which typically confront couples during each stage and offers advice on overcoming these crises and building a sound marriage.

32 Sack, Steven Mitchell. *The Complete Legal Guide to Marriage, Divorce, Custody, & Living Together*. New York: McGraw-Hill, 1987. 327 pp.

Designed as a legal guide, this work discusses the subjects mentioned in the title as well as child snatching, spouse abuse, child support, marital rape, adoption, tax considerations, and how to use a lawyer effectively.

33 Satir, Virginia M. *Peoplemaking*. Palo Alto, CA: Science and Behavior Books, 1972. 304 pp.

Contains chapters on both one-parent and "blended" families. Includes such problems as: (1) making room for previously existing family relationships, including dead spouses, both ex-spouses, parents, and grandparents, and (2) not falling victim to the "magical" presence of unrealistic expectations for the second marriage. Case studies are included.

34 Simons, Joseph. *Living Together: Communication in the Unmarried Relationship*. Chicago: Nelson-Hall, 1978. 168 pp.

Centers on unmarried couples living together. Emphasizes the underderlying emotions of relationships and how they impact communication and independence. The last three chapters are titled, "I've Got to Be Free," "It's Time to Split," and "Let's Stick Together."

35   Stinnett, Nick, and Craig Wayne Birdsong. *The Family and Alternative Life Styles*. Chicago: Nelson-Hall, 1978. 230 pp.

This work, a result of extensive studies, deals with six alternatives to traditional marriage: cohabitation, communes, swinging group marriage, extramarital affairs, and one-parent families.

36   Winfield, Fairlee E. *Commuter Marriage: Living Together, Apart*. New York: Columbia University Press, 1985. 186 pp.

Tells what commuting does to a marriage, to children, and to the commuters themselves. Information was gathered from in-depth interviews with fifty-nine spouses in commuter marriages. Twelve of the interviews included both husband and wife. Questionnaires were mailed to 100 commuter couples, and interviews were conducted with members of businesses such as IBM and General Dynamics. Biographical studies and articles from periodicals were also used.

37   Zablocki, Benjamin David. *Alienation and Charisma: A Study of Contemporary American Communes*. New York: Free Press, 1980. 455 pp.

Based on sixty rural and sixty urban communes, located throughout the country to reflect the geographical distribution of the current commune population. The authors use both observation and survey data to examine relationships among and opinions of commune members. Examines the concepts used to explain the processes by which communes reach consensus. Quantitative statistical analyses, case study material, and a bibliography are included.

B. Articles in Periodicals

38   "An Annotated Bibliography of the Remarried, the Living Together, and Their Children." Libby Walker et al. *Family Process* 18:193–222 (1979).

This bibliography was developed by the Remarried Consultation Center of the Jewish Board of Family and Children's Services of

New York City. It is divided into six sections: Demography, Remarried Couples, Stepparents and Stepchildren, Divorce as a Precursor to Remarriage, Children of Divorce in Relation to Remarriages, and Remarriage.

39   Bachrach, Christine A. "Children in Families: Characteristics of Biological, Step and Adopted Children." *Journal of Marriage and the Family* 45:171–79 (February 1983).

Presents the characteristics of children living with biological mothers, stepmothers, and adoptive mothers and the various relationships that exist between the child, the mother, and the father. Compares children living with both biological parents, children living with a biological parent and a stepparent, children with no father figure living in the home, and adopted children.

40   Bauhofer, Valerie. "Prison Parenting: A Challenge for Children's Advocates." *Children Today* 16:15–16 (January/February 1987).

Discusses the obstacles and hardships in the prison system in New York State, which discourages children from visiting their fathers in prison.

41   Brothers, Joyce. "When Unmarried Couples Live Together." *Reader's Digest* 128:11–12 (March 1986).

Reports on a study of two groups of couples married for at least one year but less than two. In one group, the couples had lived together before marriage, in the other they had not. The researcher found few differences among the couples. Thus, cohabitation prior to marriage held no particular advantage.

42   "The Changing Family." *Children Today* 13:15–16 (March/April 1984).

Reports on a study, "The Changing American Family," by Arland Thorton and Deborah Freedman, which was released by the Population Reference Bureau, Inc. It provides statistical data and information about children of divorce, divorces, households headed by women, fertility among women, women in the labor force, and other data.

43   Englund, C. L. "Parenting and Parentage: Distinct Aspects of Children's Importance." *Family Relations* 32:21–28 (January 1983).

Interviews a childless couple, adoptive couple, a blended couple, and grandparent and great-grandparent couples, to gain insight into why these couples did or did not chose to be parents.

44 Glick, Paul C. "A Demographer Looks at American Families." *Journal of Marriage and the Family* 37:15–26 (1975).

Presents data from census information collected since 1939 concerning American families. Analyzes and interprets patterns and trends in marriage, childbearing, divorce, remarriage, etc. Includes recommendations for further research and offers suggestions.

45 Greer, Kate. "Today's Parents—How Well Are They Doing?" *Better Homes and Gardens* 64:36 (October 1986).

Thirty thousand *Better Homes and Gardens* readers were surveyed to find out how this generation of parents stacks up against previous ones. Some of the areas surveyed and discussed are: what issue causes the most difficulties in families; how children fare in single-parent households; what causes conflicts with kids; do demands of job/career interfere with family; and how these parents were reared compared to how they are rearing their children.

46 Harris, Art. "Promises to Keep." *People* 26:22–27 (29 September 1986).

Tells how Terry O'Keeley, a boy of fifteen and the eldest of seven parentless brothers, took on the man-sized task of holding the family together.

47 Hedin, Tricia. "My Husband Is in Prison." *Newsweek* "108:14 (5 December 1986).

The author relates her experiences of being the wife of a husband who is in prison serving a twenty-year sentence (with a ten-year mandatory minimum) for bank robbery. She tells about the support system among inmate wives, how prison guards treat the wives as if *they* are the criminals, and the difficulties of keeping their families intact. Stresses the need for prison reform and community involvement to help form the bridge from inside the prison walls to the outside world.

48 Kenny, James, and Mary Kenny. "The Commune and the Family." *Marriage & Family Living* 57:2–7 (January 1975).

Addresses how the communal experience may help the nuclear family to regain its traditional purposes.

49 Knox, David. "Trends in Marriage and the Family—The 1980's." *Family Relations* 29:145–50 (April 1980).

Presents updated information on thirty-nine trends in marriage and the family. Some of the topics discussed are sex roles, love relationships, mate selection, dual careers, sexual fulfillment, planning children, divorce, and the later years.

50 Leigh, Geoffrey K. et al. "Correlates of Marital Satisfaction Among Men and Women in First Marriage and Remarriage." *Family Perspective* 19:139–49 (1985).

This analysis developed a model of marital satisfaction to compare male and female individuals in intact first marriages and remarriages.

51 Leonard, John. "Second Marriage, First-Class Romance." *Harper's Bazaar* 117:106 (October 1984).

Tells how second loves and marriages differ from first marriages.

52 Long, Patricia. "Growing Up Military: Separations, Moves, New Beginnings." *Psychology Today* 20:30–32 (December 1986).

Discusses the problems of military life. Although these families face a unique combination of stresses, the experts are unsure of whether these stresses make military families more troubled than most other families. Some of these stresses are the rigid class system, foreign assignments, frequent moves, special assignments, children coping with extended absences of one parent (usually the father). These separations result in what is virtually a single-parent family. Smaller children may forget what the absent parent looks like, and older children may resent the return of the parent and the unwelcome intrusion into their life's routine. Common are the fathers, who tell an eldest son, "You're the man of the house while I'm gone." Many sons resent, or are confused at, being placed in this adult role and readjust poorly to the father's return. Tells how military life often isolates family members from outside supports such as friends, family members and community groups. Positive points are also discussed, such as job security, medical services, base activities, and new experiences.

53 "Love on the Run: When Two Careers Mean Two Homes, Couples Pay the Price." *Newsweek* 106:111 (18 November 1985).

Describes how five couples maintain their life-style of living in separate cities, due to career demands, while one or both partners take turns traveling between their mate and their work. Tells under what conditions commuting marriages work best. A father can become a part-time, single parent in a biological/nuclear family. In the end, due to the emotional and financial drain, most such families decide to live in one place.

54 Rosenkrantz, Louise, and Virdia Joshua. "Children of Incarcerated Parents: A Hidden Population." *Children Today* 11:2–6 (January/February 1982).

Describes the prison program MATCH (Mothers and Their Children), at the Pleasanton Children's Center. The program was established in 1978 inside the fence of the Federal Correctional Institution in Pleasanton, California—one of the four federal prisons that house women convicted of federal crimes in the United States. The center was designed to make the visiting experience a positive one for parents, children, and staff members. Professionals work to enhance parenting skills as inmates visit children or interact with children visiting other inmates. Gives case experiences of how children live while their parent(s) are incarcerated. The experience of working in the MATCH program has enabled professionals to identify some significant concerns and their solutions.

55 Schulman, Gerda L. "Divorce, Single Parenthood and Stepfamilies: Structural Implications of These Transactions." *International Journal of Family Therapy* 3:87–112 (Summer 1981).

Focuses on changes that take place in the family structure during divorce. Discusses single parenthood and the reconstituted family. The challenges these families face are covered in various case studies.

56 Spakes, Patricia. "The Supreme Court Family Policy, and Alternative Family Lifestyles: The Clash of Interests." *Lifestyles* 7:171–86 (Spring 1985).

Reviews the basis for the judicial system's involvement in the development of a national family policy. Discusses major Supreme Court decisions in establishing the rights of the nuclear family, the extended family, foster families, communal families, homosexual couples, and unwed fathers. The implications of the Court's actions for the development of a national family policy are considered.

57 Weisner, Thomas S., and Bernice T. Eiduson. "The Children of the'60s as Parents." *Psychology Today* 20:60–66 (January 1986).

A long-term study of more than 200 families (about 50 conventional and 150 unconventional) looking at how their values differed, how they put these values to work in their actual childrearing practices, and whether these differences would affect the development of their children. The families were divided into four groups for the study: conventional, married two-parent families, and three groups of unconventional families: single mothers, unmarried "social-contract" couples, and people living in communal groups.

2
Single Parents
& Single-Parent Families

A. Books and Pamphlets

58 Adams, Jane. *Sex and the Single Parent.* New York: Coward, McCann and Geoghegan, 1978. 314 pp.

> Divorced and the mother of two children, Adams describes her "struggles to express her own sexuality; and to understand the impact her actions have on her children and the influence their presence has on her." Interviews with other single parents – divorced and widowed, male and female, homosexual and heterosexual – are included.

59 Anderson-Khleif, Susan. *Divorced But Not Disastrous: How to Improve the Ties Between Single-Parent Mothers, Divorced Fathers & the Children.* Englewood Cliffs, NJ: Prentice-Hall, 1982. 178 pp.

> Looks inside the lives of divorced mothers and examines the relationships between single-parent mothers, fathers, children, and new "relatives" who become part of their lives after divorce. The last chapter tells how these relationships can be improved. The perspectives of both mothers and fathers are included on issues concerning housing, money, custody and visitation. Offers policy proposals that could combine actions of government and the private sector.

60 Atlas, Stephen L. *The Parents Without Partners Sourcebook.* Philadelphia: Running Press, 1984. 192 pp.

> Members of Parents Without Partners, an organization for single parents, offer solutions to the questions and challenges of single parenting. This sourcebook accommodates all kinds of single

parents: men, women, custodial, noncustodial, widowed, and the never-married.

61 ———. *Single Parenting: A Practical Resource Guide.* Englewood Cliffs, NJ: Prentice-Hall, 1981. 240 pp.

Stresses that the single-parent family can be healthy, satisfying, and a complete way of life which offers unique opportunities for personal growth for each family member while providing a supportive family environment. Includes an appendix which provides resources that can help single parents and their children, such as a thorough list of organizations and publications.

62 Baruth, Leroy G. *A Single Parent's Survival Guide: How to Raise the Children.* Dubuque, IA: Kendall/Hunt, 1979. 102 pp.

A practical guide that applies Dreikurs's parenting techniques to the problems and concerns of single parents. This book is based on the belief that children raised in single-parent homes can be as happy and well adjusted as those in two-parent families.

63 Bel Geddes, Joan. *How to Parent Alone: A Guide for Single Parents.* New York: Seabury, 1974. 293 pp.

Explores the problems of single-parenthood adjustments – self-pity, guilt, loneliness, finances – and offers some solutions.

64 Bequaert, Lucia H. *Single Women Alone & Together.* Boston: Beacon Press, 1976. 256 pp.

Examines the major concerns of single women and explains the specific strategies they have devised for living as singles. It focuses on women who are single heads of households: widows, separated and divorced women, never married women, and lesbian women. Included are sections on legal and economic resources, counseling services, and information networks.

65 Cadwallader, Sharon. *Sharing in the Kitchen: A Cookbook for Single Parents and Children.* New York: McGraw-Hill, 1979. 162 pp.

Tells how to shop for and prepare simple, nutritious, good-tasting meals without spending too much time. Most of the recipes are not beyond the skills of a mature and responsible child.

66 Cashmore, Ernest E. *Having to—the World of One Parent Families.* London and Boston: Allen & Unwin, 1985. 288 pp.

The first part of this book is devoted to factors influencing the growth of one-parent families. The second part assesses the consequences of single parenthood. Some chapters cover abandoned women, schoolgirl mothers, and men alone.

67   Clay, Phyllis L. *Single Parents and the Public Schools: How Does the Partnership Work? Results of a National Survey.* Columbia, MD: National Committee for Citizens in Education, 1981. 77 pp.

The purpose of this study was to see how the partnership between the school and single-parent families is working out for single parents. The information in the study was gathered from single parents using a survey questionnaire. Suggestions are given about what single parents can do to strengthen their partnership with the schools.

68   Covington, Jim. *Confessions of a Single Father.* New York: Pilgrim Press, 1982. 181 pp.

Psychologist Covington offers a personal account of how one man comes to terms with the ups and downs of single parenting, and he gives counsel and encouragement to others in similar situations. The book does not advocate single parenting but does encourage men to share, on an equal basis, the responsibilities of child rearing.

69   Curto, Josephine J. *How to Become a Single Parent: A Guide for Single People Considering Adoption or Natural Parenthood Alone.* Englewood Cliffs, NJ: Prentice-Hall, 1983. 238 pp.

Examines the social, legal, financial, and emotional decisions faced by the growing number of singles who are considering parenthood. The author, a professor of literature and a single parent, includes information on adoption and planning a birth. Illustrated with case histories and statistics obtained from a survey of four hundred parents.

70   Davenport, Diana. *One-Parent Families: A Practical Guide to Coping.* London: Concord, 1979. 192 pp.

This book is written for families with only one *functional* parent. The vast majority of these solo parents are women who are widowed, divorced, or unmarried (having never been married). Also Considered are wives of men serving long prison sentences and women with husbands in the hospital for months or years at a time. Data and statistics are based on British families. An appendix of organizations and associations is included, and sections for further reading are provided at the end of most chapters.

71   Dietl, L. Kay, and Marsha J. Neff. *Single Parent Families: Choice or Chance?* New York: Columbia University, Teachers College Press, 1983. 110 pp.

This work is Unit 4 in the series, "Human Needs and Social Welfare Curriculum Project," designed as a guide for social studies careers in the United States. It includes current information about single-parent families: who they are, how they were formed, and what kinds of special concerns and needs they have. Study exercises and worksheets are included.

72   Duncan, Barbara. *The Single Mother's Survival Manual.* Saratoga, CA: R & E Publishers, 1984. 172 pp.

Using a reference-style format, the author spells out the problems faced by today's single mothers and how they can be handled. Some chapters included are: "Alone and Pregnant," "Sex and the Single Mother," "Being Mom and Dad," "Seeking Employment," "Living Within Your Means," and "Legal Aspects."

73   Egleson, Jim, and Janet F. Egleson. *Parents Without Partners: A Guide for Divorced, Widowed or Separated Parents.* New York: Dutton, 1961. 249 pp.

The authors base this work on the hypothesis that the "single" parent feels alone and isolated with the responsibilities of parenthood. Included are advice and suggestions for the custodial parent and a chapter on remarriage.

74   Epstein, Joyce L. *Single Parents and the Schools: The Effect of Marital Status on Parent and Teacher Evaluations.* Baltimore: Johns Hopkins University Center for Social Organization of Schools, March 1984. Report no. 353. 50 pp.

This paper uses data from a survey of 1,269 parents, 24 percent of which were single parents, to study whether single and married parents differ in their interactions with elementary schools and teachers.

75   Ferri, Elsa, and Hilary Robinson. *Coping Alone.* Windsor, England: National Foundation for Educational Research, 1976. 80 pp.

This study aims to place in some perspective the size and nature of the problems facing one-parent families by describing the experiences of a group drawn from a large, nationally representative sample. The report discusses the financial, employment, and housing situations of these families. It also looks at the difficulties parents face in caring for their children single-handedly.

76 Forman, Lynn. *Getting It Together: The Divorced Mother's Guide.* New York: Berkley, 1974. 173 pp.

A guide for divorced women that focuses on becoming your own person again, or for the first time. It deals with issues related to emotions, children, careers, dating, friendships, living together, and parent-child relationships.

77 Garfinkel, Irwin, and Sara S. McLanahan. *Single Mothers and Their Children: A New American Dilemma.* Washington, DC: Urban Institute Press, 1986. 198 pp.

This study discloses that 45 percent of white and 87 percent of black children in the United States live in mother-only families. Approximately one-half of these are at or below the government-defined poverty level. Studies also have shown correlations between low educational, economic, and social achievement, and children raised in low-income, single-adult homes. Asks what government-sponsored policies might improve this situation without encouraging more mother-only families, and gives some suggestions.

78 Gatley, Richard H., and David Koulack. *Single Father's Handbook: A Guide for Separated and Divorced Fathers.* Garden City, NY: Anchor Books, 1979. 196 pp.

The authors, both divorced, contend that it is possible for divorced fathers to nurture their children, take care of the house, and provide a second home. This guide presents methods of achieving the above along with creating loving family relationships.

79 George, Victor, and Paul Wilding. *Motherless Families.* Boston: Routledge & Kegan Paul, 1972. 229 pp.

A research study of single-parent fathers in Britain. It is based largely on interviews by social workers with six hundred families in the English East Midlands.

80 Gilbert, Sara D. *How to Live with a Single Parent.* New York: Lothrop, Lee & Shepard Books, 1982. 128 pp.

Draws upon information from teens, professionals, and the author's own experiences. The author reveals the good and bad times that single-parent families often face, and offers parents and young adults advice on ways to make that life easier and more enjoyable for everyone.

81   Greif, Geoffrey L. *Single Fathers.* Lexington, MA: Lexington Books, 1985. 194 pp.

This work grew out of the author's doctoral dissertation. It is told from the father's perspective and describes how fathers handle the various aspects of parenting: housework and child care, going to a job while raising children alone, socializing, getting along with their children and ex-wives, and dealing with the legal system.

82   Greywolf, Elizabeth S. *The Single Mother's Handbook.* New York: Morrow, 1984. 256 pp.

This book grew out of a research project in which women shared their experiences and ideas for the purpose of greater understanding. Aspects of the single mother's day—from family meals to keeping trim—are covered. The author also discusses the support and practical help of networking and how to begin to set goals for a better future.

83   Hallett, Kathryn. *A Guide for Single Parents: Transactional Analysis for People in Crisis.* Milbrae, CA: Celestial Arts, 1974. 122 pp.

This work is about saying goodbye in cases such as divorce, separation, desertion, or death. It is designed to help both adults and children learn the skills of letting go through transactional analysis.

84   Horner, Catherine Townsend. *The Single-Parent Family in Children's Books: An Analysis and Annotated Bibliography With an Appendix on Audiovisual Material.* Metuchen, NJ: Scarecrow Press, 1978. 172 pp.

Author analyzed contents of 215 books (preschool through junior high) portraying single parenthood in children's literature from 1880 to 1976. Treats causes of single-parent situations such as death, divorce, prolonged absence of one or both parents, illegitimacy, and orphans and wards of the court with a single guardian or foster parent. Includes a multimedia bibliography of related materials: filmstrips, motion pictures, video and audio tapes, slides, transparencies, and models.

85   Itzin, Catherine. *Splitting Up: Single Parent Liberation.* London: Virago Press, 1980. 231 pp.

Gives accounts of the experiences men and women have as single parents.

86   Jensen, Marilyn. *Formerly Married: Learning to Live With Yourself.* Philadelphia: Westminster Press, 1983. 116 pp.

The author shares her own experiences and those of others to illustrate how to assimilate the variety of experiences that converge on the suddenly single person, such as: making a living, finding professional counseling, enjoying new relationships, and managing one's own affairs.

87   Knight, Bryan M. *Enjoying Single Parenthood.* New York: Van Nostrand, 1980. 170 pp.

A book for all single parents: male and female, the never married, separated, divorced or widowed. Includes the opinions and experiences of the author, a single parent for nine years and social work professional, and those of about one hundred other single parents. The author offers self-awareness exercises and stresses the positive approach to single parenting, and he includes information on saving time and money, day care, sex, planning a new life-style, overcoming loneliness, and joint custody.

88   Mattis, Mary. *Sex and the Single Parent: How You Can Have Happy and Healthy Kids—And an Active Social Life.* New York: Holt, 1986. 316 pp.

The author, a family therapist, strives to help single parents establish a balance between their own sexual and social needs and the emotional and psychological health of their children. Covers homosexuals who decide to have children or who are awarded custody in divorce cases, women who choose to have children even though they have no interest in marriage, and single adults who adopt children who, in the past, would have been placed in a two-adult nuclear family.

89   McFadden, Michael. *Bachelor Fatherhood: How to Raise and Enjoy Your Children as a Single Parent.* New York: Walker, 1974. 158 pp.

A personal account of the author's experiences. This book gives advice to the single father on dealing with the divorce and custody hearing, raising small and teenage children, running a household

in the simplest way possible, cooking, and readjusting to life as a
bachelor in general.

90 Merritt, Sharyne, and Linda Steiner. *And Baby Makes Two:
Motherhood Without Marriage*. New York: Watts, 1984. 264 pp.

The authors interviewed one hundred women in their thirties
who had chosen to become mothers without being married. The
issues of single motherhood, such as adoption and choosing the
father, are presented with the intent of helping some people
make such a decision and helping others to understand why the
decision is made. An appendix provides the legal aspects of single
parenting as a life-style.

91 *Momma: The Source Book for Single Mothers*. Edited by Karol
Hope and Nancy Young. New York: New American Library,
1976. 388 pp.

Momma began as an organization of single mothers and now
includes single fathers as well. The organization published a
newspaper, and this book is a collection of some of the articles
which appeared there, as well as some new material.

92 Murdock, Carol Vejvoda. *Single Parents are People Too! How to
Achieve a Positive Self-Image and Personal Satisfaction*. New York:
Butterick, 1980. 192 pp.

Gives advice from experts and other single parents. Offers tips on
such things as money management, social life, and dealing with
ex-spouses. Some information comes from the 1979 Parents Without Partners Convention and from questionnaires distributed by
the author.

93 Reed, Bobbie. *I Didn't Plan to Be a Single Parent*. St. Louis, MO:
Concordia, 1981. 158 pp.

Reed is a single parent who relates her personal and counseling
experiences from conducting "Survival Skills for Single Parents"
workshops. Deals with all forms of custody, developing supportive networks, dating, resources for single parents, and other
topics.

94 Rejnis, Ruth. *The Single Parent's Housing Guide*. New York: M.
Evans, 1984. 218 pp.

Offers affordable housing alternatives geared to the special needs
of the one-parent family. Gives information on where to head for

housing on a tight budget. Offers advice to people who are in danger of losing their own homes because the upkeep is too high, and gives tips on decorating a matchbox of an apartment. Tells about a community complex in Colorado developed for single parents, how the government can help you, and whether to buy or rent. Lists national support groups for single parents.

95   Rekers, George Alan, and Judson J. Swihart. *Making Up the Difference: Help for Single Parents with Teenagers.* Grand Rapids, MI: Baker Books, 1984. 147 pp.

The authors, both professional counselors, offer this work, which is based on their professional and personal experiences, as a preventive approach to family-life education by pinpointing the crucial areas of need in single-parent homes.

96   Rodgers, Joann Ellison, and Michael F. Cataldo. *Raising Sons: Practical Strategies for Single Mothers.* New York: American Library, 1984. 244 pp.

Rodgers, a journalist and single mother of two sons, and Cataldo, a psychologist, advise single mothers who are raising boys to redefine traditional gender roles and to practice behavioral parenting strategies. Intersperses examples of specific techniques such as negation and modeling with comments from interviews with more than forty mothers and sons, as well as excerpts from scientific studies, expert opinions, and related books.

97   Rosenthal, Kristine M., and Harry F. Keshet. *Fathers Without Partners: A Study of Fathers and the Family After Marital Separation.* Totowa, NJ: Roman & Littlefield, 1981. 187 pp.

The authors studied 127 fathers with varying degrees of contact with their children after divorce. The authors maintain that adults experiencing divorce need children just as children need adults. Issues faced by fathers in three different situations—full custody, joint custody, and without custody—are analyzed.

98   Ross, Heather L., and Isabel V. Sawhill. *Time of Transition: The Growth of Families Headed by Women.* Washington, DC: Urban Institute Press, 1975. 223 pp.

Ross and Sawhill, economists at the Urban Institute, look at the post-World War II growth of female-headed households. They use data taken from a national sample of twenty-five hundred families to examine the growth of these households. Questions addressed are the effects of welfare, and in what ways, if any, children are harmed in these households.

99   Schlesinger, Benjamin. *The One-Parent Family: Perspectives and Annotated Bibliography*. 4th ed. Toronto: University of Toronto Press, 1978. 224 pp.

The author reviews studies on families headed by fathers, widows, unmarried women, and single parents who have adopted children.

100   Smith, Virginia Watts. *The Single Parent*. Revised, updated, and expanded. Old Tappan, NJ: Power Books, 1983. 192 pp.

Tries to identify the best in, and make the best of, family arrangements we have today, especially single-parent families. Some areas covered are: the crisis cycle, sexuality and the single parent, transition period, and society and the single parent.

101   Stafford, Linley M. *One Man's Family: A Single Father and His Children*. New York: Random House, 1978. 179 pp.

Tells of the author's experiences when his teenage son and daughter, who had been living with their mother, decide that they want to live with their father instead.

102   Staples, Robert. *The World of Black Singles: Changing Patterns of Male/Female Relations*. Westport, CT: Greenwood Press, 1981. 259 pp.

This study of black, urban, college-educated, single men and women between the ages of twenty-five and forty-five predicts that singlehood status for blacks will persist into the next century. It probes issues such as finding and keeping a mate, inter-racial relationships, and the problems of single parents.

103   Stewart, Suzanne. *Parent Alone*. Waco, TX: Ward Books, 1978. 174 pp.

This work is about a woman with three children who is left by her husband. She relates how God helped her cope, and she shares the rich rewards of being a Christian parent.

104   Weiss, Robert Stuart. *Going It Alone: The Family Life and Social Situation of the Single Parent*. New York: Basic Books, 1981. 320 pp.

Considers the family life and social situations of the woman or man who, when divorced, separated, or widowed is left to care for children.

105   ———. *Marital Separation.* New York: Basic Books, 1975. 334 pp.

Discussion and verbatim reports of the realities of parenting alone. Points out excessive sensitivity of custodial parents to signs of behavior problems. Also suggests ways to solve problems.

106   Woolley, Persia. *Creative Survival for Single Mothers.* Millbrae, CA: Celestial Arts, 1975. 144 pp.

The author discusses managing your kids in toddler, preteen and teen years; how to handle your ex; and meeting men and maintaining relationships. A strong argument for coparenting is presented, as are the legal issues of divorce.

B. Articles in Periodicals

107   Allers, Robert D. "Children from Single-Parent Homes." *Today's Education,* annual edition:68–70 (1982–83).

Provides statistical data concerning the numbers of children living in single-parent homes and discusses some of the problems these children may face, such as parents having less income, being a latchkey child, or loss of contact with an absent parent. Some of the stress symptoms, experienced by these children, that teachers should be aware of are given, as well as guidelines to help single parents in their dealings with teachers and schools.

108   Bernstein, Roslyn. "Life Without Father." *Parents* 61:111–12 (March 1986).

Author relates the experience of her forty-year-old husband's death on herself, her six-year-old daughter, and four-year-old son. She panicked at suddenly being thrust into trying to be both mother and father around the clock. Tells how her children encourage and help her to start a new life.

109   Bildner, Elisa Spunger. "Arrangements: How Single Mothers Manage 'A House Rebuilt for Two (Families That Is).'" *Working Mother* 6:50 (September 1983).

A single-parent mother tells how she renovated a single-family dwelling into two separate, but smaller, units. She preserved the single-family character of the home and was not forced, by financial need, to sell. Advice is offered for others interested in this kind of solution for single parents, and also included are: local laws and zoning code restrictions, contracting costs, and ordinances and rental arrangements.

110   Burgess, Jane K. "The Single-Parent Family: A Social and Sociological Problem." *The Family Coordinator* 19:137–44 (1970).

This article places emphasis on "marital roles" rather than the usual, traditional emphasis on "parental roles." Consideration of the problems facing single parents and possible solutions are given.

111   Delatiner, Barbara. "A Single Mother Goes Back to School." *Working Mother* 5:29–30 (September 1982).

Tells how a twenty-nine year old divorced mother, working as a forklift operator in a hospital-products plant in New Jersey, earned an associate degree in business management from a community college in two years. Others may benefit from reading her story of how she made it from a dead-end job to become more economically self-sufficient and personally fulfilled.

112   Finkelstein, Harry, Keshet Rosenthal, and Kristine M. Rosenthal. "Fathering After Marital Separation." *Social Work* 23:11–18 (January 1978).

This study deals with the experiences of a group of separated or divorced fathers who chose to remain fully involved in the upbringing of their children.

113   Gagan, Richard J. et al. "Support Networks of Single Mothers of Premature Infants." *Family Perspective* 17:117–29 (Spring 1983).

Examines the social support networks of single women who had recently given birth prematurely. The networks these women establish are described, and it is proposed that the quality of social networks has an impact on premature infants' behavior and on parent-infant interaction.

114   Gasser, Rita D., and Claribel M. Taylor. "Role Adjustment of Single Parent Fathers With Dependent Children." *The Family Coordinator* 25:397–441 (1976).

Explores the role adjustment of single-parent fathers. A structured questionnaire was administered to forty fathers who were either divorced or widowed and had at least one child under eighteen years of age living with them. The results indicated that fathers faced role adjustment in areas of home management and child care, curtailed former social activities, and shifted toward new relationships involving other single parents.

115 Greif, Geoffrey. "Children and Housework in the Single Father Family." *Family Relations* 34:353–57 (July 1985).

Findings from a sample of 1,136 fathers raising children alone following separation and divorce showed that as children grew older they participated more in housework, that fathers raising teenage girls received more help from them than fathers raising teenage boys, and that fathers may expect less from children in the way of participation in housework than was found in a study of two-parent families.Covers the fathers'use of outside help and daughters as mother substitutes.

116 Groller, Ingrid. "Jon Voight: A Father's Reflections." *Parents* 58:148 (May 1983).

The actor, divorced and a single parent of two children, gives his views on what parenting is all about.

117 Hanson, Shirley, and Jo A. Trilling. "A Proposed Study of the Characteristics of the Healthy Single-Parent Family." *Family Perspective* 17:79–88 (Spring 1983).

Investigates single-parent families and describes the characteristics which make a family unit strong and healthy. Also, a comparison is made between healthy single-parent families according to the sex of the custodial parents, and the custodial arrangements which have been made for the children.

118 Kriesberg, Louis. "Rearing Children for Educational Achievement in Fatherless Families." *Journal of Marriage and the Family* 29:288– 301 (May 1967).

Married and single mothers are compared to assess how certain conditions of fatherless families may be related to attitudes and behaviors relevant to their children's educational achievement. The analysis focuses upon neighborhood characteristics and also income and employment of the single mothers and their children.

119 Mattis, Mary. "Sex and the Single Parent." *New Woman* 16:76 September 1986).

Addresses the question of how you can have a sex life and still be a responsible single parent. Tells how to deal with your children when they ask questions about your relationships with your dates. Taken from the author's book, *Sex and the Single Parent* (Holt, 1986). See listing 88.

120 McHugh, Mary. "Diapers, Dishes and Dwindling Dollars: Mom's Struggling to Survive." *Women's World* 5:6–7 (23 October 1984).

Tells how women, with little or no skills or education, are having to cope, at the poverty level, with raising their children alone.

121 Meredith, Dennis. "Mom, Dad and the Kids." *Psychology Today* 19:62–71 (June 1985).

Describes the single father, rearing his children on his own or as a "coparent" for substantial amounts of time. Discusses the myths that seriously damage a father-child relationship when adopted by judges, lawyers and society at large. Looks at joint custody, which is one way to reduce the father's feelings of being cut off from the children. Reports on Geoffrey Greif's book, *Single Fathers* (see listing 81), and shows what happens to these fathers once they gain custody of their children.

122 "Mothers on Their Own." *Newsweek* 106:66–67 (23 December 1985).

Tells about the increasing number of single women in their thirties who have good jobs, are financially secure, and are choosing to become mothers. They adopt a child or get pregnant either through artificial insemination or with a male partner. Jane Matter, who formed the group called "Single Mothers by Choice" in 1981 (with membership now over one thousand across the country), says that women doing this should be financially and emotionally solid.

123 Orthner, Dennis K., Terry Brown, and D. Ferguson. "Single-Parent Fatherhood: An Emerging Family Life Style." *The Family Coordinator* 25:429–37 (1976).

This article explains why an increasing number of fathers are becoming the custodial parent.

124 Petronio, Sandra, and Thomas Endres. "Dating and the Single Parent: Communication in Social Network." *Journal of Divorce* 9:83–105 (Winter 1985/86).

This study was designed to assess relationship development of single parents, focusing on the communicative effects of their immediate social network (children and ex-spouses). The research used Levinger's (1983) developmental scheme to investigate the beginning phase of relationships, concentrating on dating opportunity, impressions, and interaction from the single perspective.

125 "Playing Both Mother and Father." *Newsweek* 106:42–43 (15 July 1985).

Gives current statistics and future projections for single-parent families. Addresses the number of single-parent families, families headed by females and males, and poverty-level families by race. Explains some of the positive and negative characteristics of the single-parent family life-style.

126 "Predictors of Coping in Divorced Single Mothers." L. Rebecca Propost, et al. *Journal of Divorce* 9:33–53 (Spring 1986).

Examines the effects of demographic variables, variables specific to marriage and divorce, and coping resources, on the adjustment of single mothers. The results indicate that four classes of variables have an effect on the mother's adjustment: phase of divorce and/or separtion, numbers and ages of children, style of coping, and education.

127 Richmond-Abbott, Marie. "Sex-Role Attitudes of Mothers and Children in Divorced, Single-Parent Families." *Journal of Divorce* 8:61–81 (Fall 1984).

Attempts to discover whether or not single parents and their children have nontraditional sex-role attitudes and reports on non-sex-stereotyped behavior. Study consists of a randomly selected sample of single-parent, divorced mothers and their children.

128 Rodgers, Mary Augusta. "Single Parent? Here's How to Make Christmas Merry When It's Just You and the Kids." *Woman's Day* (3 December 1985):34.

Gives nine guidelines to help singles make the holidays happy for their children. The guidelines, for example, begin with, "Don't try to keep everything the same, it isn't." The new single-parent family can start new traditions, such as preparing a special treat on Christmas Eve. Various contributors tell how they apply the guidelines.

129   Rooney, Rita. "Moving Back Home: Does It Work?" *Working Mother* 5:36 (April 1982).

Tells about divorced women who return home with their kids to live with their parents after a failed marriage. The advantages and disadvantages of this arrangement are given.

130   Rosenthal, David, Geoffrey K. Leigh, and Richard Elardo. "Home Environment of Three- to Six-Year-Old Children From Father-Asbsent and Two-Parent Families." *Journal of Divorce* 9:41–48 (Winter 1985/86).

Investigates differences in home environments between children from single- and two-parent homes. The sample contained thirty single-parent and thirty two-parent families. The data indicated similarities on all subscales between the groups studied.

131   Rossi, Mary Jane Mangini. "Single-Parent Families in Picture Books." *School Library Journal* 30:32–33 (December 1983).

An annotated bibliography of twenty-eight children's picture books which depict single-parent family styles.

132   Schlesinger, Benjamin. "Children's Viewpoints of Living in a One-Parent Family." *Journal of Divorce* 5:1–23 (Summer 1982).

Surveys forty children, aged twelve to eighteen, living in middle class, urban, separated or divorced, one-parent families in metropolitan Toronto. The children's responses to four open-ended questions relating to their feelings about living in one-parent families are given.

133   Schlesinger, Benjamin, and Rubin Todres. "Motherless Families: An Increasing Societal Pattern." *Child Welfare* 55:553–58 (1976).

This is a survey of seventy-two families, in Canada and the United States, headed by a father rearing the children in the absence of a mother. The survey indicates the need for further research in this area and the modification of social laws to meet the needs of such fathers.

134   Schlesinger, Benjamin. "The One-Parent Families in Great Britain." *Family Life Coordinator* 26:139–150 (April 1977).

Reviews the most comprehensive report on one-parent families, *The Finer Report of Great Britain* (1974). Some of its findings and recommendations are summarized.

135   "The Single Parent: Family Albums." *Newsweek* 106:44–48 (15 July 1985).

Presents five single-parent family experiences which reflect both the painful realities and the rewarding challenges of raising children alone. The families include: a father with custody of two children; a black unmarried mother of two children with different fathers; a divorced mother with two children; an unmarried mother with one child; and a twice-divorced mother, with two grown children from her first marriage and one daughter from her second marriage, who is presently planning her third marriage.

136   Stolberg, Arnold L., and Ann J. Ullman. "Assessing Dimensions of Single Parenting: The Single Parenting Questionnaire." *Journal of Divorce* 8:31–45 (Winter 1984).

This study of 239 divorced and custodial parents is an effort to develop and validate an instrument which assesses five dimensions of single parenting: problem-solving skills, parental warmth, discipline procedures, parent rules, enthusiasm for parenting, and parent support systems.

137   Strong, John. "A Human Communication Model and Its Influence on Six Single Parents." *Family Perspective* 17:67–78 (Spring 1983).

The Human Communication Model is defined, and five aspects of it are given. Six single parents were taught about the communication principles and skills, and they were asked to tell how these concepts had influenced their personal lives and their families.

138   Turner, Pauline H., and Richard M. Smith. "Single Parents and Day Care," *Family Relations* 32:215–26 (April 1983).

Addresses the day care needs, attitudes, and practices of 252 single parents with dependent children. The sample was diverse in terms of age, income, educational level, and number of children.

139   Warren, Nancy J., and Ingrid A. Amara. "Educational Groups for Single Parents: The Parenting After Divorce Programs." *Journal of Divorce* 8:79–96 (Winter 1984).

Describes a parent group for divorcing parents that is shown to be helpful and welcomed by participants. The group, part of the Parenting After Divorce (PAD) Project, was designed as an educational prevention program to help parents facilitate their children's adjustment after divorce. A session-by-session description of the program is given along with data from consumer satisfaction surveys and indications of how the model can be adapted to other settings.

140 Wedemeyer, Nancy Voight, and Jill M. Johnson. "Learning the Single-Parent-Role: Overcoming Traditional Marital-Role Influences." *Journal of Divorce* 5:41–53 (Summer 1982).

Data from previous research and from new interviews with thirty divorced custodial parents are explored to develop a model of how traditional marital roles influence the adjustment to single parenthood.

141 Weiss, Robert S. "The Contributions of an Organization of Single Parents to the Well-Being of the Members." *The Family Coordinator* 22:321–26 (1973).

On the basis of observing meetings of one chapter of Parents Without Partners, and based on interviews with members of the chapter, the contributions the organization makes to the well-being of its members are discussed. These contributions include provision of support systems and opportunities to remedy deficits prevalent in the lives of single parents.

3
Stepfamilies

A. Books and Pamphlets

142 Baer, Jean. *The Second Wife: How to Live Happily With a Man Who Has Been Married Before.* Garden City, NY: Doubleday, 1972. 269 pp.

> The author, who is a second wife, has drawn material from interviews, readings, questionnaires, and her own personal experiences and observations to write this book about how to be a second wife. Topics covered are: courtships, stepparenting, finances, and how to deal with ex-spouses and ex-in-laws.

143 Berman, Claire. *Making It As a Stepparent: New Roles/New Rules.* Garden City, NY: Doubleday, 1980. 202 pp.

> As director of public education of the North American Center for Adoption, a division of the Child Welfare League of America, the author uses interviews with hundreds of remarried men, women, and their children to look at all angles of stepfamily life. Includes the confusion of merging two or more different life-styles and the shock of a childless individual who becomes an "instant parent."

144 Bohannan, Paul, and Janice Perlman. *Stepfamilies: A Bibliography.* Baltimore: Stepfamily Association of America, 1984. 83 pp.

> A partially annotated bibliography of books, journal articles, dissertations, etc., relating to stepfamilies.

145 Burns, Cherie. *Stepmotherhood: How to Survive Without Feeling Frustrated, Left Out, or Wicked.* New York: Times Books, 1985. 228 pp.

> Based on interviews with more than forty stepmothers and on discussions with family counselors. This historical and sociologi-

cal research effort desires to help stepmothers put themselves and their experiences into focus by helping them to understand their inherent obstacles, such as constant comparisons with "moms," or being set against their husbands by stepchildren who force dad to choose between their own wishes and those of the stepmother. Topics included are visits, holidays, financial obligations, and problem stepchildren. Sections cover the special problems of being married to a widower and a stepmother's desire to have children of her own.

146 Bustanoby, Andre. *The Ready-Made Family: How to Be a Stepparent and Survive.* Grand Rapids, MI: Zondervan, 1982. 144 pp.

The author acknowledges the differences that exist in stepfamilies and places the emphasis of this book on good parenting and how to avoid making the excuse that "stepfamilies are different." The last chapter evaluates stepfamily systems.

147 Capaldi, Frederick P., and Barbara McRae. *Stepfamilies: A Cooperative Responsibility.* New York: New Viewpoints, 1979. 154 pp.

This book is written by family therapists who specialize in working with stepfamilies and addresses single parents considering remarriage and blended families. It aims to assist stepparents and stepchildren to gain a better understanding of problems that confront them, and helps to guide them toward successful solutions.

148 Currier, Cecile. *Learning to Step Together.* Baltimore: Stepfamily Association of America, 1982. 145 pp.

A leader's manual for educators and mental health practitioners in charge of courses or workshops for couples in stepfamilies.

149 Duberman, Lucile. *The Reconstituted Family: A Study of Remarried Couples and Their Children.* Chicago: Nelson-Hall, 1975. 181 pp.

A scholarly examination of reconstituted families written by a Rutgers University sociologist who presents the results of a study of eighty-eight remarried couples, in which at least one member of each couple had a child by a previous marriage. Focuses attention on the remarried family as a unit and investigates the process by which the new family obtained or failed to obtain integration. The factors which account for varying degrees of marital and parental adjustment are included.

150   Duffin, Sharyn R. *Yours, Mine & Ours: Tips for Stepparents.* Washington, DC: U.S. Government Printing Office, 1978. 27 pp.

Presents some observations made by stepparents about their experiences. It is designed to help new and future stepfamilies look more realistically at some of the problems which may confront them and suggests some steps to take, before remarriage, to ease the transistion into the new family.

151   Einstein, Elizabeth. *The Stepfamily: Living, Loving and Learning.* New York: Macmillan, 1982. 210 pp.

The author, a stepchild herself and twice a stepmother, writes about her own experiences and those reported in interviews she conducted with members of fifty stepfamilies. Offers information and advice on how this kind of family can realize its potential for happiness and fulfillment. The book is also a guide for interested persons such as grandparents, aunts, uncles, clergy, schoolteachers, and friends. *The Stepfamily* examines each family member's role within the context of the group and tries to show stepfamilies how to overcome some of the more common stresses before they become major obstacles to happiness.

152   ———. *Stepfamily Living Series.* 4 vols. Tampla, FL: Southprint Corp., 1983.

This series consists of four booklets, each of which considers one specific area of stepfamily living. The booklets are: "Preparing for Remarriage," "Pitfalls and Possibilities," "Dealing with Discipline," and "Encouragement and Enrichment." Solutions and helpful hints for the primary stepfamily problems are offered in about twenty pages of text per booklet.

153   Felker, Evelyn H. *Raising Other People's Kids: Successful Child-Rearing in the Restructured Family.* Grand Rapids, MI: Eerdmans, 1981. 164 pp.

Addresses people raising children who are not biologically their own: stepchildren, adopted children, or foster children. The author, an experienced foster parent, refers to these families as "restructured" or "functional" families. Chapters deal with topics such as bringing the child into the family and how the child adjusts to new value systems.

154   Ferri, Elsa. *Stepchildren: A National Study.* A Report from the National Child Development Study. Windsor, England: National Foundation for Educational Research-Nelson, 1984. 200 pp.

This study is based on a nationally representative sample of children living in stepfamilies. Comparisons are made between the stepchildren and equally representative groups in other types of family units. Data is also available on the various measures of psychosocial adjustment and emotional behavior, children's educational attainment and physical health, including indicators of their social and material circumstances. The study looks at changes in family structure over a period of time and attempts to relate these to other changes which took place in the environment and development of the children concerned.

155   Getzoff, Ann, and Carolyn McClenahan. *Stepkids: A Survival Guide for Teenagers in Stepfamilies.* New York: Walker, 1984. 171 pp.

The authors, who are family and child therapists, have written this work to help teenagers who are stepkids. Since being a teenager and learning how to adjust to growing up is difficult enough, being a teenager in a stepfamily can only add to these adjustment difficulties. This work addresses the feelings and confusion teens may have about their parents' divorce, adjusting to life with single parents, and trying to make the adjustment that is demanded by a parent's remarriage or close relationship with someone new. Some case histories are included along with a chapter about parents in a homosexual relationship.

156   Gruber, Ellen J. *Stepfamilies: A Guide to the Sources and Resources.* New York: Garland, 1986. 122 pp.

An annotated bibliography of books, periodicals, and journals which serves as a reference guide to research and service programs for those who work with children and families in stepfamily situations. Most materials listed were written from 1980 through 1984. Includes some dissertations, audiovisual materials, and lists of organizations and newsletters.

157   Harvey, Adell. *My Cup Runneth Over.* Nashville, TN: Nelson, 1984. 185 pp.

This book was written as a stepfamily project by Adell Harvey, a Baptist preacher's widow with three children, and her present husband, Jack Harvey, a Pentecostal preacher with four children. This work wants to disavow the pessimistic message found in many books about stepparenting by humorously covering the many problems the couple encountered in merging their two families.

158   Hill, Archie. *Closed World of Love.* New York: Simon & Schuster, 1976. 136 pp.

A personal narrative about the author's severely crippled stepson-to-be, Barry, who is fourteen years old. Through his new wife's love and encouragement, the author learns to share in the boy's care.

159   Houmes, Dan, and Paul Meier. *Growing in Step: A Christian Guide to Stepparenting*. Richardson, TX: Today Publishers, 1985. 169 pp.

A compilation of several years of counseling experience in which case experiences and problems of stepfamilies are shared. Discusses shared custody, the third parent in the family, and blending three families into one. The last chapter gives guidelines for blending families.

160   Jensen, Larry Cyril, and Janet Mitchell Jensen. *Stepping into Stepparenting: A Practical Guide*. Palo Alto, CA: R & E Research Associates, 1981. 139 pp.

Focuses on understanding the difficulties stepparents face. The final chapters offer solutions to some of the most common problems faced by stepparents. The authors point out how stepparents can develop realistic perceptions and goals for the unit. An easy-to-use system of family organization is also presented.

161   Jolin, Peter G. *How to Succeed as a Stepparent*. New York: New American Library, 1983. 175 pp.

Tells how stepparents can prevent falling into frustrating and bitter conflicts with stepchildren. Gives advice on bonding, understanding feelings, communicating, and discipline.

162   Juroe, David J., and Bonnie B. Juroe. *Successful Stepparenting*. Old Tappan, NJ: F. H. Revell, 1983. 191 pp.

Two counselors offer a collection of guidelines, based on their personal experiences and training, as preparation for the responsibilities and rewards of successful stepparenting.

163   Kalter, Suzy. *Instant Parent: A Guide for Stepparents, Part-Time Parents and Grandparents*. New York: A & W Publishers, 1979. 268 pp.

Kalter presents a guide for anyone discovering too late that marriage brought with it the totally unasked-for position of parenthood. Her discussion includes how to handle the first meeting with the child; how to live through an ongoing relationship with your partner's "ex"; how to deal with financial responsibility, vacations with children, privacy and sex; and ways to say no to someone else's child and make it stick. Also includes a child development profile for ages two to twelve.

164 Kaplan, Leslie S. *Coping With Stepfamilies*. New York: Rosen Publishing Group, 1986. 162 pp.

While the book highlights many of the things that can go wrong in stepfamilies, it maintains that stepfamilies do not have problems. People in stepfamilies make problems, and those same people can stop problems. Describes the issues that cause people in stepfamilies—along with their relatives, friends, and others in the wider community—to make mistakes.

165 Keshet, Jamie Kelem. *Love and Power in the Stepfamily*. New York: McGraw-Hill, 1987. 231 pp.

Keshet, director of the Institute for Remarriage and Stepfamilies, offers a family guide to the phases that stepfamilies live through. She starts with getting acquainted, and follows with the divorcing couple, parenting after divorce, children and new partners, the remarried couple, the divorced-remarried family, and the last phase: the new baby. The last chapter presents the stories of stepfamilies.

166 Larson, Jeffry H., James O. Anderson, and Ann Morgan. *Effective Stepparenting*. New York: Family Service America, 1984. 150 pp.

This manual is for family life educators and family therapists who are interested in stepparent education. The first five chapters prepare for the eight group-sessions which follow in chapter six. Chapter seven describes the follow-up meeting thirty days later.

167 Lewis-Steer, Cynthia. *Stepping Lightly: An A to Z Guide for Stepparents*. Minneapolis: Comp Care Publishers, 1981. 213 pp.

The author uses an A to Z dictionary format for approximately 120 random words. Each definition begins with Webster's, followed by others derived from the author's experiences.

168 Lowe, Patricia Tracy. *The Cruel Stepmother*. Englewood Cliffs, NJ: Prentice-Hall, 1970. 260 pp.

Lowe has written the story of her own remarriage, into which she brought her two sons and her husband brought his son from his first marriage. She includes personal experiences and suggestions about what might have been handled differently. The children, now grown, give their reflections on past experiences.

169 Maddox, Brenda. *The Half-Parent Family: Living With Other People's Children.* New York: M. Evans, 1975. 196 pp.

The author, a stepmother, offers a historical perspective on stepparenting. She writes about her own experiences and includes excerpts from interviews with other stepparents. Discusses the advantages and disadvantages of adoption by stepparents.

170 Mayleas, Davidyne. *Re-Wedded Bliss: Love, Alimony, Incest, Ex-Spouses and Other Domestic Blessings.* New York: Basic Books, 1977. 270 pp.

In this book the author coins the term the *synergistic* family as a family formed after divorce and remarriage, where one or both parents already have children and one parent is not the biological parent of the other's children. This is a family created by remarriage after divorce, not after death. This book, told from the author's experiences and point of view, explains how to live with the synergistic family and get the most out of it.

171 McCormick, Mona. *Stepfathers: What the Literature Reveals: A Literature Review and Annotated Bibliography.* La Jolla, CA: Western Behavioral Sciences Institute, 1974. 75 pp.

This literature review provides an essay addressing sixty subject areas, including major concepts, issues, and trends, as well as an annotated bibliography of approximately 180 articles and books.

172 Noble, June, and William R. Noble. *How to Live with Other People's Children.* New York: Hawthorn, 1977. 205 pp.

This is a book based on interviews with stepparents and stepchildren. The authors direct their book toward children's reactions. It shows how children view their parents, stepparents, and siblings; how they deal with domineering or abusive parents; and what qualities and needs they look for in a potential stepparent. It includes suggestions for step relationships.

173 Olson, Richard P., and Carole Della Pia-Terry. *Help for Remarried Couples and Families.* Valley Forge, PA: Judson Press, 1984. 159 pp.

This work grew out of a series of discussions on remarriage which were sponsored by a group of churches in the local community.

It is intended for use by the widowed or divorced person, the single person who marries either a widow(er) or someone who has been divorced, anyone considering remarriage, or the already married person.

174   Paris, Erna. *Step-families: Making Them Work.* New York: Avon, 1984. 228 pp.

The author, an ward-winning Canadian author and member of a stepfamily, has interviewed people involved in remarriage and has analyzed the successes and failures in these real stories. Information is given on the pitfalls and rewards of remarriage. Some chapters deal with false expectations, predictable problems of second marriages, joint custody of children, and accepting realities.

175   Reed, Bobbie. *Stepfamilies: Living in Christian Harmony.* St. Louis, MO: Concordia, 1980. 143 pp.

Based on the author's own experiences and her interviews with stepfamilies, counselors, pastors, educators, and lawyers. It contains discussion questions, case stories, enrichment exercises, and an appendix which lists organizations and their addresses.

176   Reingold, Carmel Berman. *How to be Happy If You Marry Again: All About Children, Money, Sex, Lawyers, Ex-Husbands, Ex-Wives, and Past Memories.* New York: Harper & Row, 1977. 220 pp. First published under the title *Remarriage,* 1976.

The author, who married a divorced man with two children after her first husband died, discusses mostly happy second marriages, including her own and those of other people she interviewed. The book encompasses the problems of dealing with stepchildren and natural parents.

177   Rice, F. Philip. *Stepparenting.* New York: Condor, 1979. 193 pp.

Dr. Rice offers a guide for those who are stepparents, or are considering becoming stepparents. Includes sections on stepsibling relationships and teenage stepchildren.

178   Roosevelt, Ruth, and Jeanette Lofas. *Living in Step: A Remarriage Manual for Parents and Children.* New York: Stein & Day, 1976. 192 pp.

Two stepmothers, founders of the Stepfamily Foundation in New York City, tell of their "step" living personal experiences, and include interviews with other stepfamilies. Defines problems and offers solutions and guidelines for stepfamilies.

179   Rosenbaum, Jean, and Veryl Rosenbaum. *Stepparenting*. New York: Dutton, 1978. 145 pp.

Gives guidance to prospective stepparents by discussing the characteristics to look for when selecting a mate. It contains a section for the weekend stepparent, and furnishes a list of guidelines for communicating.

180   Rowlands, Peter. *Love Me, Love My Kids: A Guide for the New Partner*. New York: Continuum, 1983. 150 pp.

This book is for the noncustodial parent's new partner, who is usually addressed as a female, except in the last chapter, which specifically talks to the new male partner. The recurring theme is to maintain the parent-child relationship regardless of the circumstances. The author offers suggestions for maintaining on-going relationships, and also includes case histories.

181   Silverzweig, Mary Zenorini. *The Other Mother*. New York: Harper & Row, 1982. 299 pp.

The true story of a twenty-eight-year-old businesswoman who becomes an instant parent when she marries a man, with three young daughters, who she met while he was unhappily married to a lesbian. Silverzweig describes the trials and triumphs of their relationship as they began living together including the ordeal of the divorce from his daughters' mother, and the custody fight. The details of this highly publicized New Jersey court proceeding makes it obvious that the real victims are the children.

182   Simon, Anne W. *Stepchild in the Family: A View of Children in Remarriage*. Indianapolis: Odyssey, 1964. 256 pp.

A journalistic account of the author, who has been a stepgrandparent, stepchild, and stepmother. It includes advice and case histories from studies by sociologists and psychiatrists, and will be helpful for parents and stepparents in understanding the needs and reactions of children.

183   Smart, Laura S., and Mollie S. Smart. *Families: Developing Relationship*. 2d ed. New York: Macmillan, 1980. 532 pp.

Discusses the problems of reconstituted families, including money, the real parent, hidden expectations, rivalry and competition between children and stepparent. Success in these families is also examined.

184 Smith, William Carlson. *The Stepchild*. Chicago: University of Chicago Press, 1953. 314 pp.

A sociological study of the facts and fictions of steprelationships. Explores the stepchild in folklore, literature, and other cultures. It focuses on the stepparents and also discusses the stepchild and his adjustment, which includes factors such as age, socioeconomic status, and juvenile delinquency.

185 Spann, Owen, and Nanci Spann. *Your Child? I Thought It Was My Child!* Pasadena, CA: Ward Ritchie, 1977. 176 pp.

Owen Spann, talk show host for KGO in San Francisco and his wife, Nancie, a former model and actress each brought three children to their new family. Interviews for this book were conducted with lawyers, pediatricians, psychologists and other famous and nonfamous people who have been divorced and remarried with families. A humorous account of the authors' experiences, this book offers an analysis of the problems, complexities, and fun of steprelationships. It includes sections on adoption, visitation rights, and who goes where for the holidays.

186 *Stepfather*. Compiled by Tony Gorman. Boulder, CO: Gentle Touch Press, 1983. 172 pp.

A recording of experiences told mostly by stepfathers or about stepfathers. The interviews are from people of various ages, races, occupations, and economic circumstances. Shows the way others have adapted, and the reader may find some advice and/or shared experience that may help to enhance the stepfather experience.

187 Thomson, Helen. *The Successful Stepparent*. New York: Harper & Row, 1966. 237 pp.

An early, but helpful, sourcebook on stepparenting, with advice for parents dealing with adolescents. Thomson covers such issues as discipline, jealously, custody, widows and widowers, adoptions, and children with special problems.

188 Visher, Emily B., and John S. Visher. *How to Win as a Stepfamily*. New York: Dembner Books, 1982. 196 pp.

This practical guide encompasses many aspects of the new family from dealing with former spouses and new grandparents, to legal issues involving custody, visitation, adoption, the ex-spouse, and money. Of special interest is the section on children, both those who live with you and those who visit. Rules of behavior are set for the new family during the first months of remarriage when new relations are being established.

189   ———. *Stepfamilies: A Guide to Working With Stepparents and Stepchildren*. New York: Brunner/Mazel, 1979. 280 pp.

A guide primarily for the professional, with a nontechnical style suitable for self-help reference. Separate chapters are directed to particular family members: mothers/stepmothers, fathers/step-fathers, stepchildren, and others. Relationships are explored and therapeutic techniques are discussed. The book includes an over-view, a set of guidelines for stepfamilies, a set of references for stepfamilies, and a set of general references for families.

190   ———. *Stepfamilies: Myths and Realities*. Secaucus, N.J: L. Stuart, 1980.

Originally published as *Stepfamilies: A Guide to Working with Step-parents and Stepchildren*. See listing 189.

191   Wald, Esther. *The Remarried Family: Challenge and Promise*. New York: Family Service Association of America, 1981. 254 pp.

Based on the author's experience in social work practice, this work documents the rise of divorce and remarriage rates. It also provides the basis for further examination in change of family structure and relationships.

190   Walker, Glynnis. *Second Wife, Second Best? Managing Your Mar-riage As a Second Wife*. Garden City, NY: Doubleday, 1984. 274 pp.

Addresses the following three questions: Does society relegate the second wife to an inferior status? Do the husbands, children, families, and friends do the same? Do second wives see them-selves as second best? By surveying the responses of two hundred second wives to a questionnaire, Walker examines the problems experienced by this growing segment of the population. The work tells how to prepare for marriage to men who have been married before, and includes sections on coping, feelings, sex, and par-enting.

B. Articles in Periodicals

193 Ahrons, Constance R. "The Binuclear Family: Two Households, One Family." *Alternative Lifestyles* 2:499–515 (1979).

> The author proposes a new term, binuclear family, to describe the newly emerging family form which is characterized by two nuclear households, maternal and paternal.

194 Auerbach, Stevanne. "From Stepparent to Real Parent." *Parents* 51:34 (June 1976).

> The author, a parent-child consultant, gives advice and practical insights to stepparents based on his personal and consulting experiences.

195 Auerbach, Sylvia. "Stepping into Grandparenting." *Psychology Today* 17:56–57 (April 1983).

> Explains what is it like to become an instant grandparent. Tells how to cultivate the special bond that can exist between grandparents and grandchildren.

196 Baptiste, David A., Jr. "Marital and Family Therapy With Racially/Culturally Intermarried Stepfamilies." *Family Relations* 33:373–80 (July 1984).

> Focuses on the difficulties experienced by racially and/or culturally intermarried stepfamilies, and seeks to sensitize mental health professionals to issues specific to treating such families.

197 Berman, Claire. "Learning to be a (Not-So-Wicked) Stepmother." *Woman's Day* (May 1984):54.

> Explains to the stepmother that expectations for stepfamily relations will differ from intact family relationships because of the relationships that existed before the stepmother entered the picture. Suggests solutions to the stepmother for handling some of the more common situations that may occur.

198 Bohannan, Paul J., and Rosemary J. Erickson. "Stepping In." *Psychology Today* 11:52–54 (January 1978).

> An account of research on stepfather families in the San Diego area.

199   Brockman, Elin Schoen. "A Few Kind Words in Defense of 'The Wicked Stepmother.' " *Family Circle* 100:117–20 (14 April 1987).

Tells how the author slowly gains the approval of her stepson and gives ten guidelines for stepmothers.

200   Burns, Cherie. "Travelers Without Maps in the Family Mine Field, Stepmothers Need to Stop, Look and Listen." *People Weekly* 23:47–48 (21 October 1985).

This article asks questions of Burns, whose book, *Stepmotherhood: How to Survive Without Feeling Frustrated, Left Out, or Wicked.* (see listing 145) is based on interviews of more than forty women who have taken on part of the job of raising other mothers' children. The question/answer format includes such questions as: What mistakes do stepmothers tend to make at the start? What if, in spite of your best efforts, you don't like your stepchildren? Can a new baby strengthen the family?

201   Chapman, Grace. "A Very Special Wedding." *Good Housekeeping* 199:70 (August 1984).

Tells how the author, the stepmother of four, takes the responsibility for arranging her stepdaughter's wedding, hoping to give her the wedding her late mother would have wanted for her.

202   Clingempeel, W. Glenn, Eulalee Brand, and Richard Ievoli. "Stepparent-Stepchild Relationships in Stepmother and Stepfather Families." *Family Relations* 33:465–73 (July 1984).

Assesses the quality of stepparent-stepchild relationships in stepmother and stepfather families. Findings reveal that stepparent-stepdaughter relationships in both stepmother and stepfather families have more problems than stepparent-stepson relationships.

203   Cole, K. C. "The Travails of a Part-Time Stepparent." *New York Times* 14:61 (14 May 1980).

The author, a stepmother, tells about her relationships with two stepdaughters. Her experiences, which are often strained, are told with understanding, sensitivity, and humor.

204   Coleman, Marilyn, Lawrence H. Ganong, and Ronald Gingrich. "Stepfamily Strengths: A Review of Popular Literature." *Family Relations* 34: 583–88 (October 1985).

Reviews popular literature that identifies stepfamily strengths and focuses on stepchildren. Self-help books, magazine articles, and adolescent fiction are reviewed.

205   Coleman, Marilyn, Lawrence H. Ganong, and Jane Henry. "What Teachers Should Know About Stepfamilies." *Childhood Education* 60:306–09 (June 1984).

Mentions some stepfamily stereotypes found in fairy tales and real life. Explains how schools seem to have neglected the reality of stepfamilies and gives suggestions for raising teacher awareness about stepfamilies.

206   Collins, Laura J., and Bron B. Ingoldsby. "Living in Step: A Look at the Reconstituted Family." *Family Perspective* 16:23–30 (Winter 1982).

This compilation of research by approximately thirty-three authors includes sections on children of divorce, stepmothers, stepparenting, stepchildren, and stepfamilies.

207   Crosbie-Burnett, Margaret. "The Centrality of the Step Relationship: A Challenge to Family Theory and Practice." *Family Relations* 33: 459–63 (July 1984).

Compares the relative importance of the marital relationship versus the steprelationship in predicting family happiness. It includes the self-reported behaviors and emotions of the family members in eighty-seven upper middle class, Caucasian, mother-stepfather households with one or two adolescent children, who were surveyed using questionnaires. Variables measured were family happiness, marital happiness, and aspects of the relationship between the stepparent and stepchildren.

208   Dowling, Claudia. "The Relative Explosion." *Psychology Today* 17:54–59 (April 1983).

Examines the new family in America consisting of ex-spouses and half siblings, stepchildren and former in-laws, lovers and their children, and other relative relationships. Includes a small section about stepping into grandparenting.

209   Draughon, Margaret. "Stepmother's Role of Identification in Relation to Mourning in the Child." *Psychological Reports* 36:183–89 (1975).

Discusses three models of identification for interaction between stepchild and stepmother: "primary" mother, "other" mother, and "friend". Tells how each role model effects the stepchild's mourning of the biological mother.

210   Duberman, Lucile. "Step-kin Relationships." *Journal of Marriage and the Family* 35:283–95 (May 1973).

Eighty-eight reconstituted families were studied in this article. The effects of parental age, educational level, religion and social class, children's ages, sex, residence, and the influence of a child born into the new marriage are reported.

211   Einstein, Elizabeth. "5 Myths About Stepfamilies." *Parents* 58:90 (November 1983).

The author wants to dispel five myths about stepfamilies so that the new family can be built on a foundation of realistic expectations. These five myths are: making a stepfamily is as simple as saying, "I do"; stepfamilies work like nuclear families; instant love occurs among stepfamily members; part-time stepfamily living is easier than full-time; and stepfamilies resulting from death form easier than those from divorce.

212   Fields, Terri. "Learning to Live With a Stepparent." *Seventeen* (April 1983):97.

Focuses on teenagers' reactions to their parents remarrying, including emotions of jealousy, disloyalty, insecurity, guilt, and relief. Tips for feeling happier and more accepting of parents remarrying are given by a clinical psychologist.

213   Francke, Linda Bird. "Overcoming the Myth of the Wicked Stepmother." *Harpers Bazaar* 117:134 (October 1984).

Gives four stepmother roles to avoid: the super step, who is self-sacrificing and plays the martyr; the courting step, who makes lots of promises that aren't carried out; the competitive step, who is always competing with the natural mother; and the victimized step. The last section is devoted to the perfect step.

214   Giles-Sims, Jean, and David Finkelhor. "Child Abuse in Step-families." *Family Relations* 33:407–11 (July 1984).

There is often a presumption that children are at increased risk of abuse from stepparents. The author explains five theories that have been used to explain this presumed relationship: social-evolutionary, normative stress, selection, and resource theory

215   Goldstein, Harris S. "Reconstituted Families: The Second Marriage and Its Children." *Psychiatric Quarterly* 48:433–40 (1974).

Goldstein recommends that the therapist make the difficulties commonly observed in remarried families explicit for the whole family to acknowledge and verbalize, so the family may then be able to integrate into a stable, new family structure.

216 Helgesen, Sally. "The High Cost of Secondhand Husbands." *Redbook* 164:94–95 (March 1985).

Disavows the myth of "the other woman" (also known as a home wrecker and/or gold digger) by giving some real-life experiences which illustrate: (1) the second wife who delays having children of her own because of her husband's financial obligations to his first family; (2) second wives supporting the second family; and (3) the problems encountered when children from the first marriage enter the picture. The author summarizes by saying that not only can the second wife become tolerant and understanding but she should, at the same time, make sure that she is getting the understanding, attention, and respect she requires—which is in fact necessary before the stepfamily can be successful.

217 "I Couldn't Accept My Father's Remarriage." *Good Housekeeping* 199:36 (August 1984).

Tells how the children of a first marriage try to adjust to their father's life with his new, second family. Some guidelines given are: all legal matters resulting from the divorce should be handled entirely by the lawyer; parents' former marital problems should never be discussed when the children are with their mother; and, instead of living in the memory of past family customs, create new, more flexible ways to celebrate birthdays and holidays.

218 Jacobson, Doris S. "Stepfamilies: Myths and Realities." *Social Work* 24:202–07 (May 1979).

Explores the emotional issues that often confront stepparents and stepchildren. Describes a program to help stepparents deal better with their stepchildren.

219 Johnson, Bryan R. "How Do You Treat Your Wife's Ex?" *Redbook* 163:60 (October 1984).

The author presents insight into how ex-spouses remain a part of your life when children are involved. He refers to his wife's ex as *my* ex-husband to illustrate how his life is also affected by his wife's ex-spouse. Some examples are given to show how the author fuctions in the relationship with his wife's ex.

220 Johnson, Harriet C. "Working With Stepfamilies: Principles of Practice." *Social Work* 25:304–08 (July 1980).

Examines some common characteristics of stepfamilies, and suggests relevant principles for use in practice with them.

221   Kaercher, Dan. "Making Stepchildren Part of the Family." *Better Homes and Gardens* 63:67–68 (February 1985).

Tells of the experience of one stepmother and how she is rejected by her thirteen-year-old stepdaughter. The author says that children in such families are enriched, not thwarted, by the presence of a caring stepparent. Kaercher goes on to expand on some of his "tips" for stepparents, such as having reasonable expectations, respect the child's relationship with the absent parent, and not focusing your life entirely on your stepparenting role.

222   Kargman, Marie Witkin. "Stepchild Support Obligations of Stepparents." *Family Relations* 32:231–38 (April 1983).

Explores the changing legal responsibilities of support by stepparents for stepchildren during remarriage. Includes the impact upon child support, visitation, and custody after divorce from a remarriage.

223   Kompara, Diane Reinhart. "Difficulties in the Socialization Process of Stepparenting." *Family Relations* 29:69–73 (1980).

Analyzes the stepfamily literature and highlights the socialization difficulties present in this unique adjustment process, including disciplining the children, adjusting to the habits and personalities of the children, and gaining their acceptance.

224   Lagoni, Laurel S., and Alicia Skinner Cook. "Stepfamilies: A Content Analysis of the Popular Literature, 1961–1982." *Family Relations* 34:521–25 (October 1985).

A content analysis of thirty stepparenting articles in five major parenting magazines to determine if significant changes occurred in number, content, and type of stepparenting articles appearing in these magazines over this time period.

225   Lutz, Patricia. "The Stepfamily: An Adolescent Perspective." *Family Relations* 32:367–75(July 1983).

This study investigates what adolescents believe to be the stressful and nonstressful aspects of stepfamily living.

226   Meredith, Kay. "I Married My Husband's Kids." *Parents* 58:87–88 (November 1983).

The author shares her experiences as a young woman who marries a divorced father of two young daughters and a son. Tells how she copes with the stepfamily's continuous adjustment to the divorce and new stepfamily relationships. Although aware that there are areas of the children's lives she has little influence over, and being constantly reminded that she is not biologically related to her stepchildren, Kay does realize that she plays a part in their lives, and that there is something of her, their stepmother, within her stepchildren.

227 Messer, Albert A. "The Phaedra Complex." *Archives of General Psychiatry* 21:213–18 (1969).

Opens up the issue of attraction between the stepparent and the stepchild, both pathological and nonpathological, and discusses the impact of the incest taboo.

228 Mills, David M. "A Model for Stepfamily Development." *Family Relations* 33:365–72 (July 1984).

The step-by-step model for stepfamily development proposed here is distinctly different from biological family development. The stepfamily model consists of a number of stages and tasks, including setting goals, parental limit-setting, stepparent bonding, and blending family rules. Exercises are also included.

229 Mowatt, Marian. "Group Psychotherapy for Stepfathers and Their Wives." *Psychotherapy: Theory, Research, and Practice.* 9:328–31 (1972).

Group therapy and discussion of the problems common to stepfathers (such as how far to go in taking over the role of the father) helped couples to see how each one contributed to the difficulties in their relations with each other, and with their own children.

230 Nolan, Jeanne, Marilyn Coleman, and Lawrence Ganong. "The Presentation of Stepfamilies in Marriage and Family Textbooks." *Family Relations* 33:559–66 (October 1984)

Twenty-six introductory marriage and family textbooks were reviewed for content about stepfamilies. Many textbook authors did not include the topic of stepfamilies, or included it in only a cursory fashion. Reveals that stepfamilies have been a relatively neglected family style by family researchers and educators.

231 Offit, Avodah K. "Must a Second Marriage Tear This Family Apart?" *McCall's* 113:125 (April 1986).

Explains the stepdaughter's perception of the new stepmother who intrudes on the child's private relationship with her father.

The stepchild experiences the stepmother's arrival on the scene as an emotional deprival, which, in a very real way, it is. The author suggests ways for stepdaughters to deal with stepmothers so their relationship will not tear the family apart.

232 Papernow, Patricia L. "The Stepfamily Cycle: An Experimental Model of Stepfamily Development." *Family Relations* 33:355–63 (July 1984).

Draws on family systems and the Gestalt theory, and describes the seven stages of stepfamily development. The implications for counseling and educational support for stepfamilies is discussed.

233 Parent, Gail. "The New Etiquette: How to Survive a Second Marriage." *Harper's Bazaar* 117:112 (October 1984)

A social satirist gives guidelines on how to handle the marriage-go-round and blended families, while keeping your sanity intact.

234 Pasley, Kay, and Marilyn Ihinger-Tallman. "Portraits of Stepfamily Life in Popular Literature, 1940–1985." *Family Relations* 34:527–34 (October 1985).

Discusses the results from a content analysis of popular articles on stepfamily life from 1940 to 1980. Results showed that articles were primarily directed at women or general audiences. Reports the trends across the four decades.

235 ———. "Stress in Remarried Families." *Family Perspective* 16:181–90 (Fall 1982).

Identifies and examines the amount of potential stress experiences in the three major stress domains: the merging of different family cultures and the establishment of a new family identity, differing perceptions of the rules for distributing family resources, and feelings of loyalty to previous and present family members. Gives recommendations for persons working with these families.

236 Perkins, Terry F., and James P. Kahan. "An Empirical Comparison of Natural Father and Stepfather Family Systems." *Family Process* 18:175–83 (June 1979).

This study examined the family system differences between forty volunteer natural-father and stepfather families. It was concluded that the differences between the family systems in terms of their interpersonal relations and perceptions affect the entire stepparent family system and its ability to function adequately.

237   Pink, Jo Ellen Theresa, and Karen Smith Wampler. "Problem Areas in Stepfamilies: Cohesion, Adaptability, and the Stepfather-Adolescent Relationships." *Family Relations* 34:327–35 (July 1985).

Compares twenty-eight stepfamilies with twenty-eight first-marriage families on family functioning and the quality of the stepfather-adolescent relationship. Implications of the findings are discussed.

238   Robinson, Bryan E. "The Contemporary American Stepfather." *Family Relations* 33:381–88 (July 1984).

The purpose of this study was to review and isolate stepfather findings from research on stepfamilies, and to examine inconsistencies in the literature that may stem from methodological shortcomings.

239   Rosenthal, Kristine M., and Harry F. Keshet. "The Not-Quite Stepmother." *Psychology Today* 12:82–84 (July 1978).

This article is about divorced men's relationships with their children and the women with whom they are intimate. It examines how these women become more involved in decision making as emotional closeness develops.

240   Rosin, Mark Bruce. "Instant Fatherhood: Add Kids & Shake." *Parents* 59:170 (October 1984).

Tells how a stepfather to be perceives his future "instant" stepsons, their reactions to a new father, and how they all grow to know each other.

241   Sadler, Judith DeBoard. "Stepfamilies: An Annotated Bibliography." *Family Relations* 32:149–52 (January 1983).

An annotated bibliography of twenty-one general works, three juvenile books, and ten selected articles, which all deal with the various aspects of stepfamilies.

242   Salk, Lee. "You and Your Stepchildren." *Harper's Bazaar* 108:81 (June 1975).

Dr. Salk answers questions concerning stepfamily relationships.

243   Sands, Melissa. "How Long Before You Don't Mind Sharing Him With His Children?" *Woman* 6:72–73 (June 1985).

Tells how one stepmother adjusts to her role and makes friends with her husband's children. Gives some comments from other stepmothers, and includes ten questions to ask yourself before you marry a man with children.

244   Schulman, Gerda L. "Myths That Intrude on the Adaptation of the Stepfamily." *Social Casework* 53:132–39 (March 1972).

Shows how the adjustment problems existing in the reconstituted stepfamily are complicated by the existence of certain myths, such as the "wicked stepmother" and "instant love." These myths put undue stress on stepfamilies, and the author believes that family treatment is helpful for such troubled families.

245   Stark, Gail U. "Seven on a Honeymoon." *Parents* 46:44–45 (May 1971).

Tells how one remarried couple, each with children from the previous marriage, adjusted to their new life-style. Includes five guidelines for remarried couples.

246   "Stepparenting Problems: The Best Ways to Solve Them." *Good Housekeeping* 198:192 (January 1984).

Covers the most common problems occurring in stepfamilies, with advice from experts on how to work out these problems. Some areas discussed are: replacing a lost parent, adoption and inheritance rights, grandparents' rights, and health care.

247   Stern, Phyllis Noerager. "Stepfather Families: Integration Around Child Discipline." *Issues in Mental Health Nursing* 1:49–56 (1978).

Describes the one-and-a-half to two-year integration period of the stepfather stepfamily.

248   Stuart, Richard B., and Barbara Jacobson. "Stepparenting: Everyday Myths and Avoidable Pitfalls." *Ladies Home Journal* 102:54 (October 1985).

Excerpted from the authors' book, *Second Marriage: Make It Happy! Make It Last!* (see listing 361). This article serves as a guide for second families on such issues as: how to avoid problems at the start, different parenting styles, different rules in different homes, and time alone for remarried parents.

249   Turnbull, Sharon K., and James M. Turnbull. "To Dream the Impossible Dream: An Agenda for Discussion With Stepparents." *Family Relations* 32:227–30 (April 1983).

This article was written from the authors' own experiences as stepparents and their work with stepparenting couples. Suggested guidelines to begin discussions with stepparents are included.

250   Visher, Emily B., and John S. Visher. "Children in Stepfamilies." *Psychiatric Annals* 12:832–36 (September 1982).

Describes the reactions of children to separation and divorce by age groupings. General problems are also included, such as divided loyalties and two sets of rules.

251   ———. "Common Problems of Stepparents and Their Spouses." *American Journal of Orthopsychiatry* 48:252–62 (April 1978).

Four common myths that impede family functioning are identified and described. Case examples are provided.

252   Walker, Kenneth N., and Lillian Messinger. "Remarriage After Divorce: Dissolution and Reconstruction of Family Boundaries." *Family Process* 18:185–92 (June 1979).

The nuclear and remarriage family models are compared. Discussions with remarried group members provide illustrations of this process and suggest solutions to some of the problems confronting remarried family members.

253   Watrous, Peter. "Step-etiquette." *Psychology Today* 18:80 (January 1984).

Points out that we haven't experienced the fragmented family long enough to establish a universal code of behavior based on tradition. Some references are given, however, on where to go for help on steprelation etiquette: *Miss Manner's Guide to Excruciatingly Correct Behavior*, by Judith Martin; *Class Acts*, by Eve Drobot; and of course, works by Emily Post and Amy Vanderbilt.

254   Wilson, Kenneth, Louis A. Zurcher, and Diana McAdams. "Stepfathers and Stepchildren: An Exploratory Analysis From Two National Surveys." *Journal of Marriage and the Family* 37:526–36 (August 1975).

The findings from both national surveys were merged to demonstrate that there were no substantial differences between individuals who have experienced stepfather families and individuals who have not.

4
Adoptive & Foster Care Families

A. Books and Pamphlets

255 *Adopting Children with Special Needs.* Edited by Patricia J. Kravik. Riverside, CA: North American Council on Adoptable Children, 1976. 72 pp.

> Contains one- or two-page sketches, mostly written by adoptive parents. They write about children with Downs Syndrome, children with cleft palates, and children with mental retardation or severe emotional disturbances. The stories describe adoptive parents who are middle class, lower income, or handicapped themselves. The last sections of the book contain resources for children with special needs amd definitions of some common handicapping conditions.

256 *Adopting Children with Special Needs: A Sequel.* Edited by Linda Dunn. Washington, DC: North American Council on Adoptable Children, 1983. 95 pp.

> Begins with a collection of personal narrative articles on the adoption of children with special needs, followed by a section written by the children. Includes resources for success and an annotated bibliography.

257 *Adoption: Current Issues and Trends.* Edited by Paul Sachdev. Toronto: Butterworths, 1984. 304 pp.

> Consists of twenty original essays which examine a variety of issues pertinent to the field of adoption. It is divided into four parts: "Philosophy and Concepts" provides an overview of the philosophy of adoptive services and major developments in Canadian adoption practice; "Process in Adoption, includes data from the United States and Canada, and focuses on social agen-

cies' requirements and procedures for recruiting parents for children needing adoption; "Dilemma in Adoptions"; and "The Current Scene and Future Outlook highlights some of the service areas, such as stepparent adoption, and identifies trends and developments.

258 *Adoption: Essays in Social Policy, Law and Sociology.* Edited by Philip Bean. New York: Tavistock, 1984. 313 pp.

A collection of articles by authors from the United Kingdom and the United States. It is divided into three sections: adoption and social policy, adoption and the law, and transcultural adoption. Some areas of note are: access to original birth records, adoption of older children, English position on stepparent adoptions, artificial conception, and adoption of black children by white parents in the United States.

259 Bolles, Edmund Blair. *The Penguin Adoption Handbook: A Guide to Creating Your New Family.* New York: Viking, 1984. 253 pp.

Explains adopting through adoption agencies. Covers the special problems of prospective adoptive parents who belong to ethnic or religious minorities or who are single or previously divorced. Includes an agency directory and a state-by-state listing of some legal aspects of adoption.

260 Canape, Charlene. *Adoption: Parenthood Without Pregnancy.* New York: Holt, 1986. 246 pp.

All aspects of adoption, from the decision to adopt to telling the adopted child, are covered. Offers procedural advice and emotional support for several types of adoptions, including: agency, independent, foreign, single-parent, and special–needs children. Appendixes list agencies and support groups for persons who adopt.

261 Carbino, Rosemarie. *Foster Parenting: An Updated Review of the Literature.* New York: Child Welfare League, 1980. 43 pp.

Updates Delores A. Taylor and Philip Starr, "Foster Parenting: An Integrative Review of the Literature." *(Child Welfare* 46:371– 85, July 1967.) Carbino reconsiders former issues; analyzes new issues and trends in practice, policy, and research as reflected in the literature; and presents some policy and research questions which emerge from this analysis.

262 Cautley, Patricia Woodward. *New Foster Parents: The First Experience.* New York: Human Sciences Press, 1980. 287 pp.

> Studies 115 families in Minnesota, Wisconsin, and Illinois who received their first foster children, ages six to twelve. Families were followed for eighteen months, or as long as placement lasted. Contains summaries of the natural development of foster families at one, three, and twelve months after placement. Also includes interviews with parents and caseworkers. Data is analyzed to determine which characteristics predict successful foster homes and what problems contribute to the failure of placement when parents request removal?

263 Dickerson, Martha Ufford. *Our Four Boys: Foster Parenting Retarded Teenagers.* Syracuse, NY: Syracuse University Press, 1978. 222 pp.

> Tells the story of Martha and Wade Dickerson, parents of two grown children of their own, who became foster parents to four teenage boys who had been institutionalized for most of their lives. Each boy was considered to be severely mentally retarded. Recounts the plans, joys, challenges, and frustrations of both the Dickersons and the boys, over a three-year period, while the boys learned to participate in a family and become independent.

264 DuPrau, Jeanne. *Adoption: The Facts, Feelings, and Issues of a Double Heritage.* New York: Messner, 1981. 127 pp.

> Discusses the legal and emotional aspects of the adoption process and examines the current movement for giving adoptees free access to their adoption records. Topics included are transracial adoptions, black-market babies, and hard-to-place children. Explores why people choose to adopt and why parents choose to give up a child.

265 *Foster Care: Current Issues, Policies, and Practices.* Edited by Martha J. Cox and Roger D. Cox. Norwood, NJ: Ablex Publishing Co., 1985. 245 pp.

> A collection of writings to help facilitate the understanding of, and progress toward finding solutions to some of the complex problems involved with foster care. Some topics covered are standards for judicial determination in maltreatment cases, biological families and foster care, and foster parent training.

266   Gill, Owen, and Barbara Jackson. *Adoption and Race: Black,
Asian, and Mixed Race Children.* New York: St. Martin's Press,
1983. 151 pp.

Examines the lives and experiences of children adopted by parents of a different racial origin than from their own. This work
attempts to see how racial background has been defined and dealt
with inside the families.

267   Gilman, Lois. *The Adoption Resource Book.* New York: Harper,
1984. 318 pp.

Presents adoption policies, procedures, and alternatives, along
with information about agency policies and procedures, procedures and issues related to foreign adoptions, and listings of
various agencies and support groups.

268   Hallenbeck, Carol A. *Our Child: Preparation for Parenting in
Adoption, Instructor's Guide.* Wayne, PA: Our Child Press, 1984.
230 pp.

An instructor's guide for parents planning to adopt. The first four
chapters lay the groundwork for the four sessions covered in
chapters 5 through 8. Appendixes include forms, audiovisual
aids, resources, bibliography, and notes.

269   Inglis, Kate. *Living Mistakes: Mothers Who Consented to Adoption.*
Boston: Allen & Unwin, 1984. 195 pp.

Records the experiences of women who, over a period of more
than thirty years, relinquished their parental rights and their
children through adoption.

270   Jewett, Claudia L. *Adopting the Older Child.* Cambridge: Harvard
University Press, 1978. 308 pp.

The author, a family counselor and mother of seven adopted
children, uses hypothetical case histories to present the process
of adoption, from the first tentative decision through the waiting
period, placement, and follow-up. Discusses problems encountered in rearing older children and offers solutions.

271   Johnson, Patricia Irwin. *An Adopter's Advocate.* Fort Wayne, IN:
Perspective Press, 1984. 84 pp.

Addresses adoptive issues primarily from the point of view of the
infertile couple. Highlights some of the problems the adoptive

system faces with the intent of faciliating improvements and suggesting some changes in the adoption process.

272   Kadushin, Alfred. *Adopting Older Children*. New York: Columbia University Press, 1970. 245 pp.

Reports on an extensive study of ninety-one families who legally adopted children between the ages of five and twelve. The author draws on interviews with parents and parent-response forms which focused on the satisfactions and dissatisfactions of adopting an older child.

273   Kirk, H. David. *Adoptive Kinship: Modern Institution in Need of Reform*. Toronto: Butterworths, 1981. 173 pp.

A sociological look at adoptive families and the special relationships they share. Advocates reform of adoption policies, practices, and institutional arrangements. Tells about the adoptees' search for parents, and the response to it by adoptive parents, birth-parents, social work professionals, and legislative bodies. Gives a detailed examination of the differenes between birth parenthood and adoptive parenthood.

274   Koh, Frances M. *Oriental Children in American Homes: How Do They Adjust?* Minneapolis: East-West Press, 1984. 132 pp.

Explains how Asian children's cultural differences influence adjustment in their Caucasian adoptive families.

275   Lifton, Betty Jean. *Lost & Found: The Adoption Experience*. New York: Dial Press, 1983. 303 pp.

This book is a plea for the right of the adoptees to know about their true origins. The author, an adoptee, has drawn upon her own experiences as well as those of adult adoptees, birth mothers and fathers, and adoptive parents, to trace the psychological journey of the adoptee.

276   *Long-term Foster Care*. Jane Rowe et al. New York: St. Martin's Press, 1984. 255 pp.

Reports on research which reviews the cases of two hundred children in long-term foster-family care in England. Recommendations are made in regard to both management and social work practice, but fall short of the current U.S. Adoption Assistance and Child Welfare Act of 1980 (P.L. 96–272). Discusses family contact and growing up in a foster family, relations as foster parents, and the future of long-term foster care.

277   Macmanus, Sheila. *Adoption Book.* New York: Paulist Press, 1984. 131 pp.

Written for people who wish to adopt and for others who wish to support adoption. It is divided into four parts: "Adoption Overview"; "Adoption Issues," including sections on open adoption and single parent adoption; "Adoption Resources"; and "Federal/ Corporate/State Activity, Laws and Policies." An appendix section is included.

278   Meezan, William, and Joan F. Shireman. *Care and Commitment: Foster Parent Adoption Decisions.* Albany: State University of New York Press, 1985. 247 pp.

This book poses the question of why some long-term foster parents choose to adopt their foster children, when they become free for adoption, while others do not. Points out the role played by the social worker in adoptive planning and outlines ways in which the worker can be most effective in planning permanency for children.

279   Melina, Lois Ruskai. *Raising Adopted Children: A Manual for Adoptive Parents.* New York: Harper, 1986. 288 pp.

Exploration of adoption issues including bonding and attachment, family adjustment, and contact with biological relatives.

280   Nelson, Katherine A. *On the Frontier of Adoption: A Study of Special-Needs Adoptive Families.* New York: Research Center, Child Welfare League, 1985. 110 pp.

This study's purpose is to update and broaden the knowledge about families who adopt children with special needs. It is organized into six chapters, starting with a review of the historical and research context and ending with a summary of major findings, a discussion of their implications for practice, and twenty-five recommendations.

281   Niles, Reg. *Adoption Agencies, Orphanages and Maternity Homes: An Historical Directory.* Garden City, NY: Phileas Deigh Corp., 1981. 2 vols. in 1 (478 pp).

A directory to help adoptees and natural parents discover the location of records which relate to their past. Institutions in all fifty states and Canada are included.

282   Plumez, Jacqueline Hornor. *Successful Adoption: A Guide to Finding a Child and Raising a Family.* New York: Harmony Books, 1982. 234 pp.

A step-by-step guide which covers the adoption process. Helps parents to analyze whether or not adoption is a realistic option for them. Supplemented with lists of state adoption agencies and resources for foreign adoption plus state-by-state information about adoption laws and waiting periods.

283   Powledge, Fred. *The New Adoption Maze and How to Get Through It.* St. Louis: C. V. Mosby, 1985. 314 pp.

A guide to the traditional private or agency adoption process. Discusses "open adoption" and promotes the changing of attitudes and procedures. Includes an annotated bibliography.

284   Roberts, January, and Diane C. Robie. *Open Adoption and Open Placement.* Brooklyn Park, MN: Adoption Press, 1981. 90 pp.

The authors, both adoptive parents, include in this work the results of their research, and review the studies done on all aspects of adoption. It includes a "Source Guide" and bibliography.

285   Silber, Kathleen, and Phylis Speedlin. *Dear Birthmother: Thank You for Our Baby.* San Antonio: Corona, 1983. 192 pp.

Experiences in open adoption told partly through letters between birth parents and adoptive parents. Stresses that adoption is a life-time experience for the adoptive parents, the adoptee, and the birth parents. Recommendations for a myth-free adoption program are given in the second part.

286   Smith, Dorothy W., and Laurie Nehls Sherwen. *Mothers and Their Adopted Children: The Bonding Process.* New York: Tiresias Press, 1983. 160 pp.

Data for this book came from tape-recordings of sixty interviews with mothers, fifty-seven questionnaire responses, and thirty-three questionnaires completed by adopted children over the age of ten. Asks questions about how bonding theories relate to adopted children, bonding with an older adopted child, and what happens when you adopt a child that is handicapped or racially different from oneself?

287   Sorosky, Arthur D., Annette Baran, and Reuben Pannor. *The Adoption Triangle: Sealed or Opened Records, How They Affect Adoptees, Birth Parents, and Adoptive Parents.* Garden City, NJ: Anchor Books, 1984. 237 pp.

Based on the studies of adoptees, birth parents, and adoptive parents, the authors (a child psychiatrist, a psychotherapist, and a social worker) discuss the effects of secret records on the adopted, adoptive parents, and relinquishing parents. Conclusions and recommendations for change are found in the last chapter.

288   Van Why, Elizabeth Wharton. *Adoption Bibliography and Multi-Ethnic Sourcebook.* Hartford: Open Door Society of Connecticut, 1977. 320 pp.

This partially annotated bibliography identifies books, dissertations, articles, pamphlets, and reports from agencies and conferences that deal with adoption or foster care. The Second part annotates materials likely to appeal to children.

289   Winkler, Robin, and Margaret Van Keppel. *Relinquishing Mothers in Adoption: Their Long-Term Adjustment.* Melbourne, Australia: Institue of Family Studies, 1984. 100 pp.

Focuses on women who give up their babies for adoption. Investigates the effects of relinquishing a child on the adjustment of the mother and those factors which are believed to either facilitate or impede adjustment to relinquishment.

290   Wishard, Laurie, and William Wishard. *Adoption: The Grafted Tree.* New York: Avon Books, 1981. 198 pp.

A guide to all aspects of the adoption process for birth parents, prospective adoptive parents, and adopted children and their families. Hypothetical examples illustrate the situations and options available to these families. Discusses the factors that go with making the decision to adopt a child or to put a child up for adoption, the adjustment period for adoptive parents and adoptees, and issues facing natural parents whose children have been adopted by others. A section devoted to adopted adults' curiosity about their biological roots is at the end.

B. Articles in Periodicals

291   Berman, Claire. "How Open Adoption Works Out." *McCall's* 110:56 (December 1982).

Tells how an adoptive mother and a birth mother have been handling their seven-year open adoption experience. Gives some of the advantages and disadvantages of open adoption as compared to the traditional adoption system.

292   Bunin, Sherry. "Black, White & Tan Family." *Parents* 59:88 (April 1984).

The adoptive white mother of two black children describes the challenges and rewards of raising a multiracial family.

293   Canape, Charlene. "The Forgotten Parents: When Working Women Adopt." *Working Woman* 10:136 (June 1985).

States the case for adoptive mothers and fathers who are not disabled by pregnancy and therefore do not qualify for any paid work leave under existing maternity-leave disability laws. Criticizes the Pregnancy Discrimination Act of 1978 which labels pregnancy a disability and stresses the need for a law that would guarantee both biological and adoptive mothers a reasonable leave. Names some companies that do provide adoption-subsidy programs such as IBM, Control Data Corporation, Hallmark Cards, Pitney Bowes, and Digital Equipment Corporation.

294   Churchman, Deborah. "The Debate Over Open Adoption." *Public Welfare* 44:11–14 (Spring 1986).

Discusses the pros and cons of open adoption, as well as giving statistics and information about adoptive parents, birth parents, and teenage pregnancy/parenthood.

295   Eastman, Kathleen Sampson. "Foster Families: A Comprehensive Bibliography." *Child Welfare* 64:565–85 (November/December 1985).

A bibliography of approximately 450 citations of books and periodical articles on the subject of foster families, with no annotations. Useful to social work researchers, educators, practitioners, students, and foster care families.

296   Flynn, Laurie M., and Wilfred Hamm. "TEAM: Parent-Agency
Partnerships in Adoption Services." *Children Today* 12:2–5
(March/April 1983).

Explains the TEAM Project (Training and Education in Adoption
Methods) which was funded by the Children's Bureau, Administration for Children, Youth, and Families, in 1979 as part of the
NACAC's National Partnership for Permanence Project. (NACAC
is a national organization which represents over five hundred
local adoptive parent groups, organized in 1974).

297   Frank, John K., Jr., with Laurie M. Flynn. "Group Therapy for
Adopted Adolescents and Their Families." *Children Today* 12:11–
13 (March/ April 1983).

Tells of the Tressler-Lutheran Service Associates in York, Pennsylvania, and the successes it has had in placing preadolescent and
adolescent children. Explains their group therapy program for
families and their workshop for social workers. Includes a case
example.

298   Geissinger, Shirley. "Adoptive Parents' Attitudes Toward Open
Birth Records." *Family Relations* 33:579–85 (October 1984).

Investigates the adoptive parents' attitudes toward the "open
birth record issue," which would revise current law by allowing
adult adoptees access to their previously sealed adoption records.

299   Gil, Eliana, and Karen Bogart. "Foster Children Speak Out."
Children Today 11:7–9 (January/February 1982).

The study described in this article, and undertaken by the San
Francisco Child Abuse Council allows foster children the opportunity to express their perceptions about the quality of care they
receive.

300   Hornby, Helaine. "Foster Care and the Power of the State."
Children Today 10:2–5 (March/April 1981).

This article is a result of the governor of Maine's task force to
study all phases of the foster care program by reading state laws
and policies, holding public hearings, interviewing foster children, and collecting questionnaire data from foster parents,
judges, state social workers, and foster children. The task force
report acknowledged the following items for program improve-
ment: the need for time-limited decisions, the need for more
specialized foster homes, and the need for a termination statute.

301   ———."Why Adoptions Disrupt . . . and What Agencies Can Do to Prevent It." *Children Today* 15:7–11 (July/August 1986).

Examines disrupted adoptions (defined as any adoptive placement initiated and terminated within a 2½-year period), and looks at what went wrong. Reveals differences in the history and background of the children who had disrupted adoptions versus those who did not.

302   Hudgens, Leann D. "I Gave My Daughter Away—and Found Her Again." *Ladies Home Journal* 97:23–24 (March 1980).

A mother's true story as told to her daughter, the author, about why she gave Leann up for adoption and how they were reunited after twenty-five years of separation.

303   Kantrowitz, Barbara, with Elisa Williams. "Life with Two Mothers: Some Would-Be Parents Opt for 'Open' Adoption." *Newsweek* 107:86 (12 May 1986).

Explores the new kind of extended family with the birth mother playing a small but significant role in the life of the child she gave up for adoption. The birth mother and adoptive parents form a relationship and keep in touch through letters, phone calls, and visits with the children. Professionals in social work give their views and discuss the pros and cons of the open adoption arrangement.

304   Mushlin, Michael B., Louis Levitt, and Lauren Anderson. "Court Ordered Foster Family Care Reform: A Case Study." *Child Welfare* 65:141–54 (March/April 1986).

Examines the implications of G. L. v. Zumwalt, a case which resulted in a far-reaching consent decree that mandates specific reforms in policy and practice to be implemented by a public social welfare agency in its delivery of services to foster children and their families.

305   Pannor, Reuben, and Annette Baran. "Open Adoption as Standard Practice." *Child Welfare* 63:245–50 (May/June 1984).

The authors move beyond open adoption and call for an end to all closed adoptions. They advocate that all adoptions should fall within the open adoption framework, allowing birth parents and adoptive parents to meet and exchange identifying information. Both sets of parents retain the right of continuing contact and having access to knowledge on behalf of the child.

306 Pasztor, Eileen Mayers, and Elyse M. Burgers. "Finding and Keeping More Foster Parents." *Children Today* 11:2–5 (March/April 1982).

Describes some policies and practices necessary for agency recruitment efforts to be effective, and discusses how foster parents may be encouraged to remain in a program for longer periods of time.

307 Rest, Ellen Ryan, and Kenneth W. Watson. "Growing Up in Foster Care." *Child Welfare* 63:291–306 (July/August 1984).

A survey of a small sample of adults who grew up in long-term foster care under the supervision of an agency that provided supportive counseling. Shows that the experience of "impermanence" did not impair their abilities to lead independent, outwardly satisfactory lives, but it did leave them susceptible to an impaired self-image from the deeply felt stigma of foster care, a difficulty in establishing emotional intimacy, and an unresolved sense of loss.

308 Schor, David P., and Charles M. Abel. "Back to Basics in Health Care for Foster Children." *Children Today* 14:13–16 (May/June 1985).

Discusses some of the special health care needs of children in family foster care and outlines some steps that foster parents can take to help meet these needs.

309 "Stepping Out of Foster Care into Independent Living." Eileen M. Timberlake et al. *Children Today* 15:32–35 (March/April 1986).

Describes the project, "Stepping Out of Foster Care Into a More Self-Sufficient Independent Living Network," conducted by the Baltimore County Department of Social Services and funded by the Children's Bureau. Designed to prepare older adolescents to move out of foster care into responsible living situations.

310 "Update: Adoption Opportunities Projects. O. Delmar Weathers et al. *Children Today* 12:20–23 (March/April 1983).

Explains programs and projects initiated by the Children's Bureau, Administration for Children, Youth and Families, in order to facilitate the elimination of barriers to adoption and to provide permanent and loving home environments for children with special needs. Includes the development of model state adoption legislation programs, establishment of a national adoption infor-

mation exchange system, a study of unlicensed adoption placement, and provision of technical assistance through ten adoption
resource centers.

311   Veronico, Anthony J. "One Church, One Child: Placing Children with Special Needs." *Children Today* 12:6–10 (March/April
1983).

Describes the efforts to reverse the trend and effect changes
geared to increasing the number of black adoptions in Illinois.
The "One Church, One Child" program, started by a black priest,
Father George Clements of Holy Angel Church in Chicago, urged
every black church in Chicago to accept the challenge and responsibility of having one member of each congregation adopt a black
child. Lists the positive outcomes of the project.

312   Wagner, Doris, as told to John Grossman. "1,000 Children—
And I've Loved Them All." *Redbook* 164:56 (December 1984).

The story of a childless couple who, during the last thirty-five
years, have adopted infants and acted as foster parents to orphaned children, abused children, and children of unfit parents,
including American Indian, Spanish, mulatto and black children.
They have cared for as many as seventeen kids in their home at
one time. Tells how the Wagners became involved, coped, organized the daily routine, celebrated Christmas, had a big family
reunion, and parted from their foster children.

313   Wells, Kathleen, and Paula Reshotko. "Cooperative Adoption:
An Alternative to Independent Adoption." *Child Welfare* 65:177–
88 (March/April 1986).

Describes an agency-supported independent adoption program
which may have significance for other adoption programs and
policies. Provides program assumptions and goals, key design
features, and problems experienced in implementing the program. Also discusses the program's impact upon a traditional
agency adoption program.

314   Williams, Elisa, Peter McKillop, and Diane Weathers. "Adoption vs Abortion." *Newsweek* 107:39 (28 April 1986).

The Rocky Mountain chapter of Planned Parenthood in Iowa met
to discuss adoption services. This is thought to be the first such
gathering to propose that family-planning funds be used to help
subsidize adoptions.

5
Divorce & Remarriage

A. Books

315 Albrecht, Stan L., Howard M. Bahr, and Kristen L. Goodman.
Divorce and Remarriage: Problems, Adaptations, and Adjustments.
Westport, CT: Greenwood Press, 1983. 211 pp.

> Examines the divorce experience from the perspective of the
> individual who actually experiences it. Covers how the decision
> is made to end an unsuccessful marriage, the adjustment process
> after the divorce, and remarriage.

316 Arendell, Terry. *Mothers and Divorce: Legal, Economic, and Social
Dilemmas.* Berkeley: University of California Press, 1986.
221 pp.

> Presents research literature, statistics and interviews with sixty
> divorced mothers to explore the problems divorced women expe-
> rience, such as long work days and poor pay, loneliness of being
> single, the pain of watching a child's induction into poverty, and
> finding the courage to face it all.

317 Bass, Howard L., and M. L. Rein. *Divorce or Marriage: A Legal
Guide.* Englewood Cliffs, NJ: Prentice-Hall, 1976. 209 pp.

> Offers answers to many legal questions regarding marriage, di-
> vorce, and custody. In the section on custody the authors suggest
> that parents sign a written agreement containing provisions in-
> tended to help minimize the negative effects on children.

318 Bernard, Janie, and Harold Hackney. *Untying the Knot: A Guide
to Civilized Divorce.* Minneapolis: Winston, 1983. 189 pp.

> Presents family system concepts, the divorce process with special
> attention to dealing with the legal system, making decisions about

children and coparenting, being a survivor rather than a victim, and relating to ex-spouses. Appendixes include a reference list of additional books on divorce and how to seek information on how to seek professional help.

319   *A Bibliography on Divorce.* Compiled and edited by Stan Israel. New York: Block Publishing, 1974. 300 pp.

The author provides lengthy annotations for over 150 titles published from the 1940s to the 1970s on divorce materials. It is divided into three sections: legal, sociological, and religious aspects of divorce.

320   Blades, Joan. *Family Mediation: Cooperative Divorce Settlement.* Englewood Cliffs, NJ: Prentice-Hall, 1985. 239 pp.

Written for the divorcing client, the attorney, and the mental health professional. The first section introduces the fundamentals of mediation. The second section gives information on five basic models of mediation so that both professionals and couples can select the mediation style that is best for them. The third section is a compendium of various mediators' forms, brochures, training materials, sample agreements, and referral resources.

321   Cassidy, Robert. *What Every Man Should Know About Divorce.* Washington, DC: New Republic Books, 1977. 247.

Offers practical advice and emotional support for the divorced man.

322   Cauhape, Elizabeth. *Fresh Starts: Men and Women After Divorce.* New York: Basic Books, 1983. 338 pp.

A study of the effects of divorce at midlife that also examines the opportunities for growth as well as the problems that must be solved either as remarried or single, alone or with children.

323   Cherlin, Andrew J. *Marriage, Divorce, Remarriage.* Cambridge: Harvard University Press, 1981. 142 pp.

Points out that the family, while changing its character, is as stable as ever, and that the overwhelming majority of Americans are committed to family. The author analyzes the marriage and divorce data of the 1950s baby boom—with its typical earlier marriage age and slower divorce rate—and the 1970s trends of later marriages, fewer children, and divorces. He concludes with a discussion of the changing characteristics of black and white families.

324   *The Divorce Book.* Edited by Kirk and Susan Johnson. Oakland, CA: New Harbinge, 1984. 264 pp.

Written for people who are going through a divorce and for professionals who want the tools to help them. The first section begins with emotional survival, including the stages of recovery and an exploration of the mourning process, changing relationships with friends and family, and healthy ways of resolving conflict with an ex-spouse. Section two is a legal primer of basic information about your options in a divorce – do-it-yourself, lawyer-assisted, or mediated – and how to choose the right option for you. Reviews major legal issues of divorce and how to select your attorney. Section three reviews research on the effects of divorce on children. Section four is about surviving as a single: dealing with the economics of divorce, problems of isolation, issues of sexuality, and remarriage.

325   Edelman, Alice, and Roz Stuzin. *How to Survive a Second Marriage (or Save a First One).* Secaucus, NJ: L. Stuart, 1980. 269 pp.

Personal stories, told by people who have learned to cope in a second marriage, that can help and give confidence to the remarried family.

326   Fox, Elaine. *The Marriage-Go-Round: An Exploratory Study of Multiple Marriage.* Lanham, MD: University Press of America, 1983. 187 pp.

This study examines the history of "multiple marriers" (those having more than two marriages and divorces), and investigates the early years, first and second marriages, and other aspects of persons who remarry numerous times.

327   Friedman, James T. *The Divorce Handbook: Your Basic Guide to Divorce.* New York: Random House, 1984. 170 pp.

Covers the legal aspects of divorce in a question-and-answer format with worksheets and checklists that should simplify the divorce process for a person facing the legal maze for the first time.

328   Furstenberg, Frank F., and Graham B. Spainer, *Recycling the Family: Remarriage After Divorce.* Beverly Hills: Sage Publications, 1984. 288 pp.

Assesses how family images and family relations have been altered by both the expectation and the occurrence of marital instability. Most of the chapters report on findings from a study of the transition from divorce to remarriage from 1977 to 1979 in Centre County, Pennsylvania.

329 Gettleman, Susan, and Janet Markowitz. *The Courage to Divorce.* New York: Simon & Schuster, 1974. 285 pp.

A researched look at our social biases against divorce, with an eye to helping mismatched mates feel less guilty about dissolving their poor relationships.

330 Goldstein, Sol. *Divorced Parenting: How to Make It Work.* New York: Dutton, 1984. 200 pp.

Dr. Goldstein is a psychiatrist and psychoanalyst who has counseled divorcing couples and their children for over fifteen years. He offers here solutions to the most commmon, day-in, day-out problems faced by parents and children in this troubled time of transition, such as: How to tell the children? How to handle holidays and school events? How to go beyond surivial to an enriching parent-child relationship? How to handle postdivorce dating and remarriage?

331 Goode, William Josiah. *Women in Divorce.* Westport, CT: Greenwood Press, 1978. 381 pp.

Discusses what to expect of oneself after the trauma of divorce, and how to deal with practical and psychological problems that occur after divorce.

332 Halem, Lynne Carol. *Separated & Divorced Women.* Westport, CT: Greenwood Press, 1982. 335 pp.

Examines the legal, emotional, and economic effects of separation and divorce on middle-class American women. Halem, works for a human services consulting firm. She role-plays a fictitious separated woman "Sheila Ash," whose identity has been statistically structured from divorce figures. The author, as Sheila, seeks aid through a variety of community services. She hunts for jobs, legal aid, daycare centers, and places to live. Includes interviews with divorced or separated women, and a few men going through divorce.

333 Haynes, John M. *Divorce Mediation: A Practical Guide for Therapists and Counselors.* New York; Springer, 1981. 193 pp.

Proposes that people can be empowered to negotiate their own divorce settlement outside the legal system and in a nonadversarial way. Mediation is to be viewed as an extension of the clinical resources of the family therapists. Outlines a session-by-session process, discussing such issues as legitimate feelings goal setting, and articulating hidden agendas.

334   Hocking, David L. *Marrying Again: A Guide for Christians.* Old Tappan, NJ: Revell, 1983. 157 pp.

A guide for counselors and parents which includes biblical teachings and advice. It is designed to help divorced people in decision making regarding their new lives, and advise on how to adjust.

335   Hoffman, Bob. *No One Is to Blame: Getting a Loving Divorce from Mom and Dad.* Palo Alto, CA: Science and Behavior Books, 1979. 221 pp.

Explains the therapy method for psychological and spiritual development called the Quadrinity Process.

336   Hootman, Marcia, and Patt Perkins. *How to Forgive Your Ex-Husband and Get on With Your Life.* Garden City, NY: Doubleday, 1983. 176 pp.

A guide written to help women constructively resolve anger during the critical time following a divorce. Reassures her that she is not alone.

337   Hunt, Bernice, and Morton Hunt. *Prime Time: A Guide to the Pleasures and Opportunities of The New Middle Age.* New York: Stein and Day, 1975. 225 pp.

Both of the Hunts remarried in their fifties, and they use their personal experiences and those of their friends to demonstrate that, despite widowhood and divorce, new relationships and pleasures are possible to develop in the years from forty to sixty-five.

338   ———. *The Divorce Experience.* New York: New American Library, 1979. 306 pp.

Case histories, for the divorced and remarried, of men and women and how they adapted or failed to adapt to postmarried life. The chapter "Sexual Behavior in the New World" provides insights to people who are struggling with their own sexual identity.

339   Irving, Howard H. *Divorce Mediation: A Rational Alternative to the Adversary System.* New York: University Books, 1981. 188 pp.

Offers divorce mediation as an alternative method of settling family disputes without litigation. It is a self-determining process for resolving issues resulting from divorce and is an alternative option to the adversary system. Presents a three-phase procedure of mediation and gives attention to interviewing skills. Chapters of note are included on historical custody issues and joint custody.

340   Joiner, E. Earl. *A Christian Considers Divorce and Remarriage.* Nashville, TN: Broadman's Press, 1983. 154 pp.

This book was inspired by responses received from hundreds of divorcees attending conferences on divorce and remarriage conducted by the author, who is a Christian minister. It examines what both the Old and New Testaments teach on divorce and the attitude of the Church toward divorce throughout history. The book is directed to the many persons in the process of breaking up, pastors, divorcees, counselors of divorce, and friends of divorcees.

341   Krantzler, Mel. *Creative Divorce: A New Opportunity for Personal Growth.* New York: New American Library, 1975. 240 pp.

A book which explains how to end up friends instead of enemies after the divorce. Includes a chapter on new commitments and one on seeing the person in the child.

342   Kressel, Kenneth. *The Process of Divorce: How Professionals and Couples Negotiate Settlements.* New York: Basic Books, 1985. 349 pp.

Describes ways in which couples negotiate their divorce settlements and how that process can be enhanced or hindered by various "divorce professionals," such as attorneys, therapists, and divorce mediators. Also cites the lack of child support payments as evidence of the failure of most divorce negotiations to foster cooperation in the "postdivorce" family and the deterioration of the relationship between children and their absent father.

343   Lebowitz, Marcia Lepman. *The Children's Divorce Center Reading Guide.* Woodbridge, CT: Children's Divorce Center, 1985. 31 leaves.

An annotated bibliography of books for children on all aspects of divorce and remarriage.

344 Little, Marilyn. *Family Breakup*. San Francisco: Jossey-Bass, 1982. 235 pp.

Traces the intact family through the separation phase and to its postdivorce situation. Adapted from the author's dissertation, this work includes interviews with twenty men and twenty women. The information in this study was used to create six family patterns and five types of parenting roles. The author explains how each family type copes with the developmental stresses of family life and how the children act out the roles, in the developmental process, as stabalizer, competitor, hostage, caretaker, or obstacle. The introductory chapter traces the historical changes in legalities and customs of custody. Designed for professionals working with families entering the divorce process to give a more complete view of the family system approaching the brink of breakup. The author's research suggests there is no one way to split families and that each family's unique pattern and interaction prior to the breakup calls for more flexibility from professionals working with such families. The final chapter deals with the practical and legal considerations of families facing disruption.

345 Lorimer, Anne, and Philip M. Feldman. *Remarriage: A Guide for Singles, Couples, and Families, Including Stepchildren, In-Laws, Ex-Spouses, Possessions, Housing, Finances & More*. Philadelphia: Running Press, 1980. 158.

This book is designed to free its readers from any romantic misconceptions about remarriage by concentrating on its potential problems, as listed in the subtitle, and others: sex, discipline, conflicting life styles, where to live, and overt hostility. Part 3 is devoted to stepfamilies and the dynamics of the interrelationships in these families.

346 Mackin, Theodore. *Divorce and Remarriage: Marriage in the Catholic Church*. New York: Paulist Press, 1984. 565 pp.

Examines, from its beginings to the present, the Roman Catholic doctrine and discipline concerning divorce and remarriage.

347 McKenney, Mary. *Divorce: A Selected Annotated Bibliography*. Metuchen, NJ: Scarecrow Press, 1975. 157 pp.

McKenney, a librarian, has listed and annotated 613 items, representing every significant writing on divorce that she could find in English, through 1972.

348   McNamara, Lynne, and Jennifer Morrison. *Separation, Divorce, and After.* St. Lucia: University of Queensland Press, 1982. 192 pp.

This book was written for people who are considering or are already involved in separation and divorce. Problems that lead to the ending of a marriage are discussed. It provides information about how to cope with being single again and the common problems of custody, the possibility of remarriage, and the stepfamily.

349   Messinger, Lillian. *Remarriage: A Family Affair.* New York: Plenum, 1984. 246 pp.

Describes the experiences of individuals involved in ending one marriage and beginning another. Based on a study conducted by the author and her associates at the Clarke Institute of Psychiatry in Toronto, Canada. Presents commonly experienced situations while at the same time emphasizing the uniqueness of each individual family. Discusses stepparenting, decisions regarding child custody, and the limitations of various social institutions in meeting the needs of remarried families. Offers recommendations for change.

350   Neely, Richard. *The Divorce Decision: The Legal and Human Consequences of Ending a Marriage.* New York: McGraw-Hill, 1984. 207 pp.

The author, an expert on divorce law, examines what happens when a couple ends a marriage. He paints a detailed picture of divorce, custody, alimony, property division, living together, palimony, and marriage contracts. The powers and limitations of the judge, the court, and the lawyers are explained with hypothetical examples of the author's point of view.

351   O'Brien, Judith Tate, and Gene O'Brien. *A Redeeming State: A Handbook for Couples Planning Remarriage in the Church.* New York: Paulist Press, 1983. 79 pp.

"A Redeeming State" is a program designed to help couples take an open-eyed approach to their marriages. The program involves using this handbook and meeting with a sponsor couple three times for three hours each time. Some topics are: your former spouse, stepfamily structure, stepparenting, and handling conflict.

352   ———. *A Redeeming State: Leader's Guide for Couples Planning Remarriage in the Church.* New York: Paulist Press, 1983. 37 pp.

This is a guide offered by the Catholic Church for remarried sponsor couples to help engaged couples prepare for remarriage.

It offers a training plan for sponsor couples in part 1, and part 2 outlines the topics to be covered during three meetings with the engaged couple. Some issues addressed are former spouses, stepparenting, and handling conflict.

353   Pino, Christopher J. *Divorce, Remarriage and Blended Families: Divorce, Counseling and Research Perspectives*. Palo Alto, CA: R & E Research Associates, 1981. 128 pp.

Provides practitioners and students of divorce with a set of reviews and research dealing with divorce adjustment and remarriage.

354   *Procedures for Guiding the Divorce Mediation Process*. Edited by John Allen Lemmon. San Francisco: Jossey-Bass, 1984. 89 pp.

Consists of articles taken from the December 1984 issue of the *Mediation Quarterly*. The contributors address the following questions: How does the mediation process balance the power between divorcing spouses? What are the advantages of interdisciplinary team mediation? How does a knowledge of emotional concerns the couple face help the mediator to choose techniques that facilitate agreement?

355   Rothman, Rusty. *How to Find Another Husband . . . by Someone Who Did*. Cincinnati: Writer's Digest Books, 1985. 198 pp.

Answers questions about how to be happy as a single woman and how to find the man with whom you will share a new married life. These answers come from the author's professisonal experience as a social worker and psychotherapist, as well as from her personal experience and interveiws with remarried women. Includes special problems of the single mother and how children can affect your new marriage.

356   Sands, Melissa. *Second Wife's Survival Manual*. New York: Berkley Publishers, 1982. 248 pp.

Designed for the mistress who becomes the wife. This work is divided into four sections: strategies for choosing and making decisions; strategies for living and preparing to be a second wife; new family roles and relationships; and coping with the challenges of becoming a second wife.

357   Schlesinger, Benjamin. *Remarriage: A Review and Annotated Bibliography*. Chicago: Council of Planning Librarians, 1983. 69 pp.

An annotated bibliography which covers remarriage-related topics, such as adjustment, children, counseling, divorce, education, mate selection, homosexuality, myths, older persons, religion, single persons, stepfamily therapy, and widows/widowers.

358   Sell, Kenneth D. *Divorce in the 1970's, A Subject Guide to Books, Articles, Dissertations, Government Documents, and Films on Divorce in the United States, 1970–1976.* Preliminary ed. Salisbury, NC: Catawba College, 1977. 22 pp.

List almost 4,800 items of nonfiction materials on divorce in the United States, taken from 73 indexes/abstracts and 12 unindexed periodicals. The entries include helpful features for obtaining materials, such as order numbers for dissertations available from University Microfilms.

359   Sell, Kenneth D., and Betty H. Sell. *Divorce in the United States, Canada and Great Britain: A Guide to Information Sources.* Detroit: Gale Research Co., 1978. 298 pp.

Volume one in the Gale Social Issues and Social Problems Information Guide series is not a bibliography of books and articles on divorce, but rather a guide to finding such books and articles. The Sells provide discussions of divorce in bibliographic basic reference, as well as abstracting tools, periodical indexes, legal literature, the news media, nonprint media, and fiction.

360   Stewart, Marjabelle Young. *The New Etiquette Guide to Getting Married Again.* New York: St. Martin's Press, 1980. 222 pp.

A guide for second weddings and special wedding ceremonies and receptions. Gives advice on how to cope with the problems and emotions surrounding remarriages, such as becoming a stepparent, forming new relationships with in-laws, merging two households or beginning a new one, merging two careers, making financial arrangements, and drawing up a marriage contract.

361   Stuart, Richard B., and Barbara Jacobson. *Second Marriage: Make It Happy! Make It Last!* New York: Norton, 1985. 247 pp.

Based upon the authors' many years of practicing marriage and family therapy, their own personal experiences of separation and remarriage, and a review of the marriage and family literature. Focuses on solutions rather than problems, with specific suggestions on how to avoid the mistakes and fears of second marriages, describing practical methods for making decisions about how to handle work, money, and stepchildren. Includes a chapter on stepparenting.

362 *Treating the Remarried Family.* Clifford J. Sager et al. New York: Brunner/Mazel, 1983. 388 pp.

A clinical work based on the authors' experiences. It is divided into four sections: Structure and Theory; Treatment for Remarried Families; Special Issues of Remarriage; and a review of the experiences of the authors and others in the area of prevention.

363 U.S. Department of Health, Education and Welfare. *Remarriages: United States.* Hyattsville, MD: National Center for Health Statistics, 1983.

An analysis of national trends in remarriage.

364 Weitzman, Lenore J. *The Divorce Revolution: The Unexpected Social and Economic Consequences for Women and Children in America.* New York: Free Press, 1985. 504 pp.

Based upon interviews with judges, lawyers, and divorced persons in California, and data collected from the state's court dockets. Presents an examination of the social and economic effects of divorce law reform on women and their dependent children.

365 Westoff, Leslie Aldridge. *The Second Time Around: Remarriage in America.* New York: Viking, 1977. 174 pp.

Contains interviews with men, women, and children who have gone through divorce and remarriage. It is both a guide for individuals contemplating a second marriage as well as a source of insight for others, such as in-laws, children, "ex's," and friends.

366 Wilkie, Jane. *The Divorced Woman's Handbook: An Outline for Starting the First Year Alone.* New York: Morrow, 1980. 172 pp.

Focuses on the divorced woman's first year alone, offering some practical advice on such matters as finances, how to change one's name, health, children, work, social life, and moving.

367 *Women in Transition: A Feminist Handbook on Separation and Divorce.* New York: Scribner, 1975. 538 pp.

Looks at many aspects of the separation and divorce problem and suggests solutions. Covers children in transition, what the law says, economic realities of separation and divorce, educational resources, mental health, physical health care, and consumer protection information.

B. Articles in Periodicals

368   Baer, Jean. "Is Sex Better the Second Time Around?" *Harper's Bazaar* 117:116 (October 1984).

Spells out why second marriages are stronger sexually. Includes the problems and pressures of rewedded life and has a section on "sexual etiquette."

369   Bahr, Stephen J. "Impact of Recent Changes in Divorce Laws for Women." *Family Perspective* 20:95–103 (1986)

Reviews the major changes in divorce laws and assesses their impact on women. Assesses two major changes occurring in the past two decades: no-fault divorce laws have been passed in most states, laws have become gender neutral in response to the equal rights movement. Discusses changes to help correct economic inequities faced by divorced women in laws governing child support, pensions, and nonmonetary contributions.

370   Berman, Claire. "What You Should Know Before You Remarry." *Reader's Digest* 125:167–68 (September 1984).

Five common issues that should be faced before marrying the second time are discussed: letting go of the past, sharing values, fitting in children, handling money, and finding time for intimacy.

371   Bernstein, Barton E., and Sheila K. Collins. "Remarriage Counseling: Lawyer and Therapist Help With the Second Time Around." *Family Relations* 34:387–91 (July 1985).

Problems specific to remarrying families with children are summarized from the literature, including such concerns as complex kinship networks, ill-defined rules, and financial and legal issues. Topics included are the family counselor involving an attorney to provide services to remarrying families, options and limitations in the law, premarital agreements, inventories, living trusts, estate planning and postmarital partition. Also identfied are the qualities and skills needed by both lawyers and therapists in serving remarried couples.

372 Bitterman, Catherine M. "The Multimarriage Family." *Social Casework* 49:218–21 (April 1968)

Examines the causes of divorce and reasons for remarriage after death and divorce. Problem areas of remarriage covered are: steprelations and adapting children to new family styles.

373 Brothers, Joyce. "Making a Second Marriage Work." *Good Housekeeping* 174:65 (February 1972).

Dr. Brothers tells why second marriages should not be compared to first marriages. She gives examples of how first and second marriages differ, including problems encountered by children and stepparents in remarriage situations. The last part points out how and why sexual life in second marriages is usually more satisfying than in first marriages.

374 Davitz, Lois Leiderman. "Why Men Divorce." *McCall's* 114:26 (March 1987).

The author asked four hundred divorced men between the ages of twenty and forty-five why their marriages disintergrated. The men represented a cross section of different occupations and they lived in different parts of the country. The marriages lasted anywhere from three months to twenty years, and about half of them included children. The answers given by these men dispel the prevailing beliefs that couples divorce usually because of money and/or sex problems. Although these two issues did cause some friction, few men in the study saw them as the cause of the breakup. The leading cause among most of the men interviewed was a lack of companionship.

375 Day, Randal D., and Stephen J. Bahr. "Income Changes Following Divorce and Remarriage." *Journal of Divorce* 9:75–88 (September 1986).

The purpose of this study was to determine how gender and divorce affect per capita family income.

376 Demaris, Alfred. "Comparison of Remarriages With First Marriages on Satisfaction in Marriage and Its Relationship to Prior Cohabitation." *Family Relations* 33:443–49 (July 1984).

Compares the marital satisfaction of remarried vs. first-married husbands and wives. This investigation is based on cross-sectional data from 309 recently married couples and shows no significant differences between first-married and remarried individuals in either marital satisfaction or the likelihood to cohabit before marriage.

377   "Divorce American Style." *Newsweek* 101:42–48 (10 January 1983).

Explains how divorcing couples who cannot resolve their own disputes face boundless official intrusion into their lives. Gives case examples of how custodial arrangements and property settlements decided by the courts often work against the best interests of those involved. Tells how the legal system, which has had to face an excalating number of divorces, was unprepared to deal with both the increasing number of old issues and the many new issues brought before the courts. Other case stories concerning joint custody, child snatchings, and grandparents' rights are included.

378   Duffy, Michael. "Divorce and the Dynamics of the Family Kinship System." *Journal of Divorce* 5:3–18 (Fall/Winter 1981).

Examines the dynamic patterns in relationships between members of the extended family (the grandparents) after divorce, and after subsequent remarriage.

379   Elkin, Meyer. "The Missing Links in Divorce Law: A Redefinition of Process and Practice." *Journal of Divorce* 6:37–63 (Fall/Winter 1982).

Proposes interrelated changes in the divorce process and related legal practices. This would provide for a more humanistic approach to divorce, create a system of nonadversarial practices that would enable the law itself to become a more effective support system, maximize client determination, and redefine the role of the judge and attorney in divorce.

380   Glenn, Norval D., and Charles N. Weaver. "The Marital Happiness of Remarried Divorced Persons." *Journal of Marriage and the Family* 39:331–37 (1977).

This study tested the hypotheses that divorced persons in remarriage will report less marital happiness as a whole than persons in other marriages, and that remarried females will evaluate their marriages less positively than remarried males. Tentative conclusions suggest that the increased divorce rate has not been accompanied by a significant decline in marital happiness and that prospects for divorced males to remarry successfully are better than for remarried females.

381   Glick, Paul C., and Arthur J. Norton. "Marrying, Divorcing and Living Together in the U.S. Today." *Population Bulletin* 32:complete issue (October 1977).

Analyzes figures from Censes Bureau documents and shows the changing patterns of marriage, divorce, remarriage, and living arrangements in the United States in the mid–1970s.

382   ———. "Perspectives on the Recent Upturn in Divorce and Remarriage." *Demography* 10:301–14 (August 1973).

The results of this study demonstrate that a fundamental modification of life-styles and values relating to marriage has been taking place. Covers rates on divorce, remarriage, and early marriage for women.

383   Goldman, Janice, and James Coane. "Family Therapy After Divorce: Developing a Strategy," *Family Process* 16:357–62 (1977).

A treatment article for clinicians working with divorce and remarriage families, which includes a four-part model for intervention in family therapy after a divorce to facilitate the ongoing parental relationship. A case study is also presented.

384   Hyatt, Ralph, and Florence Kaslow. "The Impact of Childrens' Divorce on Parents: And Some Contributing Factors." *Journal of Divorce* 9:79–92 (Fall 1985).

Addresses the issue of the impact of an adult child's divorce on his or her parents—their anguish, grief, concern, humiliation, or even occasional elation. How the senior parent's reactions affect their own life cycle development and the impact upon their children's, and grandchildren's, postdivorce readjustment.

385   Jones, Shirley Maxwell. "Divorce and Remarriage: A New Beginning, a New Set of Problems." *Journal of Divorce* 2:217–22 (Winter 1978).

Current trends, practices and problems of remarriage, and its impact on stepfamily members.

386   Kaslow, Florence, and Ralph Hyatt. "Divorce: A Potential
      Growth Experience for the Extended Family." *Journal of Divorce*
      5:115–140 (Fall/Winter 1981).

> Discusses some of the ways in which divorce, usually conceived
> of as a primarily negative experience, can be turned into a positive
> advantage and have a beneficial impact on the divorcing person's
> extended family.

387   Kiester, Edwin, Jr. "How Divorce Counselors Sweeten the Sour
      Taste of Separation." *Today's Health*. 53:46–50 (November 1975).

> Stresses that divorce need not be viewed as the ultimate disaster,
> but as an option to consider when trying to find solutions in a
> troubled relationship. It explains that counseling is shifting away
> from the attitude of "save the marriage at all costs" to answering
> the question, "can this marriage be saved?" Described are the
> ways counselors help couples close the door of waning relation-
> ships gradually and gently, along with some case histories.

388   Koopman, Elizabeth Janssen. "The Present and Future Role of
      Higher Education in Divorce Mediation: Problems and Promise
      in Teaching, Research, and Service." *Journal of Divorce* 8:15–32
      (Spring/Summer 1985).

> Describes the current academic developments in divorce media-
> tion and addresses issues relevant to the roles and responsibilities
> of academe in the divorce mediation field.

389   Lloyd, Sally A., and Cathleen D. Zick. "Divorce at Mid and
      Later Life: Does the Empirical Evidence Support the Theory?"
      Journal of Divorce 9:89–102 (September 1986).

> Reviews the mid- and later-life divorce literature in the context of
> two currently popular theories of divorce.

390   Messinger, Lillian et al. "Preparation for Remarriage Following
      Divorce: The Use of Group Techniques." *American Journal of
      Orthopsychiatry* 48:263–72(1978).

> This article reports on an experience of four series of weekly
> group meetings, with a total of twenty-two couples, in which at
> least one partner had children by a previous marriage. This group
> experience was found to be beneficial in clarifying roles in the
> remarriage family.

391   Messinger, Lillian. "Remarriage Between Divorced People With Children From Previous Marriages: A Proposal for Preparation for Remarriage." *Journal of Marriage and Family Counseling* 92:193–200 (1976).

Interviews with seventy couples suggest that the stress for couples and families involved in divorce and remarriage would be prevented or reduced through remarriage-preparation courses.

392   Newman, Mildred, and Bernard Berkowitz. "Making Second Marriages Work." *Harper's Bazaar* 108:80 (June 1975)

Harper's Bazaar asked one couple, Newman and Berkowitz, both twice-married and coauthors of *How to Be Your Own Best Friend*, to discuss getting over your first marriage and getting ready for your second.

393   Nichols, William C. "Divorce and Remarriage Education." *Journal of Divorce* 1:153–61 (1977).

Addresses the need for helping the many people involved in marital and family disruption and describes using an educational approach, first for those adjusting to divorce and then to those both contemplating and already in a remarriage.

394   Perlman, Judy L. "Divorce—A Psychological and Legal Process." *Journal of Divorce* 6:99–114 (Fall/Winter 1982).

The role of mental health professionals, lawyers, and courts in a divorce are discussed in terms of individual contributions as well as interdisciplinary "team" approaches.

395   Poussaint, Ann Ashmore. "Are Second Marriages Better?" *Ebony Magazine* 30:55–56 (March 1975).

Stresses the success of second marriages and gives examples of celebrity couples and why their second marriages work.

396   Rydman, Edward J. "Advice to Second Wives." *Harper's Bazaar* 106:104–05 (April 1973).

Dr. Rydman, former executive director of the American Association of Marriage and Family Counselors, answers questions concerning the odd threesome that is created when a man gains a second wife and can't completely erase the first wife from his life.

397   Streshinsky, Shirley. "How Divorce Really Affects Children: A Major Report." *Redbook* 147:70 (September 1976).

Reports on a study conducted by Judith Wallerstein and Joan Kelly, which involved 60 families and 131 children in these families, in an attempt to find out how children really feel about their parents' divorce.

398   Torrey, Joanna. "Double Beds, Separate Bank Accounts." *Harper's Bazaar* 117:122 (October 1984).

Cautions women who have been burned once in their first marriage to get something in writing before remarrying. Discusses marriage contracts, prenuptial counseling, and financial advice.

399   Vinick, Barbara H. "Remarriage in Old Age." *Family Coordinator* 27:359–63(1978).

Explores some social, situational, and personal factors associated with remarriage in old age, and focuses on role changes associated with remarriage.

400   Walker, Kenneth N., Joy Rogers, and Lillian Messinger. "Remarriage After Divorce: A Review." *Social Casework* 58:276–85 (1977).

Reviews the literature and research on remarriages and advocates ongoing research into the issues involved, in particular: demographic characteristics of remarriages, the consequences for children living in remarriage households, and the rate of divorce for remarriages compared to first marriages.

6
Custody & Child Support

A. Books

401 Bertin, Emanuel A. *Pennsylvania Child Custody: Law, Practice, and Procedure, Including Using Expert Witnesses in Custody Cases.* Philadelphia: George T. Bisel, 1983. 475 pp.

Comprehensive source book, written by a Pennsylvania family-law specialist, which includes the structuring of a case from the initial interview to preparation and presentation of evidence. It is divided into three parts: child custody law, child custody practice and procedure, and the use of experts in child custody cases. Contains a definitive treatment of Pennsylvania's child custody techniques and procedures to guide attorneys and judges, as well as comments of a psychiatrist, psychologist, and a social worker. Also includes a sample custody evaluation.

402 Bienenfeld, Florence. *Child Custody Mediation: Techniques for Counselors, Attorneys, and Parents.* Palo Alto, CA: Science and Behavior Books, 1983. 192 pp.

The author, a counselor/mediator, illustrates how to use the power of the court to facilitate mediation and how to develop the psychological pressure to help parents settle child custody issues. Includes explanations for handling special situations with fourteen different case methodologies and the techniques for resolving each problem effectively. The final part presents five case studies.

403 Cassetty, Judith. *Child Support and Public Policy: Securing Support from Absent Fathers.* Lexington, MA: Lexington Books, 1978. 171 pp.

This analysis and discussion focuses on the issue of child support enforcement policy as it relates to the female-headed family and the absent father.

404   Chambers, David L., and Terry K. Adams. *Making Fathers Pay: The Enforcement of Child Support*. Chicago: University of Chicago Press, 1979. 365 pp.

> This is the first book to appear on child support enforcement. It is a statistical analysis of procedures in Michigan, the state that collects the highest percentage of child support in the United States. It covers reasons for divorce, payment histories, collection techniques, punishment for nonpayment, and the financial impact of divorce on both parents and children.

405   Chesler, Phyllis. *Mothers on Trial: Battle for Children and Custody*. New York: McGraw-Hill, 1986. 651 pp.

> This work is an indictment of how the modern justice system is treating mothers seeking custody. The author charges that the "fathers' rights" movement and the double standard in our patriarchal society are governing the rights of women, children, and child custody. Because of this, unfit fathers are now granted custody with increasing frequency. She has drawn together mythology, historical research, case studies, and an analysis of what constitutes "fit" parents to support her claims.

406   *Child Custody Disputes*. Edited by Gary E. Stollak and Michael G. Lieberman. New York: Irvington Publishers, 1985. 528 pp.

> Examination of current law and research, and discussion of joint custody and mediation, which points toward a legal system which makes cooperative postdivorce parenting possible in the best interest of the children. Some articles address visitation rights of a grandfather over the objections of a parent, when a father gets custody, joint custody, and proper roles of legal and mental health professionals.

407   Foster, Henry, and Doris Jonas Freed. *Current Development in Child Custody*. New York: Law Journal Seminars Press, 1978. 603 pp.

> Provides a general overview of the law, and articles on custody, visitation, child support, child napping, the rights of grandparents, and custody and visitation in nonmarital cases.

408   Franks, Maurice R. *Winning Custody*. Englewood Cliffs, NJ: PrenticeHall, 1983. 192 pp.

> Written to help men get fair treatment in child custody and child support cases. Promotes the understanding of the problems fa-

thers must face in winning custody, and describes how fathers should go about trying to win custody. Some chapters included are: "Finding the Right Lawyer," "Factors in Obtaining Custody," "The Custody Evaluation," and "Trial Strategy."

409   Galper, Miriam. *Co-Parenting: A Source Book for the Separated or Divorced Family*. Philadelphia: Running Press, 1978. 158 pp. (1980 edition published under the title: *Joint Custody and Co-Parenting.*)

Contains accounts of shared custody by parents experiencing it, with special stress on how and why it works for them. Tells parents how to develop and maintain a coparenting arrangement.

410   ———. *Joint Custody & Co-Parenting*. Philadelphia: Running Press, 1980. 207 pp.

See listing 409.

411   Gardner, Richard A. *Family Evaluation in Child Custody Litigation*. Cresskill, NJ: Creative Therapeutics, 1982. 360 pp.

Explains the role that mental health professionals should play in child custody cases. States that not only should the mental health professionals furnish information to the courts, but also advocates that these professionals are better prepared, by training and experience, than judges to make custody recommendations to the courts. Selected chapters deal with "The Adversary System vs. The Impartial Expert," "Evaluation of the Children," "The Final Recommendations," "Providing Testimony in Court," and "Interviews with parents

412   Goldstein, Joseph, and Anna Solni. *Beyond the Best Interest of the Child*. New ed. New York: Free Press, 1979. 203 pp.

Written from a psychoanalytical perspective, which discusses child custody, foster placement, and adoption. The authors emphasize the importance of maintaining continuity in a child's relationships and surroundings. A number of the arguments against joint custody have come from ideas presented in this work.

413   Goldzband, Melvin G. *Consulting in Child Custody: An Introduction to the Ugliest Litigation for Mental-Health Professionals*. Lexington, MA: Lexington Books, 1982. 183 pp.

A guide for specialists written to alleviate the fears of most mental-health experts who avoid the legal arena, especially in child custody cases. It provides information about the law, how lawyers think and plan their cases, and especially how lawyers, courts, and litigants all need the help of expert witnesses.

414 Group for the Advancement of Psychiatry. Committee on the Family. *Divorce, Child Custody, and the Family.* San Francisco: Jossey-Bass, 1981. 180 pp.

This report considers two types of divorces: the amicable ones, in which parents are able to come to an agreement about the care and custody of the children; and the contested ones, in which differences are irreconcilable and decisions about child custody have to be made by the courts. Special attention is focused on current thinking in psychiatry, and the potential contribution of mental health professionals to custody determination.

415 Haddad, William F., and Mel Roman. *No-Fault Custody: Special Report to Honorable Speaker Stanley Steingut.* Albany: The Assembly of New York State, 1978. 34 pp.

A paper prepared for the New York State hearings on custody matters. Discusses the issues of joint custody, the history of custody determination, and the removal of custody disputes from the adversary system.

416 Horowitz, Robert M., and Diane Dodson. *Child Support: An Annotated Legal Bibliography.* Washington, DC: U.S. Department of Health and Humman Services, Office of Child Support Enforcement, 1984. 1 vol. (various paging).

An annotated bibliography of all major legal literature on child support issues published since 1975.

417 *Interstate Child Custody Disputes and Parental Kidnapping: Policy, Practice and Law.* Patricia M. Hoff et al. Washington, DC: Legal Services Corporation, American Bar Association, 1982. 1 vol. (various paging).

A joint project of the Child Custody Project, American Bar Association, National Center for Women and Family Law, and National Center for Youth Law under a grant from the Legal Services Corporation. This manual discusses existing laws, suggests strategies for litigating interstate jurisdictional disputes and ties both law and strategy to the policies underlying the Uniform Child Custody Jurisdiction Act (UCCJA) and Parental Kidnapping Prevention Act (PKPA).

418   *Joint Custody: A Handbook for Judges, Lawyers and Counselors.*
      Edited by Ann L. Milne. Ft. Lauderdale: Prepared by the
      Association of Family Conciliation Courts, Nova University Law
      Center, 1979. 1 vol. (various paging).

      Provides a comprehensive exploration of the advantages and
      disadvantages of joint custody; and presents research findings,
      case law, and joint custody agreements.

419   *Joint Custody and Shared Parenting.* Edited by Jay Folberg. Wash-
      ington, DC: Bureau of National Affairs, 1984. 350 pp.

      A collection of writings which brings together a diversity of views
      that examine both the pros and cons of joint custody. Issues
      presented are the changing joint custody law, child development,
      counseling, and legal and research writings.

420   Kiefer, Louis. *How to Win Custody.* New York: Cornerstone
      Library, 1982. 308 pp.

      Written by a lawyer as a response to his own custody experiences
      and those of his clients. He strives to: make judges more sensitive
      to their roles, give parents a philosophy to use in resolving their
      own differences, provide attorneys with more insight into the
      feelings and emotions of their clients, and show how the legal
      system really works.

421   Kram, Shirley Wohl, and Neil A. Frank. *The Law of Child
      Custody: Development of the Substantive Law.* Lexington, MA:
      Lexington Books, 1982. 176 pp.

      Analysis of the conceptual evolution of judicial and legislative
      policy toward the resolution of disrupted child custody proceed-
      ings.

422   Krause, Harry D. *Child Support in America: The Legal Perspective.*
      Charlottesville: The Michie Co., 1981. 700 pp.

      Describes, analyzes, and evaluates child support enforcement
      laws and practices, regulations, and working procedures at the
      state and federal levels, and their interactions. The establishment
      of the paternity of children born to unmarried parents, and data
      on the "medical proof" that is increasingly determinative in
      paternity actions, are covered. Intended for the state's attorney,
      the private attorney, and the judge, who all deal with child
      support problems and also directed to other public aid officials.

423   Luepnitz, Deborah Anna. *Child Custody: A Study of Families After Divorce.* Lexington, MA: Lexington Books, 1982. 191 pp.

The author compares the postdivorce experience of families in three custody patterns. In a nonclincial sample of sixteen maternal, sixteen paternal, and eleven joint custody families, she explores the psychological adjustment of children and parents to divorce as well as family functioning in five areas: economics, authority, domestics, child care, and social support. The findings illustrate the strengths and weaknesses of the three custody types experienced by the families, and comparisons are made between traditional sole custody families and the more innovative joint custody families. Leupnitz concludes that "joint custody at its best is better than sole custody at its best." Her results suggest that joint custody is a viable alternative to sole custody, and that social scientists should examine under what conditions it will work best.

424   Maidment, Susan. *Child Custody and Divorce: The Law in Social Context.* London: Croom Helm, 1984. 324 pp.

The author's contention is that the nature of custody decision-making can only be understood when the legal structure is firmly placed within its social context. She includes observations about the exact social context of the law, describes the legal processes involved in both terms of procedure and substantive law, and investigates the rules and interpretations of the child welfare principle in a social context.

425   Matthews, Joseph L. *After the Divorce.* Rev. ed. Berkeley, CA: Nolo Press, 1983. 156 pp.

Explains to lay people how to change child support orders, custody/visitation matters, and spousal support. Sample legal forms are provided. The original edition was intended for California.

426   Morgan, Elizabeth. *Custody: A True Story.* Boston: Little, Brown, 1986. 254 pp.

The author, a successful plastic surgeon, tells her own story of how she, a single mother, had to defend her morals and fitness in court in order to bring up her child.

427   Morgenbesser, Mel, and Nadine Nehls. *Joint Custody: An Alternative for Divorcing Families.* Chicago: Nelson-Hall, 1981. 168 pp.

Discusses joint custody, a nontraditional form of custody, which may be desirable and appropriate for some divorcing families.

The authors explain what joint custody is, and how to decide if it is an appropraite alternative to sole custody by one parent. Benefits and problems involved in making a custody decision, information about how to implement the custody decision, and interviews with men and women who presently have joint custody are included.

428   Musetto, Andrew P. *Dilemmas in Child Custody: Family Conflicts and Their Resolution.* Chicago: Nelson-Hall, 1982. 216 pp.

A report of the author's clinical efforts with families involved in custody and visitation disputes. The theme of the book is that custody and visitation problems are family problems and will be successfully resolved only with the involvement of the entire family.

429   Noble, June, and William Noble. *The Custody Trap.* New York: Hawthorn Books, 1975. 163 pp.

Examines problems in the present custody system. Case examples are used to illustrate the adversary nature of custody decision making. The authors conclude with a recommendation of joint responsibility for children following marital dissolution.

430   *The Parental Child-Support Obligation: Research, Practice, and Social Policy.* Edited by Judith Cassetty. Lexington, MA: Lexington Books, 1983. 300 pp.

A collection of papers presented at the Wisconsin workshop on child support, research, and social policy, held at the University of Wisconsin-Madison, spring 1981. A number of scholars from diverse disciplines explore the economic consequences of a rapidly growing number of female-headed families in the United States. From this inquiry the issue of parental liability for child support in such families emerged as a focal point of interest as did questions about how best to improve the system for establishing and enforcing the parental support obligation.

431   Paskowicz, Patricia. *Absentee Mothers* New York: Universe Books, 1983. 248 pp.

Paskowicz, an "absentee mother" herself, tries to bring her readers to a deeper empathy with mothers who have chosen and/or been forced to relinquish custodial parenting, thus becoming the noncustodial parent after separation or divorce. She integrates personal experiences, responses from others in similar circumstances and interviews with professional consultants.

432 Ramos, Suzanne. *The Complete Book of Child Custody.* New York: Putnam, 1979. 330 pp.

Comprehensive book which examines all the possible child custody arrangements for parents to consider. The author cites many case histories that illustrate how one form of custody works for some and not for others.

433 Ricci, Isolina. *Mom's House, Dad's House: Making Shared Custody Work.* New York: Collier Books, 1982. 270 pp.

Based on eight years of research on divorce, custody, and single parenting, this handbook discusses all the stages of divorce. It serves as a guide on how divorced parents can develop a working relationship that is in the best interests of their children, even under the most strained circumstances and regardless of the custody situation. Although the emphasis is on shared parenting, the book includes many problems common to the stepfamily and offers compassionate advice on such topics as parenting agreements, remarrying, and where to spend the holidays.

434 Roman, Mel, and William Haddad. *The Disposable Parent: The Case of Joint Custody.* New York: Holt, 1978. 215 pp.

A research work which looks at the professional, political, and economic bias against shared custody, and makes a strong argument for reassessing both our custody practices and our family law system. The authors uphold that joint custody is the best optional post divorce arrangement, and that courts should begin with a presumption for joint custody.

435 Saposnek, Donald T. *Mediating Child Custody Disputes.* San Francisco: Jossey-Bass, 1983. 326 pp.

This is a guide, written by a clinical child psychologist, for professionals who want to learn how to resolve custody disputes. Techniques explained are intended for a wide range of practitioners who work with custody or visitation matters. Information for mediators specializing in the financial aspects of divorce settlements, and some of the more difficult challenges encountered in mediation are included.

436 Schnell, Barry T. *Child Support Survivor's Guide.* Salem, NJ: Consumer Awareness Learning Lab, 1984. 96 pp.

Provides parents with information about their child support rights. Gives guidance in resolving child support problems, enforcing the order, and protecting the economic and emotional needs and rights of the dependent children. Some topics included are: how to determine the support amount, provisions that may be included in support orders, grandparents' rights, and the non custodial mother. Supportive organizations, state agencies administering child support programs, and resource publications are listed at the end.

437   Silver, Gerald A., and Myrna Silver. *Weekend Father: For Divorced Fathers, Second Wives and Grandparents: Solutions to the Problems of Child Custody, Child Support, Alimony and Property Settlements.* Los Angeles: Stratford Press, 1981. 236 pp.

This work was generated by the authors' anger at a family-law system that favors mothers over fathers. The Silvers call for a presumption of joint custody, and for a major overhaul of the adversary legal system.

438   Skafte, Dianne. *Child Custody Evaluations: A Practical Guide.* Beverly Hills: Sage Publications, 1985. 215 pp.

Primarily for the custody evaluator. Covers separating the roles of therapists and evaluator, preparing the final report, interviewing litigants, the home visit, working with children, interviewing collaterals, organizing everything for a final judgement, drafting a visitation plan, and writing the final report.

439   Takas, Marianne. *Child Support: A Complete, Up-to-Date, Authoritative Guide to Collecting Child Support.* New York: Harper & Row, 1985. 219 pp.

Provides laws and services now available to help collect child support. Chapters address different family situations, for example chapter 8 is specifically for single mothers, while chapter 12 is for married mothers considering divorce or separation. Special aspects, such as establishing paternity and methods of detecting hidden assets, are included. A resources section lists agencies as well as parents' support enforcement groups.

440   Victor, Ira, and Win Ann Winkler. *Fathers and Custody.* New York: Hawthorne Books, 1977. 209 pp.

Describes the father's role in different custody arrangements, and includes a chapter on joint custody. Other issues related to fathers and custody are also discussed, such as parental kidnapping, joint custody, visitation, and the custodial father. The appendix lists three types of resources: divorced-fathers groups, single-parent and child-help groups, and legal advice referrals.

441   Ware, Ciji. *Sharing Parenthood After Divorce: An Enlightened Custody Guide for Mothers, Fathers, and Kids.* New York: Viking, 1982. 349 pp.

The author, a radio/TV journalist and a divorced parent who is sharing joint custody wrote this guide "to show parents how to stop fighting over their offspring and negotiate a sharing arrangement." She argues for mediation rather than litigation, and for allowing children free access to parents and extended family. She presents various options for sharing time and space, and appends a list of mediating agencies, existing laws, a sample sharing agreement, and suggested further readings.

442   Wheeler, Michael. *Divided Children: A Legal Guide for Divorcing Parents.* New York: Norton, 1980. 224 pp.

Informs readers about the legal aspects of divorce as applied to children. In addition to the question of custody and child support, the author covers such areas as grandparents' rights and ownership of property.

443   Woody, Robert Henley. *Getting Custody: Winning the Last Battle of the Marital War.* New York: Macmillan, 1978. 178 pp.

Brings together information on the history and status of child custody in America, the legal factors prescribed by state child custody statutes, and the criteria that will be applied in evaluating whether you or your ex-spouse should be awarded custody. Focuses upon professionals such as lawyers, psychiatrists, psychologists, social workers, etc. who can be brought into the custody proeedings to evaluate parents' abililty for fulfilling the best interests of the child.

444   Woolley, Persia. *The Custody Handbook.* New York: Summit Books, 1979. 350 pp.

A handbook on custody which presents and weaves together the various subjects of divorced parents, child custody, and the ways and means to help parents establish what is best for their own families. Alternatives to the traditional custody arrangements, such as coparenting, are included, along with the legal issues and the legal statutes in the more progressive areas of the country.

B. Articles in Periodicals

445 Abarbanel, Alice R. "Shared Parenting After Separation and Divorce: A Study of Joint Custody." *American Journal of Orthopsychiatry* 49:320–29 (April 1979).

> Overview of the research on children and divorce which includes the results of in-depth interviews with four joint-custody famlies.

446 Ahrons, Constance R. "Joint Custody Arrangements in the Postdivorce Family." *Journal of Divorce* 3:189–205 (1980).

> Describes the shared parenting arrangements of forty-one divorced parents with court-awarded joint custody.

447 Alexander, Sharon J. "Protecting the Child's Rights in Custody Cases." *The Family Coordinator* 26:377–82 (1977).

> Provides guidelines for use by both parents and the courts to assist in appropriately weighing the factors that determine custody. When parents choose mediation, a specialist in child custody is appointed to educate and assist in the decision-making process; when parents choose litigation, counsel is appointed to represent the child.

448 Baroni, Barry J. "Conflict of Laws—Child Custody—Theory of Concurrent Jurisdiction." *Loyola Law Review* 12:147 (1965).

> Discusses what criteria should be used in situations where two states have concurrent jurisdiction over a custody dispute.

449 Baum, Charlotte. "Best of Both Parents: Joint Custody." *New York Times Magazine* (31 October 1976): 44–98.

> The author discusses her experiences with joint custody and the arrangements with her children and former husband.

450 Berkman, Barbara Gerber. "Father Involvement and Regularity of Child Support in Post-Divorce Families. *Journal of Divorce* 9:67–74 (September 1986).

> Examines the relationships between twenty divorced, non-custodial fathers and their children from the perspective of both the mother and the father. Results indicate parental agreement over the perceived consistency of child support but disagreement over

the amount of influence the fathers had in the area of financial affairs.

451 Black, David. "The Weekend Parent." *Apartment Life* 13:64–65 January 1981).

Gives some examples of how divorced parents, single and remarried, are experiencing joint custody arrangements with their children.

452 Bodenheimer, Brigitte M. "Progress Under the Uniform Child Custody Jurisdiction Act and Remaining Problems: Punitive Decrees, Joint Custody and Excessive Modifications." *California Law Review* 65:978–1,014 (1977).

The Uniform Child Custody Jurisdiction Act, adopted by eighteen states, facilitates the solution of many of the interstate problems of child custody litigation by introducing greater predictability into the enforcement of out-of-state decrees. The author discusses problems of interpretation of the act and explores three areas of acute difficulty: punitive decrees, joint custody decrees, and excessively modified custody decrees.

453 Bowman, Madonna, and Constance R. Ahrons. "Impact of Legal Custody Status on Fathers' Parenting Post Divorce." *Journal of Marriage and the Family* 47:481–88 (May 1985).

Compares the parenting, one year after divorce, of twenty-eight joint custody fathers with fifty-four noncustodial fathers. The study evaluates contact and activities with the children, as well as shared responsibility and decision making.

454 Branson, Mary Lou. "Resource Management: Divorced Custodial Fathers Compared to Divorced Custodial Mothers." *Family Perspective* 17:101–07 (Spring 1983).

This study was designed to represent areas in which economizing is most often attempted, as self-reported by a random sample of thirty unmarried males with custody of children under twenty-one, as compared to a like sample of unremarried custodial females.

455 Bruch, Carol. "Making Visitation Work, Dual Parenting Orders." *Family Advocate* 1:22 (1978).

Argues that continued contact with both parents is important for the child of divorce. The author offers suggestions about how this can be accomplished.

456   Cox, Mary Jane Truesdell, and Lary Cease. "Joint Custody, What Does It Mean?" *Family Advocate* (Summer 1978): 10–13.

Definitions and issues related to joint custody are discussed. The benefits of this custody arrangement are also described.

457   Dancy, Elizabeth. "Who Gets the Kids, New Solutions for the Big Dilemma." *Ms.* 5:70–72 (September 1976).

Writer tells of her own divorce battle over custody of her daughter, and interviews other couples who have arranged to share custody of their children.

458   Druckman, Joan M., and Clifton A. Rhodes. "Family Impact Analysis: Application to Child Custody Determination." *Family Coordinator* 26:451–58 (1977).

Examines current changes in child study determination policies and related programs. Family Impact Analysis, a framework for assessing the impact of legal and social policy on the family, is described as an objective approach for investigating the implementation of family legal policy. The utility of Family Impact Analysis is illustrated by its application to an analysis of child custody policy and a recently developed "mediation counseling" program used in child custody determination cases in the family court service of Hennepin County (Minneapolis), MN.

459   Dullea, Georgia. "Custody and the Legal Clashes." *New York Times* (23 July 1981): 1.

The story of a fifteen-year-old boy who, because he preferred to live with his dad, defied the court orders that awarded custody to his mother. This article questions the vaguely defined rights of children in such cases and attributes this situation, at least in part, to the growing number of children, aged six and older, who are leaving home.

460   ———. "Half-Time Fathers Know Best." *Chicago Tribune* (19 March 1978): Section 5, p.6.

Compares the father who shares custody with his counterparts: the weekend father and the full-time father. The author concludes that the father who shares custody is happier and has the lowest level of conflict with his former mate.

461   ———."Joint Custody: Is Sharing the Child a Dangerous Idea?" *New York Times* (24 May 1976): Section 1, p.24.

Defines joint custody and explains why some couples are deciding on this arrangement. It includes personal examples of joint custody life-styles shared by divorced parents and their children.

462   Eckman, Fern Marja. "Joint Custody, Does It Work?" *Working Mother* (September 1981): 72.

Explains what "joint custody" means, ranging from parents sharing their children by splitting the week, or alternating either weekends, two-week periods, and, in rare cases, years. In some situations the child remains at "home base" while the parents take turns moving in and out. Some study results are also included.

463   Eider, Vicki. "Shared Custody—An Idea Whose Time Has Come." *Conciliation Courts Review* 16:23–25 (June 1978).

A review of the Oregon statutee on joint custody. Contains criteria for joint custody and a summary of the arguments for and against joint custody.

464   Elliott, Elizabeth, and Wendy Susco. *"Kramer vs. Kramer* and Other Child Custody Cases." *Working Woman* 5:12 (April 1980).

A review of the movie, *Kramer vs. Kramer*, which was adapted from a novel by Avery Corman. Although the movie may deserve awards for acting, writing and direction the reviewers disagree with the outcome of the custody case in the movie, and believe that this would be an unlikely outcome in a real-life custody situation. Offers examples of some other custody situations.

465   Ellsworth, Phoebe C., and Robert J. Levy. "Legislative Reform of Child Custody Adjudication: An Effort to Rely on Social Science Data in Formulating Legal Policies." *Law and Society Review* 4:167–233 (1969).

A survey of child custody cases drawn from a report entitled "Uniform Marriage and Divorce Legislation: A Preliminary Inquiry," prepared for the National Conference of Commissioners on Uniform State Laws. The report, of which this article is a part, was the initial product of a conference endeavor to promulgate a uniform marriage and divorce law.

466 Folberg, Jay. "Joint Custody Law—The Second Wave." *Journal of Family Law* 23:1–55 (1984/85).

Explains how child custody law following divorce is being recast in state legislatures and courtrooms throughout the United States, and how the law is changing to reflect the new postdivorce family patterns and sensitivity to issues of gender equality. The changes in the law of custody are part of a second wave following the nofault divorce movement of the past decade. Although recasting of custody law is not yet complete, the emerging trends and issues are covered. A state-by-state chart is included which illustrates the considerable variation that exists among states regarding the law of joint custody and shared parenting.

467 Foster, Henry, and Doris Jonas Freed. "Life With Father: 1978." *Law Quarterly* 11:321–42 (Winter 1978).

Gives a complete accounting of the history and court cases involving child custody from English law through the industrial revolution and the advent of the "tender years" doctrine to the concept of joint custody. Includes state statutes relevant to child custody cases and significant court decisions.

468 Gaddis, Stephen M. "Joint Custody of Children: A Divorce Decision Making Alternative." *Conciliation Courts Review* 16:17–22 (June 1978).

Explores why joint custody is a viable alternative, and when it should be considered. Terms are defined and suggestions for joint custody arrangements are provided.

469 Girdner, Linda K. "Adjudication and Mediation: A Comparison of Custody Decision-Making Processes Involving Third Parties." *Journal of Divorce* 8:33–47 (Spring/Summer 1985).

Child custody adjudication and mediation are compared as processes of dispute settlement and conflict resolution involving divorcing parents and third parties. Adjudication of the custody issue fosters conflicts and competitive interactions between parents, whereas mediation fosters cooperative and interdependent interactions. The implications of this to the emotional process of divorce and directions for future research are discussed.

470 Grief, Judith Brown. "Fathers, Children and Joint Custody." *American Journal of Orthopsychiatry* 49:311–19(1979).

A research study of forty middle-class, separated and divorced fathers, some of whom share custody of their children.

471   Grote, Douglas F., and Jeffrey P. Weinstein. "Joint Custody: A Viable and Ideal Alternative." *Journal of Divorce* 1:43–55 (Fall 1977).

Suggests that joint custody is an ideal alternative for families in divorce because it allows for ongoing parental and parent-child relationships.

472   Holly, Marcia. "Joint Custody: The New Haven Plan." *Ms.* 5:70–71 (September 1976).

Describes the New Haven Plan, a concept of shared custody for divorced parents that lets the children spend half-time with each parent. The author tells how she and her former husband have adjusted to the weekly version of the plan with their child.

473   Isaacs, Marla Beth, George H. Leon, and Marsha Kline. "When Is a Parent Out of the Picture? Different Custody, Different Perceptions." *Family Process* 26:101–10 (March 1987).

An investigation of how two hundred children from mother-, father-, or joint-custody arrangements perceived their divorced families. The authors maintain that it is not the type of custody that shapes the child's view of whether one parent is peripheral but, rather, the nature of relationships within the various custody arrangements.

474   Jenkins, R. L. "Maxims in Child Custody Cases." *The Family Coordinator* 26:385–89 (1977).

The author, an expert witness in many child custody cases, offers advice to behavioral scientists who will be in similar roles. One of his suggestions is to "not divide the child." He argues against joint custody arrangements, feeling that they invite conflict.

475   Kellogg, Mary Alice. "Joint Custody." *Newsweek* 89:56–57 (24 January 1977).

Interviews with parents who share their children half-time, and the opinions of legal and mental health professionals about such arrangements.

476   Lawrence, W. "Divided Custody of Children After Their Parents Divorce." *Journal of Family Law* 8:56–68 (1968).

Covers some of the literature on psychological problems of children after divorce and reviews case law regarding joint custody.

477 Lowery, Carol R. "Child Custody in Divorce: Parents' Decisions and Perceptions." *Family Relations* 34:241–49 (April 1985).

Interviews and questionnaire data regarding the factors considered in reaching a decision about the custody of children. The results are discussed in the context of their implications for clinical work with divorcing families.

478 Luepnitz, Deborah Anna. "A Comparison of Maternal, Paternal, and Joint Custody: Understanding the Varieties of Post-Divorce Family Life." *Journal of Divorce* 9:1–12 (Spring 1986).

Forty-three families with either maternal, paternal, or joint custody were studied an average of 3.5 years after divorce. It appears that joint custody at its best is superior to single parent custody at its best. The author cautions against a legal presumption for the joint award.

479 Magid, Ken, and Parker Oborn. "Children of Divorce: A Need for Guidelines." *Family Law Quarterly* 20:331–41 (Fall 1986).

Offers a set of guidelines for governing the implementation of shared parental responsibility for parents and professionals who consider bonding and attachment issues important and who want to implement a low-risk program to minimize subsequent trauma in future generations of children of divorce. Determination of what solution is in the best interest of the children and what is the most equitable custody arrangement for the parents would also be an outcome.

480 "Men's Lib Movement Trains Its Guns on Divorce Courts." *U.S. News and World Report* 7:42 (12 September 1977).

A number of men and men's groups protest custody and alimony procedures they feel favor women.

481 Moramarco, Sheila Sobell. "Crimes of the Heart." *Redbook* 64:136–37 (February 1985).

Discusses two custody cases: the first case tells how a disabled father wins custody of his two sons, and the second case tells why and how the judge sets a visition schedule for two grandparents and their granddaughter whose parents have divorced.

482 Nehls, Nadine, and Mel Morgenbesser. "Joint Custody: An Exploration of the Issues." *Family Process* 19:117–25 (1980).

The authors discuss the potential positive and negative effects of joint custody decisions by reviewing relevant research and theoretical concepts.

483 Noble, Dorinda N. "Custody Contest: How to Divide and Reassemble a Child." *Social Casework* 64:406–13 (September 1983).

Reviews historical attitudes toward child custody. Discusses the custody options of sole or joint custody and the parental kidnapping phenomena which has increased in recent years.

484 Ralston, Jeannie. "Child Support: Getting Tough With Fathers Who Don't Pay." *McCall's* 112:69–70 (February 1985).

Explores automatic income-withholding legislation, which went into effect in October 1985. This legislation requires states to order a delinquent parent's employer to begin taking out of the parent's paycheck the amount owed in child support each month. Lists recommendations for the custodial parent to follow in order to receive support payments.

485 Roman, Mel, and William Haddad. "The Case for Joint Custody." *Psychology Today* 12:96–105 (September 1978).

Describes several joint custody arrangements and responses to the criticism of joint custody.

486 Rooney, Rita. "When Dad is Given Custody." *Parade* (24 February 1980): 4–5.

Explains why more mothers are voluntarily relinquishing custody of their children to their husbands.

487 Santrock, John W., and Richard A. Warshak. "Father Custody and Social Development in Boys and Girls." *Journal of Social Issues* 35:112–25 (1979).

A study of the effects of father custody on children's social development by comparing children whose fathers have been awarded custody, children whose mothers have been awarded custody, and children from intact families. Of special note is that children living with the opposite-sex parent are less well adjusted than children living with the same-sex parent. Authoritative parenting and contact with other adult caretakers yielded positive results in both father- and mother-custody families.

488 Settle, Shirley A., and Carol R. Lowery. "Child Custody Decisions: Content Analysis of a Judicial Survey." *Journal of Divorce* 6:125–38 (Fall/Winter 1982).

This study presents the findings of a content analysis of responses to open-ended questions from a survey of judges and trial commissioners regarding child custody decisions in divorce.

489   Stack, Carol B. "Who Owns the Child? Divorce and Custody Decisions in Middle-Class Families." *Social Problems* 23:505–15 (1976).

This article stems directly from the publication of *Beyond the Best Interest of the Child*, by Goldstein, Freud, and Solnit (see listing 412). The authors argue that the parent awarded custody in divorce proceedings should have the right to allow or refuse the other parent access to the child. It is Stack's contention that these guidelines are not in the best interests of children. This paper proposes the adoption of uniform statutes regarding child custody in divorce cases. In the event of a divorce, it is proposed that children be given to the joint custody of both parents provided the courts find no overriding reason why it would be in the best interests to award custody of the child to only one parent.

490   Stewart, James R., Andrew I. Schwebel, and Mark A. Fine. "The Impact of Custodial Arrangement on the Adjustment of Recently Divorced Fathers." *Journal of Divorce* 9:55–65 (Spring 1986).

Explores the impact of custodial arrangement on the adjustment of recently divorced fathers. Testing of three groups of men— divorced fathers with custody, divorced fathers without custody, and a comparison group of married fathers—provides statistically significant findings indicating that divorced fathers with custody of their children exhibited less depression and anxiety, and fewer problems in general adjustment, than those without custody. Implications for research and clinical intervention are discussed.

491   Trombetta, Diane. "Custody Evaluation and Custody Mediation: A Comparison of Two Dispute Interventions." *Journal of Divorce* 6:65–76 (Fall/Winter 1982).

A description and comparison of two changes currently being addressed in custody mediation: to improve the existing family law courts or to take custody determination out of the courts altogether and rely instead on professional custody evaluations by behavioral scientists and other consultants. Discusses new custody legislation, emerging in states such as California, New York and Oregon, which demonstrates the extent to which public pressure can change the policies and practices commonly applied to custody dispute processing.

492 Turner, Michelle. "Unhappy Families: Special Considerations in Custody Cases Involving Handicapped Children." *Journal of Family Law* 24:59–69, (1985/86).

Discusses current statistics which reveal that half of all existing American marriages will end in divorce, and that marital breakdown occurs more frequently in families with disabled children. Explains how attorneys making cases for the custody of handicapped children should stress such factors as parent's ability to provide superior educational opportunities, the parent's knowledge of the child's disability and prognosis, and the parent's ability to provide a stable environment.

7
Parental Kidnapping

A. Books and Pamphlets

493 Abrahms, Sally. *Children in the Crossfire: The Tragedy of Parental Kidnapping.* New York: Atheneum, 1983. 297 pp.

Combines advice to parents, advocacy for stricter laws, and profiles of kidnappers, with emphasis on how kidnapping affects the children involved. Texts of recent federal laws are included.

494 Agopian, Michael. *Parental Child-Stealing.* Lexington, MA: Lexington Books, 1981. 147 pp.

Agopian reviews cases in Los Angeles in which a parent denied custody of his or her own child took the child away from the law-designated custodian. Ninety-one instances fell into this study during the initial year of operation of a California statute that significantly tightend up the definition and control of child stealing. These cases provided a study group that allows a thorough consideration of the demographics and dynamics of child stealing.

495 Arenberg, Gerald S., Carmella R. Bartimole, and John E. Bartimole. *Preventing Missing Children: A Parental Guide to Child Security.* Hollywood, FL: Compact Books, 1984. 93 pp.

This official guide was prepared by the National Asssociation of Chiefs of Police in order to share their professional child security advice with parents, thus helping to prevent children from being abducted or exploited. Topics included are missing children; parental kidnapping; child abuse; what to do if your child is missing, drugs, alcohol and school, and how to insure identification of your child.

496 Black, Bonnie Lee. *Somewhere Child*. New York: Viking, 1981. 293 pp.

After a short and unhappy marriage, Black left with her daughter, Whitney. This book recounts the fight between Black and her former spouse over custody of Whitney, and Black's search for her daughter after her "ex" illegally flew away with Whitney to Rhodesia.

497 Cook, Earleen H., and Karen F. Harrell. *Parental Kidnapping: A Bibliography*. Monticello, IL: Vance Bibliographies, 1984. 11 pp.

A bibliography of approximately 130 items, including professional journals, magazines, books, and government documents. There are no annotations.

498 Demeter, Anna. *Legal Kidnaping: What Happens to a Family When the Father Kidnaps Two Children*. Boston: Beacon Press, 1977. 148 pp.

Both parents in this book are physicians, one a cardiologist and the other a family expert, who are both better prepared than most to anticipate the effects of kidnapping on their children. This work gives a personal account of what happens to their family when the father kidnaps two of his children. Also brings to the forefront and examines father's rights, mother's rights, and the rights of the children.

499 Froncek, Thomas. *Take Away One*. New York: St. Martin's/ Marek, 1985. 357 pp.

This is the purportedly true story of Sarah Stefanovic, who hired a professional agent to kidnap her son, Joey, and smuggle him out of Yugoslavia where her estranged husband had kidnapped and taken him. The story traces the couples courtship and marriage and gives an account of Joey's rescue from his father's home in central Belgrade.

500 Gill, John Edward. *Stolen Children: How and Why Parents Kidnap Their Kids—And What to Do About It*. New York: Seaview Books, 1981. 260 pp.

Explains the problem of child stealing. The legal rights that parents do have, and how to exercise them to the fullest, are covered. Also the author analyzes the child-stealing law of 1980, explaining what it can and cannot do for the victimized parents. Offers advice on how parents should conduct their own search for their children: whether to locate the children on their own or use private investigators, how to recover the children once they are found, and how to prevent a second snatch. Based on hundreds of interviews with parents of stolen children, lawyers, psychologists, private detectives, police, and the children themselves.

501   Hoff, Patricia M. *Parental Kidnapping: How to Prevent an Abduction and What to Do If Your Child Is Abducted.* 2d ed. Washington, DC: National Center for Missing and Exploited Children, 1985. 40 pp.

This handbook describes the actions parents can take and the laws that may help them when their children are the victims of parental kidnapping. It also explains how to prevent abductions and outlines the rights of noncustodial parents. Includes a list of selected parental kidnapping support groups throughout the country.

502   *Interstate Child Custody Disputes and Parental Kidnapping: Policy, Practice and Law.* Patricia M. Hoff et al. Washington, DC: Legal Services Corporation, American Bar Association, 1982. 1 vol. (various pagings).

For annotation see listing 417.

503   Katz, Sanford N. *Child Snatching: The Legal Response to the Abduction of Children.* Chicago: Section of Family Law, American Bar Association, 1981. 206 pp.

Presents an analysis of the problems of parental kidnapping of children in the United States after or during divorce and separation. This book is based on a study prepared for the National Institute of Justice under P.O. no. 0-0608-JARS. The Uniform Child Custody Jurisdiction Act (UCCJA) is analyzed, and cases decided under the Act are interpreted and compared with one another. The final chapter discusses the remedies available to aggrieved parents in the state courts and gives the variations of the remedies from state to state.

504   Lawrence, Bobbie, and Olivia Taylor-Young. *The Child Snatchers.* Boston: Charles River Books, 1983. 259 pp.

This book begins with the story of one child snatching and the second part gives the reader advice on how to prevent child snatching. It includes case histories of child snatching by divorced or separated parents.

505 *My Child Is Not Missing: A Parents' Guidebook for the Prevention and Recovery of Missing Children.* Plantation, FL: Child Safe Products, 1984. 169 pp.

Contains portrayals of missing and exploited children, including parental kidnaps, runaways, criminal abductions, and child abuse. Includes information about prevention, the first missing hours, recovery, involving the community, and where to turn for help.

506 *Parental Kidnapping: A Handbook and Directory of Resources in the Denver Metropolitan Area.* Compiled by Susan M. Black, Barbara K. Lindauer, and Janet A. Buxton. Denver: Social Systems Research and Evaluation Division, Denver Research Institute, University of Denver, August 1983. 45 pp.

Contains information about what to do once you suspect your child is missing, whom to contact for help in finding your child, what you can do to help find your child, what to do when your child is located, what to do when your child has been returned, and how you can prevent a parental kidnapping incident. Also included is a directory of resources providing legal and mental health services.

507 Redpath, Peter A. *Help Me! My Child Is Missing! A Missing Child Handbook and Child-Saver Guide for Parents and Children.* New York: Child-Savers, Inc., 1984. 106 pp.

Offers advice to parents and children on how to best protect themselves from becoming another statistic in a lost-persons case. This handbook is divided into three parts. "Prevention Tips" describes ways to prevent an abduction, a child snatching, and a runaway. "Action Tips" gives advice on precise steps to take in the event of an abduction, a child snatching, and a runaway. "Material Aids in Dealing with the Missing Children Problems" contains such aids as fingerprint ID programs, missing-child network of concerned citizens organizations, runaway hotlines, a list of detectives who specialize in missing person cases, and cult-awareness group organizations which can provide information regarding religious cults.

508 Schaefer, Michael W. *Child Snatching: How to Prevent It From Happening to Your Child.* New York: McGraw-Hill, 1984. 112 pp.

Schaefer, director of the K.I.D. Fingerprint Identification program, covers what to do if a child is missing, if one's spouse or ex-spouse snatches a child, and if a child runs away or is abducted by a stranger. A section is devoted to safety-awareness instructions for children, and the author emphasizes the importance of fingerprinting children.

509 Strickland, Margaret. *Child Snatched: The Danny Strickland Case.* Moore Haven, FL: Rainbow Books, 1979. 109 pp.

This story is a classic case of child snatching. The author writes about the experiences of her grandson, who was kidnapped from the custody of her son by his ex-wife.

510 ————. *How to Deal With a Parental Kidnapping.* Moore Haven, FL: Rainbow Books, 1983. 263 pp. With her *Child Snatched: The Danny Strickland Case,* 1979. See listing 509.

Serves as a guide to any person involved in a child-snatching case. It is a directory of organizations that provides advice and other assistance to parents whose children have been abducted or retained in child custody disputes.The Uniform Child Custody Jurisdiction Act and the Missing Children Act are also discussed.

511 Tresidder, Alan. *Child Snatching.* Salem, OR: Legislative Research, 1981. 14 leaves.

In this work, Legislative Research was asked to describe Oregon's law relating to custodial interference (child snatching), compare it with other states, and describe the Canadian program. This is prefaced with a discussion of the increasing problem of child snatching.

B. Articles in Periodicals

512 Abrahms, Sally, and Joseph N. Bell. "Have You Seen the Children?" *Ladies Home Journal* 98:77 (April 1981).

Pictures seven children who have been kidnapped by parents and gives some of their personal experiences. Includes sources of help for parents seeking kidnapped children, discusses the Parental Kidnapping Prevention Act of 1980, and gives tips on how parents can protect against child snatching.

513   Barrett, Katherine. "I Always Knew You'd Find Me, Mom."
(Custody case of James Kennedy). *Ladies Home Journal* 98:86
(August 1981).

> This article is the result of the *Ladies Home Journal* story in April
> 1981 of ten-year-old James Kennedy, who was pictured with seven
> other children, all of whom had been kidnapped by one of their
> parents. Although he had been missing for over two and a half
> years, a reader recognized him and he was recovered by his
> mother. This is the story of his rescue and reunion with his
> mother.

514   "Child Custody Disputes and Parental Kidnapping: A Conference Report." *Children Today* 12:32–33 (January/February 1983).

> Overview of the First National Conference on Interstate Child
> Custody and Parental Kidnapping Cases, held in Arlington, Vir-
> ginia, and sponsored by the Child Custody Project and the Family
> Law Section of the American Bar Association. The conference
> offered a review of state and federal civil and criminal laws and
> procedures applicable to interstate child custody and parental
> kidnapping cases, as well as private and governmental resources
> available to help in cases of parental kidnapping.

515   "Child Snatching." *Children Today* 10:30–31 (March/April 1981).

> Announces the passage of the Parental Kidnapping Prevention
> Act of 1980 (P.L. 96–611) and explains its provisions.

516   Crowley, Eileen. "I Found My Kidnapped Daughter." *Good
Housekeeping* 197:117 (August 1983).

> The true story of the parental kidnapping of Robin, who was four
> years old when snatched by her father and was finally returned
> to her mother seven years later. Tells of the mother's struggles
> through the courts in two states, the hiring of private investigators
> to retrieve Robin, and how the organization Child Find helped to
> reunite mother and daughter.

517   Davidson, Joanne. "When Parents Kidnap Their Own Children." *U.S. News and World Report* 90:66–67 (30 March 1981).

> Tells of the tragic experiences of some children kidnapped by a
> parent and how the kidnapping trauma affects the lives of both
> the children and the custodial parents who have lost them.
> Children may be afraid to play outside for fear that they may be
> kidnapped again, they may start carrying a safety pin for protec-

tion, or they may not be able to sleep soundly. Also provides the names of organizations that locate stolen children.

518 Gelles, Richard J. "Parental Child Snatching: A Preliminary Estimate of the National Incidence." *Journal of Marriage and the Family* 46:735–39 (August 1984).

Reports the results of a preliminary survey which measures the incidence of parental child-snatching.

519 Hammer, Joshua. "The Struggle for Custody of a 7-Year-Old Boy Ends in an Explosion of Gunfire and Death." *People Weekly* 25:28–40 (24 February 1986).

Tells of a struggle for custody which resulted in parental kidnapping and death for the mother, who was killed by her former husband, and also the death of her former husband, who was killed by the mother's second husband in self defense.

520 "Kidnappings: A Family Affair." *Newsweek* 88:24 (18 October 1976).

Gives the personal experiences of noncustodial parents kidnapping their children from the custodial parent. Tells of one such case which ended in death for both the child and the kidnapping parent. Also explains briefly the Uniform Child Custody Jurisdiction Act which helps to eliminate jurisdictional disputes between states that have awarded custody to different parents.

521 Leo, John. "Kidnaped by Mom or Dad." *Time* 116:41 (14 July 1980).

Gives the personal experiences of parental kidnapping and examples of the psychological effects of the experience on children. Tells how Children's Rights, Inc., an organization with chapters across the country, cooperates in order to locate abducted children.

522 Most, Bruce W. "The Child-Stealing Epidemic or Parent Against Parent: The Child-Stealing Epidemic." *Nation* 224:559–61 (7 May 1977).

Tells of the experiences of custodial parents, both men and women, who have had their children kidnapped by their former spouses. Explains corrective legislation including the Uniform Child Custody Jurisdiction Act (UCCJA): its pros and cons.

523   "Moving to Stop Child Snatching." *Time* 111:85 (27 February 1978).

> Examines what can be done about parental kidnapping, such as the Uniform Child Custody Jurisdiction Act, which provides respect for custody terms worked out in other states, and considers subjecting parental child snatchers to federal kidnapping laws.

524   Ralston, Jeannie. "The Search for Kathey and Debbie." *McCall's* 113:71 (October 1985).

> As a result of Janet Hick's story on the TV documentary, "Missing: Have You Seen This Person?" 29 April 1985 her two daughters, Kathey and Debbie, who had been kidnapped by their father when they were 5 and 7, were reunited with their mother. This article traces what Janet did to try and find her two daughters. Tells of their reunion and life together after being apart for ten years, lists child-protection guidelines and information parents should have readily available, and also lists organizations to contact for help in missing children.

525   Spangler, Susan E. "Snatching Legislative Power: The Justice Department's Refusal to Enforce the Parental Kidnapping Prevention Act." *Journal of Criminal Law and Criminology* 73:1176–1203 (1982).

> Examines the legislative history of the Parental Kidnapping Prevention Act of 1980 (P.L. 96-611) to determine how its drafters hoped to solve the problem of child snatching and how recently issued Justice Department regulations frustrate parents who request governmental assistance, thus weakening the law's impact.

526   Tunley, Roul. "I'll Never Give Up." *Reader's Digest* 117:90–94 (September 1980).

> Tells about Vince Paris's personal experience when his daughter, Missy, was kidnapped by his ex-wife, and how, after an eighteen-month search, Missy was found.

527   Van Gelder, Lindsy. "Beyond Custody: When Parents Steal Their Own Children." *Ms.* 6:52–53 (May 1978).

> Tells of divorced women's experiences involving the kidnapping of their children by their ex-spouses, and examines legislation to prevent and aid custodial parents in reuniting with their children.

528   Van Rooyen, Deborah Steiner. "How Could You Do This to My Baby?" *Redbook* 165:46 (September 1985).

Recounts the author's experience when her ex-husband kidnapped their nineteen-month-old daughter and hid her in another country. Although Kierie was found after two months, she suffered emotionally and psychologically from the abduction. The author formed the International Child Abduction Information and Search Agency (ICAISA), a nonprofit organization, to provide on-the-spot information to parents looking for their children in foreign countries.

8
Children of Divorce

A. Books

529 Allers, Robert D. *Divorce, Children & the School.* Princeton, NJ: Princeton Book Co., 1982. 158 pp.

School is a large part of a child's life and can provide the security needed to help children of divorced parents adjust to the rapid changes occurring in their homes. The responsibilities and implications for educators are many, affecting attitudes, curriculum, and methods of dealing with parents as well as children. This book explains the events occurring in the child's life at this crucial time, describes typical reactions of the child to the situation and provides suggestions and guidelines for educators.

530 Barnett, Peter, Christine P. Gaudio., and Margaret G. Sumner. *Parenting Children of Divorce.* New York: Family Service Association of America, 1980. 107 pp.

This is a manual, in a workshop format, which serves as a training mechanism and basic framework for group leaders involved in Family Life Education workshops. Consists of five sessions which cover expressing feelings, self-worth, changing roles and needs of parents, the divorce triangle, and relationships with persons of the opposite sex. Provides outlines for all sessions, assignments, and handouts.

531 Berger, Stuart. *Divorce Without Victims: Helping Children Through Divorce With a Minimum of Pain and Trauma.* Boston: Houghton-Mifflin, 1983. 194 pp.

Psychiatrist Berger addresses concerned parents, emphasizing the resources needed to ease childrens' stress reactions to divorce, knowledge of child development, emotional self-control, and access to good professional help if necessary. Case examples are discussed along with such topics as: defense mechanisms, custody, visitation, parental dating/marriage, homosexuality, and incest.

532 Bernstein, Joanne E. *Books to Help Children Cope With Separation and Loss.* 2d ed. New York: Bowker, 1983. 439 pp.

This new edition critically annotates four hundred additional titles includes a selection of the best in-print titles from the first edition (1977). It includes books designed to help children from ages three to sixteen overcome the grief of loss in whatever form it takes death, separation, divorce, or hospitalization.

533 Buchanan, Neal C., and Eugene Chamberlain. *Helping Children of Divorce.* Nashville, TN: Broadman, 1981. 154 pp.

This book is a result of a church seminar for elementary-age children whose parents were divorced or were in the process of divorcing. Designed as a tool for adults to help children and families in the crisis of divorce.

534 *Children of Separation and Divorce: Management and Treatment.* Edited by Irving R. Stuart and Lawrence Edwin Abt. New York: Van Nostrand, 1981. 365 pp.

This anthology of fifteen articles explores a variety of issues related to management and treatment of children affected by divorce and separation. The section on joint custody provides an overview of this social issue from both a family and policy perspective.

535 Ciborowski, Paul J. *The Changing Family.* Vol. 1, *Group Manual.* Vol. 2, *Leader's Guide.* New York: Stratmar Educational Systems, 1984.

These resource manuals, which can be used by counselors and teachers, include over thirty small-group and classroom activities for children, ages eleven to seventeen, from divorced homes.

536 Despert, Juliette Louise. *Children of Divorce.* Garden City, NY: Doubleday, 1962. 298 pp. Originally published in 1953.

Dr. Despert was one of the first professionals to speak of divorce as not necessarily traumatic and destructive for children. She feels it is ". . . the emotional situation in the home, with or without divorce, that is the determining factor in a child's adjustment."

Case studies, a step-by-step guide for divorcing parents, and a chapter on remarriage are included.

537   Diamond, Susan Arnsberg. *Helping Children of Divorce: A Handbook for Parents and Teachers.* New York: Schocken, 1985. 115 pp.

The author draws on fifteen years of experience as a counselor and includes interviews with parents, children, lawyers, psychiatrists, social workers, clergy, and school personnel. She offers recommendations on sensitizing teachers to the nontraditional family rights of the noncustodial parent, and ways the schools can help children of divorce.

538   Duncan, T. Roger, and Darlene Duncan. *You're Divorced But Your Children Aren't.* Englewood Cliffs, NJ: Prentice-Hall, 1979. 236 pp.

Explores the problems divorce creates and offers insights into dealing with them. Activities for self-evaluation which can help readers explore emotions that they are experiencing are included, and ways are offered to help children through the transitional period which follows divorce. Areas of note are the legal aspects of divorce, custody and visitation, the kidnapping parent, and therapy and counseling.

539   *Explaining Divorce to Children.* Edited by Earl A. Grollman. New York: Beacon Press, 1972. 272 pp.

Nine writers offer their points of view and advice about divorce and its effects on children. Attention is given to personality development, parental relationships, and the legal complications and requirements. The final chapter is a panel discussion in which six teenagers whose parents are divorced answer the question, "Would a broken home break you?"

540   Francke, Linda Bird. *Growing Up Divorced.* New York: Simon & Schuster, 1983. 303 pp.

This work grew out of a 1980 *Newsweek* cover story. It details the effects of divorce on children by providing statistics, interviews with about one hundred boys and girls, and quotes from specialists. Also separate chapters discuss the behavior patterns exhibited at different stages of child development, how schools help students cope with divorce, and the trauma of custody battles.

541   Gardner, Richard A. *The Parents' Book About Divorce.* Garden City, NY: Doubleday, 1977. 368 pp.

The author addresses parents about how to deal with difficulties of a separation in ways that are most likely to protect their children from psychological disturbance. Guidance is given on such problems as counseling, effects of divorce on children, early postseparation adjustment, and dealing with feelings such as anger, grief, depression, abandonment, shame, and guilt.

542 ———. *Psychotherapy With Children of Divorce.* New York: J. Aronson, 1976. 534 pp.

Addresses therapists who work with children of divorce. It contains specific techniques for working through the feelings aroused by the divorce such as guilt, anger, abandonment, grief, depression, and is useful for diagnostic understanding. There is a short section on remarriage.

543 Goldstein, Sonja, and Albert J. Solnit. *Divorce and Your Child: Practical Suggestions for Parents.* New Haven, CT: Yale University Press, 1984. 135 pp.

Focuses entirely on children's needs and perceptions during separation, divorce, and remarriage, with suggestions for parents. Custody is covered throughout the book. Chapters deal with stepfamilies, the custodial and the noncustodial parent.

544 Hart, Archibald D. *Children and Divorce: What to Expect, How to Help.* Waco, TX: World Books, 1982. 157 pp.

Addresses the issues which confront children of divorce, such as what it feels like to be a child of divorce. It offers suggestions for alleviating the damaging consequences divorce is likely to have on children, and it includes chapters on the question of remarriage.

545 Inglis, Ruth. *Must Divorce Hurt the Children?* London: Temple Smith, 1982. 176 pp.

The author speaks of seeking the "least detrimental available alternatives" in this child-centered study of divorce. Some chapters deal with laws and customs, the preschool child, primary and junior school age, the adolescent, absent fathers, and achieving a "good divorce."

546 Jackson, Michael, and Jessica Jackson. *Your Father's Not Coming Home Anymore.* Edited by Bruce Jackson. New York: Richard Marek, 1981. 320 pp.

Records interviews with teenagers in which they discuss how they coped with their parents' divorce and its many aspects, such as stepparents, custody, and the reasons for divorce.

547   Jewett, Claudia L. *Helping Children Cope With Separation and Loss.*
      Boston: Harvard Common Press, 1982. 146 pp.

      Authored by a child-and-family therapist, this book focuses on
      the effects of major loss (through death, divorce, hospitalization,
      etc.) on children. Outlines specific methods to be used in dealing
      with a mourning child.

548   Laiken, Deidre S. *Daughters of Divorce: The Effects of Parental
      Divorce on Women's Lives.* New York: Morrow, 1981. 201 pp.

      Laiken, the daughter of divorced parents, writes about the long-
      term effects of divorce on women, and how living in a divorced
      family alters a girl's dreams and expectations. Chapters of note
      are "The Daddy Game" and "Stepmother/Stepdaughter."

549   List, Julie Autumn. *The Day the Loving Stopped: A Daughter's
      View of Her Parents' Divorce.* New York: Seaview Books, 1980.
      215 pp.

      List describes how her happy childhood, in a middle-class home,
      was disrupted by her parents' divorce when whe was nine years
      old.

550   Robson, Bonnie. *My Parents are Divorced Too: Teenagers Talk About
      Their Experiences & How They Cope.* New York: Everest House,
      1980. 208 pp.

      Interviews, with twenty-eight young people, about their parents'
      divorce; what caused it, their feelings about it, and how they
      coped with it.

551   Salk, Lee. *What Every Child Would Like Parents to Know about
      Divorce.* New York: Harper & Row, 1978. 149 pp.

      Suggests ways that parents can approach the subject of divorce
      with their children, what pitfalls to avoid, and how to reassure
      the children that they are still loved. Includes a chapter about
      custody.

552   Spilke, Francine Susan. *What about the Children? A Divorced
      Parent's Handbook.* New York: Crown Publishers, 1979. 81 pp.

      A manual for parents that answers questions raised by divorce,
      such as how to tell your child about the divorce, dating, and
      remarriage.

553 Tessman, Lora Heims. *Children of Parting Parents.* New York: J. Aronson, 1978. 604 pp.

> The author, a therapist who has worked extensively with children and their parents, uses material from more than fifty cases to illustrate the child's experience of separation from a parent through either death or divorce.

554 Troyer, Warner. *Divorced Kids: Children of Divorce Speak Out and Give Advice to Mothers, Fathers, Lovers, Stepparents, Brothers and Sisters, Boyfriends and Girlfriends, Each Other.* New York: Harcourt, 1979, 175 pp.

> From hundreds of interviews with American and Canadian children, Troyer, the divorced father of eight, gives us a child's-eye view of divorce that ranges from deep emotional trauma to apparent resilience. The bulk of the interviews were with children from five to fifteen years of age, and some were with adults who were children of divorce themselves.

555 Turow, Rita. *Daddy Doesn't Live Here Any More* Garden City, NY: Anchor Books, 1978. 222 pp.

> Written to help parents experiencing divorce answer questions raised by their children and deal with the most common situations involving their children. Chapters are included on how to tell about divorce, custody, planning holidays, playing one parent against the other, grandparents, lower finances, working mothers, stepparents, discipline, and the need for professional help. Material is taken from a survey of divorced parents as well as from personal interviews conducted by the author.

556 Vigeveno, H. S., and Anne Claire. *Divorce and the Children.* Glendale, CA: Regal Books, 1979. 127 pp.

> Interviews with over one hundred children, ages six to twenty, tell how children are affected by divorce and how parents can help them and themselves. Includes dealing with divorce, building a single-parent family, adjusting in a stepfamily, and pulling together.

557 Walczak, Yvette, with Sheila Burns. *Divorce: The Child's Point of View.* London: Harper & Row, 1984. 156 pp.

> Based on the experiences of one hundred children, conveying their points of view on divorce. Some of the areas explored are memories of the predivorce family, how children learned about

divorce and their immediate reactions to the news, custody and access immediate financial consequences, and parental remarriage. Ends with conclusions which summarize the findings, compares them with those of others, and makes recommendations about who can help and how.

558   Wakerman, Elyce. *Father Loss: Daughters Discuss the Man That Got Away and the Impact of His Absence.* Garden City, NY: Doubleday, 1984. 282 pp.

Explores the effect that the early loss of a father through death, divorce, or abandonment has on the psychological development of a woman.

559   Walker, Glynnis. *Solomon's Children: Exploding the Myths of Divorce.* New York: Arbor House, 1986. 200 pp.

Based on questionnaires completed by people whose parents divorced an average of eleven years ago. The author wants to dispel the "myth" that children of divorce are an army of walking wounded whose lives are laid waste. Instead, he concludes, it is the fathers who are the real victims of divorce.

560   Wallerstein, Judith S., and Joan Berlin Kelly. *Surviving the Breakup: How Children and Parents Cope With Divorce.* New York: Basic Books, 1980. 341 pp.

Reports on a five-year study of the children from sixty divorced families in Marin County, California. Covers the children's feelings and the parent-child relationship after separation.

B. Articles in Periodicals

561   Burchinal, Lee G. "Characteristics of Adolescents from Broken, Unbroken and Reconstituted Families." *Journal of Marriage and the Family* 26:44–51 (1964).

In this investigation, nonsignificant differences were found for the majority of adolescent relationships tested pertaining to the detrimental effects of divorce upon children.

562   Cantor, Dorothy W. "The Psychologist as Child Advocate With Divorcing Families." *Journal of Divorce* 6:77–86 (Fall/Winter 1982).

Proposes that psychologists assume an active role as child advocates with divorcing families to reduce the stress for the children. Describes ways in which psychologists can intervene both indirectly (with significant adults in the children's lives), and directly with children.

563   Green, Virginia P., and Lyn Schaefer. "The Effects of Personal Divorce Experience on Teacher Perceptions of Children of Divorce." *Journal of Divorce* 8:107–10 (Winter 1984).

This investigation determines that teachers with personal divorce experience were more likely to encourage teacher and school involvement with children of divorce than teachers without personal divorce experience.

564   Gunther, Max. "Who Gets the Kids This Christmas?" *Families* December 1981): 11–16.

Explains how divorced parents can help their children get the most out of the holiday season. One little girl, instead of feeling only sadness because her family would be split apart at Christmas, informed her schoolmates that this year she would have two Christmases—one with each parent. Her parents help her to find the pluses in a disadvantaged situation. Included are general guidelines for working out the best Christmas holiday arrangements.

565   Kalter, Neil. "Children of Divorce in an Outpatient Psychiatric Population." *American Journal of Orthopsychiatry* 47:40–52 (1977).

Kalter found that there was a greater tendency for children of divorce, living in both single-parent and stepfamilies, to manifest aggression toward their parents, compared with children of intact families.

566   Kaplan, Stuart L. "Structural Family Therapy for Children of Divorce: Case Reports." *Family Process* 16:75–83 (1977).

Describes structural family-therapy techniques for treating families of divorce. Five case reports, each representing a different stage in divorce, are presented.

567   Katz, Lilian G. "Telling Children about Divorce." *Parents* 61:152 (July 1986).

> Tells how to help children understand the meaning of divorce, such as how and what to tell them, and how to help parents acknowledge and accept children's feelings of grief, anger, and fear.

568   Kelly, Joan B., and Judith S. Wallerstein. "Brief Interventions With Children in Divorcing Families." *American Journal of Orthopsychiatry* 47:23–39 (1977).

> Preventive clinical interventions developed for children of various ages are described. Formulations regarding assessment, strategies, and the limitations of brief interventions with children at the time of divorce are presented.

569   Lowery, Carol R., and Shirley A. Settle. "Effects of Divorce on Children: Differential Impact of Custody and Visitation Patterns." *Family Relations* 34:455–63 (October 1985).

> Reviews the research literature on children's experience of the restructuring of the family following divorce. Custody arrangements and visitation patterns potentially minimizing the harmful effects related to these variables are identified.

570   Parish, Thomas S., and Judy W. Dostal. "Relationships Between Evaluations of Self and Parents by Children from Intact and Divorced Families." *Journal of Psychology* 104:35–38 (1980).

> This study surveyed 639 fifth- through eigth-grade boys and girls from a total of 14 school districts across the state of Kansas in each of the following areas: yourself, mother, father, and (when applicable) stepfather. Children from divorced families were found to have self-concepts that correlated significantly with their ratings of their mothers and stepfathers, but not with their natural fathers.

571   Parish, Thomas S., and Terry F. Copeland. "The Relationships Between Self-Concepts and Evaluations of Parents and Stepfathers." *Journal of Psychology* 101:135–38 (1979).

> This study surveyed 206 male and female college students in the following areas: yourself, mother, father, and (when applicable) stepfather. Students from father-absent families tended to demonstrate self-concepts that correlated significantly with how they

evaluated their mothers and stepfathers, but not their natural fathers.

572 Pett, Marjorie G. "Correlates of Children's Social Adjustment Following Divorce." *Journal of Divorce* 5:25–39 (Summer 1982).

Examines family correlates of children's social adjustment following divorce. Data was collected concerning 411 children from interviews with 206 randomly selected custodial parents.

573 "Reading, Writing and Divorce." *Newsweek* 55:74 (13 May 1985).

Tells how some school systems have initiated programs for students from broken homes, such as weekly counseling sessions or an hour of shopping, play, or lunch. California's Hermosa Valley School offers a stop-by center which provides supervised exercise and crafts. Denver public schools has workshops and some Michigan schools have group-discussion programs known as "The Divorce Club."

574 Salk, Lee. "Helping Children Deal With Divorce." *McCall's* 111:88 (October 1983).

Discusses four questions: whether or not couples in a troubled, loveless marriage should stay together; dating after divorce; effects of the divorce in a child having nightmares; and children accepting the new mate.

575 Skeen, Patsy, Bryan E. Robinson, and Carol Flake-Hobson. "How Teachers Can Help Children From Stepfamilies." *Education Digest* 50:54–57 (November 1984).

Explains some of the techniques teachers can use to facilitate a child's adjustment to divorce. These techniques are also appropriate for use with children in stepfamilies.

576 Wallerstein, Judith S., and Joan B. Kelly. "The Effects of Parental Divorce: Experiences of the Child in Early Latency." *American Journal of Orthopsychiatry* 46:20–42 (1976).

Examines seven- to eight-year-old children's initial reactions to marital breakup, and the effect of expectations placed upon them by new stepparents.

577 ———. "The Effects of Parental Divorce: Experiences of the Child in Later Latency." *American Journal of Orthopsychiatry* 46:356–69 (1976).

Children, ages nine to ten years, were studied at the time of divorce and one year later. At follow-up, fifty percent of the children were significantly worse. Angry feelings expressed in the initial study continued, with one-third of the children remaining enraged with the noncustodial parent.

578 ———. "The Effects of Parental Divorce: Experiences of the Preschool Child." *Journal of the American Academy of Child Psychiatry* 14:600–16(1974).

Considers the responses of thirty-four preschool children to their parents' separation and divorce, and fifteen children who deteriorated psychologically at the end of one year.

579 Weisfeld, David, and Martin S. Laser. "Divorced Parents in Family Therapy in a Residential Treatment Setting." *Family Process* 16:229–36 (1977).

A treatment article emphasizing the importance of including the divorced or separated parents in the treatment of their child.

580 Weissbourd, Bernice. "When Parents Separate." *Parents* 58:100 (May 1983).

Discusses the behavior of two-year-olds and how to help them adjust to life in the single-parent household.

9
Fathers

A. Books

581 Adams, Paul L., Judith R. Milner, and Nancy A. Schrepf. *Fatherless Children*. New York: Wiley, 1984. 407 pp.

Starts with a plea for better research on the effects of father absence. Explains how father absence affects family functioning and child development in a variety of ways, such as economic or socioemotional stress, social isolation, lack of parenting support, and the absence of a male sex-role model. Summarizes much of the literature on father absence.

582 Atkin, Edith Lesser, and Estelle Rubin. *Part-Time Father*. New York: New American Library, 1977. 182 pp.

The authors, two psychotherapists, deal with a variety of problems a divorced custodial or noncustodial father faces with his children at different stages of their development, from infancy through adolescence, and also at different stages of the divorce – from the breakup of the family to the evolving relationship of father and child as they both adjust to the divorce situation. They also try to deal not only with the problems of the part-time father, but with his potentialities and opportunities for a fulfilling and gratifying relationship with his children. There is a chapter about the father as the custodial parent and a brief critique of divided custody arrangements.

583 Biller, Henry B. *Father, Child, and Sex Role: Parental Determinants of Personality Development*. Lexington, MA: Heath Lexington Books, 1971. 193 pp.

Begins with an examination of the relationship of father absence to sex-role development and considers next the variation in the father-son relationship. Other chapters deal with the mother-son relationship and the father-daughter relationship. The final chapter is devoted to an evaluation of the research, suggestions for further investigations, and possible applications of the findings.

584   Biller, Henry, and Dennis Meredith. *Father Power*. New York: McKay, 1975. 376 pp.

Classic work on the importance of fathers highlights their importance to their children's development in such areas as competence and intelligence, sexuality, body image, self-confidence, and achievement. Includes chapters on divorced fathers, stepfathers, and single fathers.

585   *Dimensions of Fatherhood*. Edited by Shirley M. H. Hanson and Frederick W. Bozett. Beverly Hills: Sage Publications, 1985. 464 pp.

Consists of nineteen chapters by twenty-seven contributors distributed over a number of disciplines: family studies, psychology, sociology, nursing, social work, education, and therapy. The first nine chapters each represent a developmental stage in the life cycle, beginning with men and family planning and ending with men as grandfathers. The last half of the work presents fathers in a variety of circumstances: in dual-income families, in the military, as househusbands, stepfathers, gay men, adolescent fathers, single custodial fathers, noncustodial fathers, and widowers.

586   *Fatherhood and Family Policy*. Edited by Michael E. Lamb and Abraham Sagi. Hillsdale, NJ: L. Erlhaum, 1983. 276 pp.

Brings together the scholarly literature and contemporary social policy concerns to review the evidence concerning: the factors that limit or constrain male involvement in child care; the ways in which some of these factors are being or might be changed; and the effects of traditional and increased paternal involvement on men, women, and children. Chapter 5 is entitled, "The Father's Case in Child Custody Disputes: The Contributions of Psychological Research."

587   *Fathers, Husbands, and Lovers: Legal Rights & Responsibilities*. Compiled by Sanford Katz and Monroe L. Inker. Chicago: American Bar Association, 1979. 318 pp.

A collection of professional articles that have appeared in the *Family Law Quarterly* about the man's legal role in formal and informal marital relationships. Includes essays on the establishment of paternity, paternal support and the father's right to custody, test tube babies, unwed fathers' paternal rights, and changes in custody laws.

588 Ferrara, Frank. *On Being Father: A Divorced Man Talks About Sharing the New Responsibilities of Parenthood.* Garden City, NY: Doubleday, 1985. 175 pp.

This book is for divorced fathers and tells how they can maintain a vital relationship with their children regardless of the less-than-ideal visitation arrangements. Some areas discussed are: getting through the period between the separation and divorce, helping children adjust, finding support groups, dealing with feelings such as guilt and depression, running a home as a single father, and celebrating holidays.

589 Green, Maureen. *Fathering.* New York: McGraw-Hill, 1976. 230 pp.

Advocates a redefinition of the father's role. It offers suggestions for fathering children within the nuclear family, fathering natural children separated from one parent by divorce, assuming the role of stepfather, father-son relationships, and father-daughter relationships.

590 Hamilton, Marshall L. *Fathers' Influence on Children.* Chicago: Nelson-Hall, 1977. 203 pp.

Reviews relevant research concerning the influence of fathers on children. The author emphasizes the need for recognition and examination of the father's contribution to parenting.

591 Kahan, Stuart. *For Divorced Fathers Only.* New York: Monarch, 1978. 179 pp.

Brings together the basic facts and feelings involved in being a divorced father. It is written for, about, and by divorced fathers. Chapters deal with "The New Life," "Child Relationships," "Adult Relationships," and "The Financial/Legal Relationships." Chapter topics include custody and remarriage.

592 Klinman, Debra G., and Rhiana Kohl. *Fatherhood U.S.A.: The First National Guide to Programs, Services, and Resources For and About Fathers.* New York: Garland, 1984. 321 pp.

The Fatherhood Project was started in 1981 at the Bank Street College of Education, New York City, with the goal of encouraging the development of a wide range of options for male involvement in child rearing. The Project has produced this directory of organizations which are described by state in the following subject areas: health care, education, social and supportive services, family law and employment. Bibliographical resources on such topics as single fathers, stepfathers, gay fathers, father involvement in schools, child support enforcement, and paternity benefits are included as well as alphabetical and geographical listings of programs and organizations for fathers.

593 Levine, James A. *Who Will Raise the Children? New Options For Fathers (and Mothers)*. Philadelphia: Lippincott, 1976. 192 pp.

Presents current social changes in the relationship between fathers and children. Although this book is not specifically about divorce, a full chapter is devoted to fathers and custody. Promotes the idea that fathers are as adept at child rearing as mothers. Chapter 2, "Confronting Fatherhood: Men and Custody," contains information regarding shared custody and discusses needed reform to make shared custody an option available to more separated or divorced parents.

594 Newman, George. *101 Ways to Be a Long-Distance Superdad*. Mountain View, CA: Blossom Valley Press, 1981. 108 pp.

A guide to help divorced and noncustodial fathers keep in touch with their children who may be miles away.

595 Oakland, Thomas. *Divorced Fathers: Reconstructing a Quality Life*. New York: Human Sciences Press, 1984. 201 pp.

Written for fathers experiencing divorce-related difficulties who want to fashion a better life for themselves and their children. It explains how a father's adjustment and that of his children are inseparably intertwined, and offers suggestions to help fathers and children develop healthy, happy, and productive lives. It includes chapters that deal with custody, legal issues, and household management.

596 Parke, Ross D. *Fathers*. Cambridge: Harvard University Press, 1981. 136 pp.

Provides a discussion of fathering in its many forms: the divorced father, the stepfather, the father surrogate, the absent father, the dead father, and the househusband.

597 Robinson, Bryan E., and Robert L. Barrett. *The Developing Father: Emerging Roles in Contemporary Society.* New York: Guilford Press, 1986. 224 pp.

Presents research findings about fatherhood using case studies from the author's inteviews with a wide range of fathers and nonfathers. Provides special sections in each chapter on "Suggestions to Professionals" and "Professional Resources for Working with Fathers." Section 1 examines four major topics: theories about fatherhood, choosing and preparing for fatherhood, traditional and newly emerging models of the father role, and fathering across the life span. Section 2 presents the findings about different kinds of fathers that have become prevalent in American family life: never-married single and adoptive fathers, fathers of broken homes (divorced and widowed) or blended families, gay fathers, and teenage fathers of disabled children (those with physcial, emotional, intellectual handicaps).

598 *The Role of the Father in Child Development.* Edited by Michael E. Lamb. New York: Wiley, 1981. 582 pp.

A collection of articles which focus on the effects fathers have on the psychological development of children.

599 Rowlands, Peter. *Saturday Parent: A Book for Separated Families.* New York: Continuum, 1982. 143 pp.

There have been many books written for the parent who, as a result of separation or divorce, is bringing up a family single-handedly. This is a book for the other parent, the "Saturday parent," who lives apart from his or her children and sees them only occasionally. The author has written several books about children and is also a Saturday parent himself. He has conducted interviews with many Saturday parents and their children in order to write this book. This work will be helpful not only for Saturday parents but for anyone whose job it is to look after the children of these parents, such as teachers or social workers, and for grandparents and others closely involved with families that separate.

600 Shepard, Morris A., and Gerald Goldman. *Divorced Dads: Their Kids, Ex-Wives, and New Lives.* Radnor, PA: Chilton Book Company, 1979. 154 pp.

Two divorced fathers, who wanted their relationships, with their children to be more than "father as visitor" or "father as Sunday hero," have written this book which describes the development of a child-sharing plan that allowed them to remain involved in their children's lives. Both authors discuss their own experiences of sharing the care and responsibility for their children with their former wives. Other issues include how to: negotiate with your former spouse; plan a new social life; and adjust, emotionally and financially, to divorce.

601   Sifford, Darrell. *Father & Son.* Philadelphia: Westminster Press, 1982. 270 pp.

Personal recounting of the relationship that evolves between a father and his two sons after separation and divorce.

602   Sturner, William. *Love Loops: A Divorced Father's Personal Journey.* New York: Libra Publishers, 1983. 229 pp.

Personal experience, written in diary form, of one father's struggle to adjust to divorce and then to relate in meaningful ways with his two daughters.

603   Wishard, William R., and Laurie Wishard. *Men's Rights: A Handbook for the 80's.* San Francisco: Cragmont Publications, 1980. 264 pp.

This father-daughter writing team covers a variety of legal issues as advocates of the male point of view on such issues as living together, marriage, separtion and divorce, child custody, visitation rights, and financial support.

604   Woolfolk, William, with Donna Woolfolk Cross. *Daddy's Little Girl: The Unspoken Bargain between Fathers and Their Daughters.* Englewood Cliffs, NJ: Prentice-Hall, 1982. 220 pp.

This father-daughter author team interviewed fathers and daughters from middle- and upper-middle income classes for an honest account of the relationship between fathers and daugters. Stresses that the relationship may be subject to parents' divorce, handicapped daughter, infirmity, and death of the father.

605   Yablonsky, Lewis. *Fathers and Sons.* New York: Simon & Schuster, 1982. 218 pp.

Explains the normal conflicts that may exist between fathers and sons. Includes interviews and references to the professional literature with chapters on such topics as the father's role, father styles, and the life phases of father-son interaction.

B. Articles in Periodicals

606 Hetherington, E. Mavis. "Divorced Fathers." *The Family Coordinator* 25:417–28 (1976).

> Presents the results of a two-year study following divorce. Forty-eight divorced parents and their preschool children and a matched group of forty-eight intact families were studied through observational interviews, self-reports, rating scales, and standardized test measures at two months, one year, and two years following divorce. The process of disruption, coping, and adjustment by fathers to the crisis of divorce is examined.

607 ———. "Effects of Father Absence on Personality Development in Adolescent Daughters." *Developmental Pyschology* 7:313–26 (1972).

> Investigates the effects of father absence due to divorce or death on adolescent girls. Differences among divorcees, widows, and mothers of intact families on various personality measures, on childrearing attitudes, and on relations with their daughters were also investigated.

608 ———. "Effects of Paternal Absence on Sex-Typed Behavior in Negro and White Pre-adolescent Males." *Journal of Personality and Social Psychology* 4:87–91 (1966).

> Investigates the effects of race, father absence, and time of departure of the father on sex-typed behavior of preadolescent males.

609 Keshet, Harry F., and Kristine M. Rosenthal. "Fathering After Marital Separation." *Social Work* 23:11–18 (January 1978).

> A study of 128 separated men who chose to remain fully involved in the upbringing of their children. The study examines how being an involved parent contributes to the stability and personal growth of the fathers and their relationship with their children.

610 Koch, Mary Ann, and Carol R. Lowery. "Visitation and the Noncustodial Father." *Journal of Divorce* 8:47–65 (Winter 1984).

> Thirty noncustodial fathers were interviewed with regard to their satisfaction with the amount and quality of visitation. Information was also obtained about the amount of child support payments, the typical visitation schedule, and the relationship between the former spouses.

611   Leader, Arthur L. "Family Therapy for Divorced Fathers and Others Out of the Home." *Social Casework* 10:13–19 (1973).

A treatment article advocating the inclusion of separated members of the family in family therapy.

10
Working Parents
& Latchkey Children

A. Books

612 Bodin, Jeanne, and Bonnie Mitelman. *Mothers Who Work: Strategies for Coping.* New York: Ballantine Books, 1983. 259 pp.

The author surveyed 442 working mothers and interviewed 25 more. Suggestions for long-range changes of attitude are presented. The book communicates a strong sense of fellowship among working mothers who are experiencing stressful situations.

613 Chaback, Elaine, and Pat Fortunato. *The Official Kids' Survival Kit: How to Do Things on Your Own.* Boston: Little, Brown, 1981. 222 pp.

An alphabetical handbook giving practical advice to help in coping with everyday situations and routines as well as handling accidents and common medical emergencies.

614 Curtis, Jean. *Working Mothers.* Garden City, NY: Doubleday, 1976. 214 pp.

A discussion of the emotional aspects of being a working mother. The author interviewed some two hundred working mothers, and through their shared experiences she explores how women find ways to be good mothers and have careers at the same time.

615 Greenleaf, Barbara Kaye, and Lewis A. Schaffer. *Help: A Handbook for Working Mothers.* New York: Crowell, 1978. 296 pp.

Addresses the wide variety of pressures confronting the fifteen million mothers who work outside the home. Some areas considered are the pitfalls of nonsupportive husbands, children who require day care, housekeeping, and menu planning. Appendixes offer time-management techniques and other resource aids.

616 Grollman, Earl A., and Gerri L. Sweder. *The Working Parent Dilemma: How to Balance the Responsibilities of Children and Careers.* Boston: Beacon Press, 1986. 190 pp.

Grollman, a Massachusetts rabbi, lecturer, and writer on family issues, and Sweder, a child-development specialist and teacher, interviewed one thousand youngsters from two-job families to find out how children of employed parents fare and what their attitudes are. Among the book's suggestions, many relate to safety precautions at home and outside. Advice on how to prepare a child to be alone at home, which includes handling emergencies and illness, is important for latchkey children.

617 Kyte, Kathy S. *In Charge: A Complete Handbook for Kids With Working Parents.* New York: Knopf, 1983. 115 pp.

Advice for children who must take care of themselves in the morning or after school, on dealing with organizing time, first aid, cooking, laundering and mending clothes, and other helpful information for getting through the day.

618 Long, Lynette, and Thomas Long. *The Handbook for Latchkey Children and Their Parents.* New York: Arbor House, 1983. 316 pp.

The Longs, she a school principal and he a counselor, summarize their research findings from feedback of five hundred interviews with school personnel, parents, and the kids, about the "latchkey" phenomen of regularly leaving children unattended before and after school. Chapters deal with siblings, fears and dangers, stresses, time-fillers (e.g., TV, chores). Case histories dramatize short- and long-term effects, and examine the positive and negative results of self-care.

619 Long, Thomas. *Safe at Home, Safe Alone.* Alexander, VA: Miles River Press, 1985. 64 pp.

Designed to teach coping and survival skills to the eleven million school-aged children, ages seven to eleven, who spend time at home without adult supervision. Includes colorful illustrations with charts, games, and activities. Stresses responsibility and communication between child and parent. Gives insights into such issues as home safety, planning daily activities, nutrition, and learning to solve problems and make compromises.

620 Olds, Sally Wendkos. *The Working Parents' Survival Guide*. New York: Bantam Books, 1983. 318 pp.

Stresses the importance to the family of working together toward common goals to achieve a healthy, cooperative family, and gives ideas on balancing many parent roles. Discusses child care arrangements, home management, and most importantly the possibilities for growth of child, marriage, and family in the working parents' situation. Includes a section for the single, employed parent.

621 Robinson, Bryan E., Bobbie H. Rowland, and Mick Coleman. *Latchkey Kids: Unlocking Doors for the Children and Their Families*. Lexington, MA: Lexington Books, 1986. 220 pp.

Drawn from a survey of 1,806 families, travel to national child care programs for school-age children, conversations with leaders in the field of school-age child care, and correspondence with people who are coping with the latchkey situation. Includes the latest research about latchkey kids and examines actual case studies for the effects latchkey arrangements have on children, parents, and the family. Presents policies and programs that have been established in many states identifying what families, schools, business, industry, and government still need to do to come to grips with this growing social trend. Suggestions are also included for parents, teachers, school administrators, children in self-care, and researchers in the field of child development on how to cope with the latchkey situation.

622 Scott, Lucy, and Meredith Joan Angwin. *Time Out for Motherhood: A Guide for Today's Working Woman to the Financial, Emotional, and Career Aspects of Having a Baby*. Los Angeles: J. P. Tarcher, 1986, 253 pp.

Deals with the finances and challenges of single motherhood. despite the title, fathers receive attention also. Chapters of note are: "Single Mothers by Choice," " The Older Mother," and "Fathering the Working Family."

623 Swan, Helen L., and Victoria Houston. *Alone After School: A Self-Care Guide for Latchkey Children and Their Parents*. Englewood Cliffs, NJ: Prentice-Hall, 1985. 200 pp.

Written to help families whose children are alone after school develop a self-care plan to meet their needs and which will safeguard their children emotionally and physically as the number of latchkey children rapidly increases.

B. Articles in Periodicals

624 Berman, Eleanor. "Make Sure Your Child is Safe Alone: Suggestions for Those After-School Hours." *Working Mother* 9:143–144 (November 1986).

> Discusses what factors to consider before leaving children to care for themselves while parents are away at work, such as neighborhood and ages of the children. Other issues included are after-school care programs, ways to help your children feel safe, and tapping community resources. Gives the results of a survey of kids who are left alone and provides a reading list.

625 Bodley, Margaret J. "Family Resources Database: Latchkey Children." *Family Relations* 36:113–15 (January 1987).

> A bibliography, with no annotations, taken from the on-line Family Resources Database, of four books, thirteen articles, eight documents and reports on the subject of latchkey children.

626 Cole, Cynthia, and Hyman Rodman. "When School-Age Children Care for Themselves: Issues for Family Life Educators." *Family Relations* 36:92–96 (January 1987).

> Reviews several of the major questions parents, researchers, and family-life educators may have about self-care. Includes five related research studies. The following topics are covered: defining the self-care arrangement, the number of children in self-care, impact of self-care on children's development, and guidance for parents and children.

627 Enos, Forsyth. "The Secret World of Latchkey Kids." *Ladies' Home Journal* 103:63–66 (September 1986).

> A photo essay of three families offering a glimpse of latchkey children and what they do after school when they are alone. Although not an ideal solution, millions of working and/or single parents do leave young children alone, and this article tries to focus on making the experience as positive as possible. Tells how the children, ages nine to fifteen, feel about being left alone, how they spend their time, and offers safety advice.

628 Galamabos, Nancy L., and Roger A. Dixon. "Toward Understanding and Caring for Latchkey Children." *Child Care Quarterly* 13:116–25 (Summer 1984).

> This paper summarizes and compares the various opinions held on the treatment of latchkey children, and offers suggestions for their care and understanding.

629   Galambos, Nancy L., and James Garbarino. "Identifying the Missing Links in the Study of Latchkey Children." *Children Today* 12:2–4 (July-August 1983).

This study builds upon the existing work by answering the following question; How does a lack of supervision affect a child's school adjustment, academic achievement, orientation to the classroom, and fear of going outdoors alone?

630   Garbarino, James. "Latchkey Children: How Much of a Problem?" *Education Digest* 46:14–16 (February 1981).

Discusses the reasons for leaving children alone to care for themselves and what the effects of being alone may have on these children. Offers some possible alternatives/solutions, such as flexible work hours for parents, after-school programs, community projects like HELP (Homemaking Elementary Learning Procedures) which help children care for themselves, and lists ways human-service agencies can help.

631   Gillis, Phyllis. "Survival Guides for Working Moms: The Best Books Around on Balancing Child Raising, Work, and Marriage." *Parents* 56:30 (October 1981).

Six books are reviewed for working mothers, and one, *The Fathers' Almanac*, is for fathers. Information is included for single, separated, or divorced parents.

632   Guerney, Louise, and Leila Moore. "PhoneFriend: A Prevention-Oriented Service for Latchkey Children." *Children Today* 12:5–10 (July/August 1983).

Tells how an after-school telephone service for children, left to care for themselves, was initiated in the Pennsylvania State University area. Covers the planning phase, setting up operations, training volunteers, and implementing the pilot program. Gives an evaluation, expansion plan, and future plan. After a year's experience this telephone project proved to be an effective way of providing emotional support to children alone after school.

633   Hawkes, Ellen. "Working Moms: Job Security." *Parade* (26 April 1987): 18.

Contrasts countries that have national policies insuring paid and unpaid leaves for 8 to 52 weeks (and where in most cases, the job is protected) to the United States, where only five states have legislation requiring employers to provide pregnant workers with a job-protected unpaid leave of absence. The Family and Medical Leave Act, introducted in Congress in 1987, would provide employees up to 18 weeks of unpaid leave for birth, adoption, or serious illness of a child, and up to 26 weeks of unpaid leave for a serious illness (including pregnancy). This legislation would insure that employees' jobs are guaranteed upon their return. Fathers would also be eligible.

634   Marzollo, Jean. "Don't Call Me Supermom." *Parents* 59:59–63 (April 1984).

The author resents being called "supermom," a term used by men as a put-down implying that such a woman is foolish enough to go beyond her abilities by trying to work outside the home and care for a family. She sees the term as a slur to sling at women because it fuels their guilt, especially since the insult comes from men, whom most women are trained from childhood to please. This article tries to help release working women from feelings of guilt by dispelling the myth of the "supermom."

635   McCurdy, Jack. "Schools Respond to Latchkey Children." *School Administrator* 42:16–18 (March 1985).

Gives background, statistics, and definiton of latchkey children. Presents the role schools and private industry can play in working with latchkey children. Provides examples of four school programs for latchkey children.

636   Robinson, Bryan E., Bobbie H. Rowland, and Mick Coleman. "Taking Action for Latchkey Children and Their Families." *Family Relations* 35:473–78 (October 1986).

A summary of research findings about latchkey situations is presented, followed by suggestions for activities and programs which involve parents, schools, and community. Potential resources for programs are provided for use by practitioners.

637   Scherer, Marge. "Loneliness of the Latchkey Child. *Instructor* 91:38–41 (May 1982).

Stresses the need for teacher sensitivity in dealing with the latchkey parent as well as the latchkey child. Gives classroom experiences that could benefit children in isolated situations.

638   Stroman, Suzanne Higgs, and R. Eleanor Duff. "Latchkey Child: Whose Responsibility?" *Childhood Education* 59:76–79 (1982).

Presents the positive and negative consequences of being a latchkey child, as well as the concern for safety and the mental attitudes of the children. Offers classroom experiences that can benefit children in isolated situations. Closes on stressing the need for organized community action from school-sponsored community-sponsored programs, church programs, family day care, civic organizations, senior citizen groups, and community volunteers.

639 Strother, Deborah Burnett. "Latchkey Children: The Fastest-Growing Special Interest Group in the Schools." *Journal of School Health* 56:13–16 (January 1986).

Poses the following questions: Should parents be solely responsible for the before-school and after-school care of their children? What role might the schools play in providing this supervision for youngsters of working parents? How does self-care before and after school affect children's school performance? How can teachers help latchkey children and their parents? Addresses the role of the school, effects of self-care, and offers advice.

11
Teen Pregnancy & Parenthood

A. Books and Pamphlets

640 *Adolescent Abortion: Psychological and Legal Issues.* Edited by Gary B. Melton. Lincoln: University of Nebraska Press, 1986. 152 pp.

> Report of the Interdivisional Committee on Adolescent Abortion, American Psychological Association. Reviews the psychological issues that have been central to the Supreme Court's analysis of adolescent abortion policy and provides guidelines to psychologists involved in counseling minors about abortion or conducting research on the issue.

641 *Adolescent Fatherhood.* Edited by Arthur B. Elster and Michael E. Lamb. Hillsdale, NJ: L. Erlbaum Associates, 1986. 204 pp.

> This work is divided into four sections, each containing a set of chapters focused on similar themes covering adolescent development. The first section is an overview of key issues in the study of adolescence and a review of research on sexuality and contraceptive use by adolescents. Section 2 focuses on those adolescents who become fathers and the effects of adolescent fatherhood on individual males. The third section considers the effects of stress and economic constraints on the ability of adolescent fathers to fulfill their responsibilities. The final and fourth section covers intervention strategies, reviewing considerations relevant to the behavior of individual clinicians, and programs, as well as the development of national policies concerning teen fathers.

642 *Adolescent Parenthood.* Edited by Max Sugar. New York: SP Medical & Scientific Books, 1984. 237 pp.

> A collection of writings by fourteen authors covering a broad range of topics. There is an overview of perceptions of adolescent

pregnancy in nineteenth-century English novels; discussions of facets of decision making related to adolescent sexual behavior, contraception, and pregnancy resolutions; explorations of the psychodynamics of teenage development, pregnancy, and motherhood; observations on male roles and ethnic factors. Includes profiles of black and hispanic adolescent mothers, mental health services, parenting perceptions, the extended family context, and the legislative history of federally funded adolescent pregnancy programs.

643   Alan Guttmacher Institute. *Teenage Pregnancy: The Problem That Hasn't Gone Away.* New York: The Institute, 1981. 79 pp.

Gives the rising statistics of teenage pregnancy births and how many teenage mothers elect to keep their babies. In addition to presenting information on teenage sexual activity, the consequences of early childbearing, and efforts to solve the problem, the report discusses the needs that are still left unsatisfied. Calls for more emphasis on reaching young people with information about sex, reproduction, contraception, and the responsibilities of parenthood.

644   Anastasiow, Nicholas J. *The Adolescent Parent.* Baltimore: P. H. Brookes, 1982. 142 pp.

Begins with a review of the worldwide problem of adolescent pregnancy and a summary of knowledge about physical and intellectual development in adolescents. Presents studies on the effect of parenthood on teenage mothers, their offspring, and effect of parenting styles on children. Describes, evaluates, and suggests methods for strengthening programs aimed at improving the life chances and health of teenage-parent offspring. Some programs addressing adolescent pregnancy are presented and data evaluating such programs are reviewed. Project FEED, (Facilitating Environments Encouraging Development), designed to teach adolescents child-development and parenting skills, is described.

645   Baum, Daniel Jay. *Teenage Pregnancy.* New York: Beaufort Books, 1980. 157 pp.

Examines the many aspects of teenage pregnancy and births, from what can be done to prevent it to how we can help the young mother make a good life for herself and her child. This overview discusses the role of the boy father; the availability of birth control; how parents can help; choosing between adoption, abortion, and keeping the baby; the confusion of the law; the role of the commmunity; and the challenge of education.

646   Bedger, Jean E. *Teenage Pregnancy: Research Related to Clients and Services*. Springfield, IL: Charles C. Thomas, 1980. 203 pp.

In 1966 the Florence Crittenton Association of America entered into a contract with the Chicago Board of Health (now the Department of Health) to administer a program for unwed teenage mothers in Chicago. During the years 1965–77, over eight thousand young women went through this day care program for pregnant teenagers. This work evaluates the effectiveness of this program in order to determine the extent to which services help the young women make better plans for themselves and their children.

647   Buntman, Peter H., and Eleanor M. Saris. *How to Live With Your Teenager: A Survivor's Handbook For Parents*. New York: Ballantine Books, 1982. 169 pp.

Provides guidelines for parents to use in helping their adolescents through the teen years.

648   Cannon-Bonventre, Kristine, and Janet R. Kahn. *The Ecology of Help-Seeking Behavior Among Adolescent Parents: Final Report*. Cambridge, MA: American Institutes for Research, 1979. 99 pp.

Prepared for the Department of Health, Education and Welfare Administration for Children, Youth, and Families, grant no.: 90-C-1342. This study was undertaken to understand teenage parents' own definitions of their needs and problems as parents and of their definitions of acceptable sources and forms of help. Includes interviews with over one hundred black, Hispanic and white teenage parents, in the Boston area, about their problems as parents, their experiences with feelings about helping networks, and their unmet needs. Also interviewed service providers about the problems teenage parents encounter, the special issues involved, and the successes and failures of programs offered by the agencies.

649   Corsaro, Maria, and Carol Korzeniowsky. *A Woman's Guide to Safe Abortion*. New York: Holt, 1983. 100 pp.

Since one out of four pregnant teens (and half of those under fifteen) choose abortion, and since there is no young adult guide to abortion, this work serves a need for pregnant teens. It deals with the legal, medical, and psychological aspects of abortion.

Also includes a chapter which walks the reader through a first trimester abortion in a typical clinic.

650 *Crisis of Adolescence, Teenage Pregnancy: Impact on Adolescent Development.* Formulated by the Committee on Adolescence of the Group for the Advancement of Psychiatry. New York: Brunner/ Mazel, 1986, 81 pp.

Presents an overall view of the dimensions of the teenage pregnancy problem followed by brief summaries of biological, psychological, and social characteristics of teenage sexuality in contemporary America. Some problems discussed are: consequences of teenage pregnancy and subsequent effects on girls' education, future marriage stability, income potential and costs to society in increased AFDC (Aid to Families with Dependent Children). A final section focuses on interventions and recommendations.

651 Ewy, Donna, and Rodger Ewy. *Teen Pregnancy: The Challenges We Faced, the Choices We Made.* Boulder, CO: Pruett, 1984. 188 pp.

A guide for teenagers facing pregnancy, including information on nutrition, exercise, childbirth, infant care, birth control, relinquishing for adoption, and the need for contraceptives. Also provides first-person narratives of white, black, Hispanic, and Asian teenage mothers, emphasizing their disillusionment with the boys who ran out on them and ending with what it means to be a teenage parent.

652 *Factbook on Teenage Pregnancy: Tables and References for Teenage Pregnancy: The Problem That Hasn't Gone Away.* Prepared by Joy G. Dryfoos and Nancy Bourque-Scholl. New York: Alan Guttmacher Institute, 1981. 124 pp.

Presents tables and references for teenage pregnancy on sexual activity and marriage, contraceptive use, teenage pregnancy and its resolution, adolescent births, consequences of teenage childbearing, sex education, family planning services, contraceptive research and abortions, and other services to pregnant teenagers, adolescent parents, and their babies.

653 Frank, Daniel B. *Deep Blue Funk & Other Stories: Portraits of Teenage Parents.* Chicago: University of Chicago Press, 1983. 194 pp.

Set in a community center in a predominantly black section of Evanston, Illinois, this work provides insight into the expressed social and psychological needs of young parents. The author interviewed black teenage mothers ages thirteen to twenty. The final chapter contains interviews with teenage fathers.

654 Furstenberg, Frank F. *Unplanned Parenthood: The Social Consequences of Teenage Childbearing*. New York: Free Press, 1976. 293 pp.

An account of the social, economic, and psychological consequences of adolescent motherhood based on the experiences of a group of young women from pregnancy through the first five years of motherhood.

655 Hansen, Caryl. *Your Choice: A Young Woman's Guide to Making Decisions about Unmarried Pregnancy*. New York: Avon, 1980. 190 pp.

The pros and cons of the options available to single pregnant women are discussed: abortion, single parenting, adoption, and marriage. Sources of information and assistance are cited throughout and appendixes list agencies and additional information.

656 Lindsay, Jeanne Warren. *Pregnant Too Soon: Adoption is an Option*. St. Paul, MN: EMC Publishing, 1980. 204 pp.

The author coordinates a teen-mother program for a school district in southern California. This book tells the stories of the young women who have taken part in this program with fact-filled discussions of the legal and psychological complexities of adoption.

657 ———. *Teenage Marriage: Coping With Reality*. Buena Park, CA: Morning Glory Press, 1984. 206 pp.

Encourages teens contemplating marriage to take a realistic look at their future. Having interviewed fifty-five teens (the majority were women), Lindsay incorporates their own words into the development of this work. She stresses the communication between young couples, touches on areas couples should consider (including similar interests), family background, changes after marriage, sexual feelings, pregnancy and child care, marital roles, and financial aspects.

658 ———. *Teens Parenting: The Challenges of Babies and Toddlers*. Burena Park, CA: Morning Glory Press, 1981. 312 pp.

A guide to the development and care of children from birth to two years old. Discusses the day-to-day business of coping happily with a baby while also coping with school, limited money, and sharing living quarters.

659 McGurie, Paula. *It Won't Happen to Me: Teenagers Talk About Pregnancy.* New York: Delacorte, 1983. 234 pp.

Presents the stories of fifteen pregnant teenagers in their own words as told to the author. Intermingled with these stories are interviews with one doctor and three social workers. Stresses the important change in attitudes about the confidentiality of adoption records and the rights of birth parents. Includes a listing of nationwide agencies involved in counseling teenagers with unwanted pregnancies and related problems.

660 Miller, Shelby H. *Children as Parents: A Final Report on a Study of Childbearing and Child Rearing Among 12- to 15-Year Olds.* New York: Research Center, Child Welfare League, 1983. 117 pp.

A study on the sexual and childbirth experiences of a sample of 183 young mothers, of which one-fifth had or were expecting a second child. Most girls were heavily dependent on their families. More than half were still in school. Gives a composite of the adolescent father and of the mother's parents from low-income families and families subsisting on an uncertain mixture of low-paying employment and public assistance. Frequently the girl's mother is single and was also an adolescent mother. Notes the policy issues that must be addressed if the problems of children as parents are to be improved.

661 Miner, Jane Claypool. *Young Parents.* New York: J. Messner, 1985. 159 pp.

A guide for pregnant teenagers becoming parents. Discusses such questions as, "Is marriage the answer?" and "How does a good parent act?" Gives suggestions on how to involve the father in child rearing, if he is around. Includes statistics and stories of young mothers told in their own words.

662 Oettinger, Katherine Brownell. *Not My Daughter: Facing Up to Teenage Pregnancy.* Englewood Cliffs, NJ: Prentice-Hall, 1979. 184 pp.

Outlines various support groups, such as innovative community programs on birth control and peer counseling, while stressing the teaching of healthy, responsible attitudes toward sexuality from birth. Includes statistics, case histories, and a resource guide to books, articles, films, directories, and organizations.

663 *Patchwork Programs: Comprehensive Services for Pregnant and Parenting Adolescents.* By Richard A. Weatherley et al. Seattle, WA: Center for Social Welfare Research, School of Social Work, University of Washington, 1985. 264 pp.

> Addresses two central questions about adolescent pregnancy and parenthood: (1) How and why have local programs for pregnant and parenting adolescents been developed and maintained? and (2) What accounts for the development and maintenance of comprehensive programs in some communities and not in others that appear to be equally or more needy? To answer these questions, ten local programs were studied in California, Massachusetts, Michigan, and Tennessee.

664 *Pregnancy in Adolescence: Needs, Problems and Management.* Edited by Irving R. Stuart and Carl F. Wells. New York: Van Nostrand, 1982. 441 pp.

> A collection of nineteen original papers by thirty-seven contributors covering a wide range of complex issues relevant to adolescent sexuality, fertility, and pregnancy resolution. Focuses on applied research and program planning, emphasizing material that is useful to professionals working with teenagers. Areas included are discussions of legal rights and responsibilities, the epidemiology of adolescent pregnancy, and diverse medical and psychosocial risk and management factors.

665 Richards, Arlene Kramer, and Irene Willis. *What to Do If You or Someone You Know Is Under 18 and Pregnant.* New York: Lothrop, 1983, 256 pp.

> Each chapter starts with a short fictionalized vignette, followed by explanations of what happened, basic medical information, services available, and emotional aspects. The last chapter gives names, addresses, and phone numbers of various agencies, state by state, throughout the United States, with a brief explanation of services and how to find further help.

666 Ross, Anne. *Teenage Mothers/Teenage Fathers.* Toronto: Personal Library, 1982. 128 pp.

> The first section of this work deals with the problem of teen sexuality and includes a short-birth control guide which lists the advantages and disadvantages of various forms of contraception. The second section deals with the pregnant teenager and the pressures on her and the father of the unborn child. The final

part deals with what to do with the child after the birth. Ends with some recommendations for changing the situation.

667   *Services to Teen Mothers in New York City: Needs, Resources, Issues and Trends.* Prepared by Diana Tendler. New York: Research and Program Planning Information Department, Community Council of Greater New York, 1982. 16 leaves.

Describes the needs of teenage parents, the resources available to them, current issues which must be addressed, and possible future trends in provisions for this group.

668   Shapiro, Constance Hoenk. *Adolescent Pregnancy Prevention— School-Community Cooperation.* Springfield, IL: Charles C. Thomas, 1981. 129 pp.

Emphasizes the importance of school and community involvement in efforts at adolescent-pregnancy prevention. Each chapter contains a list of resource materials for a more in-depth exploration of the chapter's topic, such as sexual learning, and peer support networks.

669   *Teenage Parents and Their Offspring.* Edited by Keith G. Scott. New York: Grune & Stratton, 1981. 328 pp.

Discusses three major consequences of teenage pregnancy. Part 1 covers epidemiology, with additional chapters on cost to the government, legal issues, psychological factors, and nutrition. A second section assesses outcomes for the children, and the final section reviews the advantages to be gained from interventions.

670   *Teenage Pregnancy in a Family Context: Implications for Policy.* Edited by Theodora Ooms. Philadelphia: Temple University Press, 1981. 425 pp.

An examination of how policies for pregnant teenagers of school age affect families. A collection of essays by fourteen contributors given at an October 1978 Invitational Conference convened by the Family Impact Seminar of the Institute for Educational Leadership at George Washington University. Discusses a broad range of background data, planning available resources, and policy issues from sex education and family planning to health care, economic support and social services for the pregnant adolescent and young parent.

671   *Teenage Pregnancy in Industrialized Countries* By Elise F. Jones et al. New Haven: Yale University Press, 1987. 31 pp.

This book is the report of a 1985 study by the Alan Guttmacher Institute. Compares information on teenage sexual activity, pregnancy and abortion rates, and contraceptive use. Provides a summary report of data for thirty-seven nations that is followed by case studies of five countries plus the United States. Contraceptive services, sex education, societal and religious values, economic and educational opportunities, and governmental policies are given for each country.

672   *Teenage Sexuality, Pregnancy and Childbearing.* Edited by Frank F. Furstenberg, Jr. et al. Philadelphia: University of Pennsylvania Press, 1981. 423 pp.

These articles are organized around four basic themes: historical trends regarding teenage sexual activity, contraception, pregnancy, abortion, and childbirth; consequences of early childbearing; the choices available to teens wanting to avert pregnancies; and an evaluation of current programs and materials for pregnant teens. Also includes a review of laws about abortion and pregnancy. All articles originally appeared in *Family Planning Perspectives.*

673   Walsworth, Nancy, and Patricia Bradley. *Coping with School Age Motherhood.* New York: Rosen Publishing Group, 1979. 115 pp.

An account of the authors' year on the staff of a special educational program in California for school age mothers (S.A.M.). The girls' stories show the variety of problems encountered by teenage pregnancy.

674   Wilson, Barbara Foley. *Teenage Marriage and Divorce: United States, 1970–81.* Hyattsville, MD: U.S. Department of Health and Human Services National Center for Health Statistics, 1985. 23 pp.

Analyzes the trends in teenage marriage and divorce in the United States from 1970 to 1981. Includes information on geographic variations, marriage laws, age differences between spouses, previous marital status, race, educational attainment, duration of marriage and children involved in divorce.

675   Zelnik, Melvin, John F. Dantner, and Kathleen Ford. *Sex and Pregnancy in Adolescence.* Beverly Hills: Sage Publications, 1981. 272 pp.

Based for the most part on two national surveys of young women ages fifteen through nineteen. The first survey (conducted in 1971), and the second survey (conducted in 1976), both studied group differences in premarital sex, contraceptive use, and and pregnancy related behavior, and the probability of the occurrence of these events. The last chapter looks at the changes since 1976 as revealed by a third, yet-to-be analyzed survey conducted in 1979. Examines the fertility of young American women and the decisions individual women, especially unmarried women, make preceding childbearing. These decisions include whether or not to have sex, to use contraception, to have an abortion, and whether or not to marry before the birth. These matters are discussed in the world of the teenager as they are influenced in part by race, family, friends, age, religion, social life, and perceptions of society. Provides results, summary, conclusions, and three appendixes.

676   Zitner, Rosaline, and Shelby Hayden Miller. *Our Youngest Parents: A Study of the Use of Support Services by Adolescent Mothers.* New York: Child Welfare League of America, 1980. 88 pp.

Explores the relation of access to specialized services during pregnancy and immediately after delivery to the young mothers' need for and use of support services. Interviews with 185 mothers, conducted about a year after discontinuation of service from one of the Child Welfare League of America (CWLA) institutions in the following cities: Charlotte, NC; Detroit, MI; Houston, TX; and Toledo, OH. Identifies young mothers' perceptions of the services they received and the variation in need for, and use of, services with age, race, and socioeconomic status.

B. Articles in Periodicals

677   Adler, Emily Stier, Mildred Bates, and Joan M. Merdinger. "Educational Policies and Programs for Teenage Parents and Pregnant Teenagers." *Family Relations* 34:183–87 (April 1985).

The policies and programs of the local school systems in Rhode Island are examined in light of the implications for the women's labor force based on the level of education completed.

678   Baptiste, David A. "Counseling the Pregnant Adolescent Within a Family Context: Therapeutic Issues and Strategies." *Family Therapy* 13:163–76 (1986).

Presents a family-focused approach to counseling pregnant adolescents and their families instead of the current individual-focused approach. Counseling strategies are offered.

679   Barrett, Robert L., and Bryan E. Robinson. "A Descriptive Study of Teenage Expectant Fathers." *Family Relations* 31:349–52 (1982).

Reports demographic data on a sample of twenty-six adolescent expectant fathers and information about their relationships with the expectant mothers and their families. Results indicate that young fathers maintained positive relationships with their girlfriend's family, maintained contact with the expectant mother, and desired to participate in the naming of the child and to meet certain responsibilities toward mother and child.

680   ———. "Teenage Fathers: A Profile." *Personnel and Guidance Journal* 60:226–28 (December 1981).

Addresses the problem of neglect of teenage fathers. For the most part, human-services support programs and literature written for counselors have been centered exclusively around adolescent females. The 1972 Supreme Court's ruling, *Stanley* vs *Illinois*, established equal protection and involvement, under the law, to unmarried, natural fathers in custody decisions. The few agencies that have designed creative approaches to begin to respond to the needs of these men can draw on the list of seven suggestions made by the authors in this article, which are directed to teachers, counselors, and educational programs.

681   Berman, Claire. "When Children Bear Children." *Reader's Digest* 122: 132–36 (May 1983).

Reveals that 1.1 million adolescents, more than 1 out of every 10 teenage girls, become pregnant each year, and that unplanned pregnancy no longer can be dismissed as something that happens to disadvantaged teens from minority groups. The steepest rise in out-of-wedlock births (a jump of 75 percent since 1961) has been among 15-to 17-year-old whites. Teens describe how they participated in premarital sex and give various reasons such as loneliness; friends saying, "what do you mean, you're still a virgin?"; and some girls getting pregnant to gain a commitment from boyfriends. Most girls do not enter an out-of-wedlock pregnancy on purpose. They lack information and are afraid to ask questions for fear of looking dumb. Learning the facts of life by experience means many teens must make a decision that will affect them the rest of their lives. Most teens choose abortion. There are three live births for every five abortions. Ninety-six percent of those giving birth now choose to keep their babies – thus, children raising children. Tells how teens solve the problem of teen pregnancy: some marry (among teen marriages there is the highest divorce rate); some teen mothers try to make it alone by living in a residential facility, returning to live with parents, or adoption. In the 1960s more than 80 percent chose adoption, today only 40 percent do. None of the solutions are painless or problem free. Professionals list suggestions for education in the home and school.

682 Card, Josefina, and Lauress L. Wise. "Teenage Mothers and Teenage Fathers: The Impact of Early Childbearing and the Parents' Personal and Professional Lives." *Family Planning Perspectives* 10:199–205 (1978).

Tells how teenage parents are affected by childbearing—they have less education, they are limited to less prestigious jobs (and women to dead-end ones), and they can expect to have more children than they want. They experience unstable marriages because of these problems and this results in having been married several times. This article is based on a research effort, Project TALENT. A study of high school boys and girls analyzed to document the long-term and the short-term impact of adolescent childbearing on the parents' future educational, occupational, marital, and childbearning lives. The study makes it possible to look at the consequences for the young father and young mother in regards to socioeconomic status and academic aptitude, expectations and achievement, and race.

683 "Children Having Children." *Newsweek* 126:76–77 (9 December 1985).

Tells about the growing number of teenage pregnancies in America and the more disturbingly faster growing number in America's urban ghettos. Gives the experiences of young teenage mothers and mothers-to-be, including the prototypical adolescent, a black, an American Indian, and others. States the reasons for the increasing numbers along with comparisons of the number of white and black teenage pregnancies, nonmarital and marital births, and the number of teenage pregnancies in the United States as compared with five other countries. Covers the many reasons for the growth in teenage pregnancies, such as changes in attitudes and social mores, lack of sex education or access to birth control, as well as the influence of TV rock music, videos, the movies,and the sense of worthlessness felt by these girls. Recounts one social worker, "The girls tell me, 'Before I was pregnant I was nothing, now I'm a mother.' "

684   Folkenberg, Judy. "Teen Pregnancy: Who Opts for Adoption?" *Psychology Today* 19:16 (May 1985).

States the reasons why more unmarried pregnant teenagers don't relinquish their babies for adoption. Explains that the girls who do opt for adoption have self-esteem and plans for the future, and have it together mentally and cognitively.

685   Gallagher, Michael, as told to Kate Manning.. "Am I Old Enough to Be a Parent?" *Redbook* 179:34 (May 1987).

The story of a teenage boy who gave up the pursuit of his goals and instead married his high school girlfriend who was the mother of his two-month-old son. Tells how his parents helped the young family get started.

686   Gunnerson, Ronnie. "Parents Also Have Rights." *Newsweek* 109:10 (2 March 1987).

The author writes of her experience as the stepmother of a sixteen-year-old pregnant teenager. The author feels that teenagers have the right to choose whether or not to have the baby and whether or not to keep the baby after it is born. The parents of the pregnant teenager have no rights in this decision, but will bear all the responsibility for the teenager and her baby. If a pregnant teenager's parents are ultimately responsible for the teenager and her baby then the author believes that parents should have the right to decide whether or not the teenager keeps her baby. Gunnerson tells of her stepdaughter's situation, which worked out to a happy ending. Her stepdaughter, a wife and mother, reflects on her actions as a sixteen year old.

687   "Kids and Contraceptives." *Newsweek* 109:54–58 (16 February 1987).

Due to the alarming rise in the rate of teenage pregnancy and the ever increasing spread of AIDS, this article addresses the new urgency to the debate over moral questions involved when searching for solutions on how to protect our children. Presents the problems confronting teenage pregnancy such as teenagers fast becoming the next high-risk AIDS group, popular misconceptions teenagers have about sex, and lack of sex and birth control information. Covers TV advertising of condoms, case stories, and teenagers from low-income families. Provides statistics, with illustrated charts and graphs.

688 Mech, Edmund V. "Pregnant Adolescents." *Child Welfare* 65:555–67 (November/December 1986).

Reports of an investigative study, using a twenty-item, self-report inventory, of the extent to which pregnant adolescents express interest in various aspects of adoption.

689 Moore, Kristin A. "Teenage Childbirth and Welfare Dependency." *Family Planning Perspectives* 10:233–35 (July/August 1978).

Summarizes the results of a study commissioned by a congressional committee to estimate the cost of teenage childbearing to the government through one specific welfare program, Aid to Families with Dependent Children (AFDC). Concludes by stating that a major program to help teenagers avoid pregnancies and births, that they themselves wish to postpone, clearly would be of great benefit to the young people, their families, and society.

690 Olsen, Joseph A., and Stan E. Weed. "Effects of Family-Planning Programs for Teenagers on Adolescent Birth and Pregnancy Rates." *Family Perspective* 20:153–69 (1986).

Provides estimates of how adolescent family-planning programs impact both pregnancy and birth rates among teenagers.

691 Robinson, Bryan E., and Robert L. Barrett. "Teenage Fathers." *Psychology Today* 19:66–70 (December 1985).

Gives the young unwed father's point of view when his girlfriend becomes pregnant. Notes that young men go through the same emotional struggle and confusion that young mothers do, and want to be included in the decision process of what to do about it. States the reasons why a growing number of teenage fathers are choosing not to abandon their babies.

692 Schmidt, Ann V. "School-Based Care Puts Diploma in Reach for Teenage Mothers." *Children Today* 14:16–18 (July/August 1985).

Since 80 percent of teenage mothers do not graduate from high school, there is a need for programs which will allow these young mothers to remain in school while they adjust to their new roles. Tells about the Adolescent Parenting Program, in which young mothers learn about child development and the best way to care for their children. Also describes the parenting program at Groveton High School in Fairfax County, northern Virginia, where teenage mothers leave their babies while they attend classes, anticipating completion of their high school work. Tells how the program is organized and financed, and gives some case examples of how the program has benefited teen mothers.

693   Tietz, Christopher. "Teenage Pregnancies: Looking Ahead to 1984." *Family Planning Perspectives* 10:205–07 (July/August 1978).

Seeks to estimate how many of today's fourteen year olds are likely to experience one or more pregnancies, births, abortions, and miscarriages before they reach the age of twenty, assuming that there is no change in the level or timing of sexual activity among teenagers, or in their use of contraception or abortion.

694   Weed, Stan E., and Joseph A. Olsen. "Effects of Family-Planning Programs on Teenage Pregnancy—Replication and Extension." *Family Perspective* 20:173–95 (1986).

Summarizes the findings of the authors' original paper, "Effects of Family-Planning Programs for Teenagers on Adolescent Births and Pregnancy Rates." Provides additional data and analysis to substantiate and extend this original research.

12
Homosexual Relationships

A. Books and Pamphlets

695 Borhek, Mary V. *Coming Out to Parents: A Two-Way Survival Guide for Lesbians and Gay Men and Their Parents.* New York: Pilgrim Press, 1983. 208 pp.

> The author draws on her own experiences as mother of two straight daughters and a gay son. She presents stories of other parents and gay children. One chapter gives suggestions on how homosexuals can tell their parents about their life-styles, and another chapter covers religious issues and biblical themes.

696 ———. *My Son, Eric.* New York: Pilgrim Press, 1979. 160 pp.

> Tells how the author, through counseling and faith, learned to cope with her son's homosexuality.

697 Curry, Hayden, and Denis Clifford. *Legal Guide for Lesbian & Gay Couples.* Edited by Ralph Warner. 2d ed. Reading, MA: Addison-Wesley, 1984. 236 pp.

> This book, written by two attorneys, deals specifically with legal matters that concern lesbian and gay couples. It discusses such areas as raising children (custody, support, living with a lover), buying property together, wills, and includes a "living-together contract" and other sample agreements and contracts.

698 *Different Daughters: A Book by Mothers of Lesbians.* Edited by Louise Rafkin. Pittsburgh: Cleis Press, 1987. 153 pp.

> A collection of stories by mothers of lesbians with different racial, class, and religious backgrounds.

699   Fairchild, Betty, and Nancy Hayward. *Now That You Know: What Every Parent Should Know About Homosexuality.* New York: Harcourt, 1981. 227 pp.

>   Gives personal experiences of parents and their children. Includes information on how to set up a local chapter of a nationwide support group called Parents of Gays.

700   Gantz, Joe. *Whose Child Cries: Children of Gay Parents Talk About Their Lives.* Rolling Hills Estates, CA: Jalimar Press, 1983. 245 pp.

>   Looks at gay parenting primarily by interviewing the children being raised in families with gay parents. Tells how these children, ages seven to nineteen, cope with the more than usual pressures faced by most families.

701   Gay Fathers of Toronto. *Gay Fathers: Some of Their Stories, Experiences, and Advice.* Toronto: Gay Fathers of Toronto, 1981. 74 pp.

>   Written for gay fathers so that they may better understand what is happening to them and deal with their situation honestly. Some of the questions addressed are: Can I face this? What should I do with my life? Should I try again to forget it, or go on with the lies? How do I tell my wife? What about the kids? Should I tell the kids?

702   Griffin, Carolyn Welch et al. *Beyond Acceptance: Parents of Lesbians and Gays Talk About Their Experiences.* Englegood Cliffs, NJ: Prentice-Hall, 1986. 199 pp.

>   Twenty-three members of Parents and Friends of Lesbians and Gays, a national organization, describe the complicated process of coming to terms with the knowledge that their child is gay. Terms are defined and issues addressed, such as religion and AIDS.

703   Harry, Joseph. *Gay Couples.* New York: Praeger, 1984. 152 pp.

>   Explores the characteristics of male same-sex relationships to see how they may differ from opposite-sex ones, which are traditionally structured around gender roles.

704   Jay, Karla, and Allen Young. *The Gay Report: Lesbians and Gay Men Speak Out About Sexual Experiences and Life Styles.* New York: Basic Books, 1979. 816 pp.

>   The authors draw their material from more than four thousand questionnaires returned by lesbians and gay men. The book

combines authors' comments on the summaries of the responses as well as excerpts from the questionnaires. Among the subjects explored are sexual feelings experienced in childhood, self-image and the socializing process, the frustrations of role-playing, sexual acts and orgasm, incest, fantasies, and society's prejudice against gay people.

705   Jullion, Jeanne. *Long Way Home: The Odyssey of a Lesbian Mother and Her Children.* San Francisco: Cleis Press, 1985. 261 pp.

The documentation of the late 1970s legal battle in the San Francisco Bay area that involved Jullion, a lesbian mother, who fought for custody of her sons.

706   Maddox, Brenda. *Married and Gay: An Intimate Look at a Different Relationship.* New York: Harcourt, 1982. 220 pp.

This study deals with homosexuals that are married to members of the opposite sex. Includes case histories.

707   ———. *The Marrying Kind: Homosexuality and Marriage.* London: Granada, 1982. 208 pp.

Information for this book was drawn from forty-seven interviews with homosexuals, and with present and past wives or husbands of homosexuals.

708   McWhirter, David P., and Andrew M. Mattison. *The Male Couple: How Relations Develop.* Englewood Cliffs, NJ: Prentice-Hall, 1984. 341 pp.

A study of 156 male couples in loving relationships lasting from one to thirty-seven years.Addresses questions such as how do they live, handle work, chores, money and their sexuality? How do they deal with lovers, families, former wives, children, parents and friends? How are they like heterosexual couples and how are they different? The authors identify six developmental stages among these men, each possessing a set of characteristics with both positive and negative features.

709   Muller, Ann. *Parents Matter: Parents' Relationships With Lesbian Daughters and Gay Sons.* Tallahassee, FL: Naiad Press, 1987. 240 pp.

The author interviewed sixty-one lesbians and gay men and ten parents in the Chicago area, to tell the story of the relationships between adults and their homosexual children.

710 Parker, William. *Homosexuality Bibliography*. Metuchen, NJ: Scarecrow, 1971. 323 pp.

――――. *Homosexuality Bibliography*. Supplement, 1970–1975. Metuchen, NJ: Scarecrow, 1975. 337 pp.

――――. *Homosexuality Bibliography*. Second Supplement, 1976–1982. Metuchen, NJ: Scarecrow, 1985. 395 pp.

This bibliography on the subject of homosexuality, in three volumes, covers the years 1969 through 1982, and lists over ten thousand items: books, pamphlets, doctoral dissertations, court cases, articles in books, newspapers, journals, and popular magazines. It is a selective bibliography with no annotations.

711 Ross, Michael W. *The Married Homosexual Man: A Psychological Study*. Boston: Routledge & Kegan, 1983. 184 pp.

The author, a psychiatrist at an Australian medical school, did two studies concerning married homosexual men. One study uses 63 male homosexuals from Australia and New Zealand and compares questionnaire respondents who had never married with those who had married, but later separated, and those who were still married at the time of the study. The second study was on 163 Australians, 176 Swedish, and 149 Finish male homosexuals to discover the effects of culture on marriage by homosexual males. The central questions of this work are: Why do homosexual men marry? How do they cope? How can others understand them better? Some interviews and case studies are included.

712 San Francisco Bay Area National Lawyers Guild. *A Gay Parent's Legal Guide to Child Custody*. San Francisco: The Guild, n.d.

A pamphlet with information for both gay mothers and fathers.

713 Scanzoni, Letha, and Virginia Mollenkott. *Is the Homosexual My Neighbor? Another Christian View*. San Francisco: Harper & Row, 1978. 159 pp.

Presents a case for shifting Christian attitudes and practice regarding homosexuality and gay persons. Assesses the gay situation within the Christian framework of ethical values.

714 Schulenburg, Joy A. *Gay Parenting*. Garden City, N.Y.: Anchor Press, 1985. 177 pp.

Schulenburg, a lesbian, is raising her daughter (now four years old) in a household with two friends, both gay men, who act as coparents. She offers advice and support to other lesbians and gay men who are raising children. From her own experiences, conversations, and questionnaries completed by hundreds of gay parents, the author surveys the major issues of concern to lesbians and gay men who have children or who want to have them. Information covered includes being married and gay, AIDS, adoption and foster parenting, and obtaining sole or joint custody after divorce.

B. Articles in Periodicals

715 Bozett, Frederick W. "Gay Fathers: Evolution of the Gay-Father Identity." *American Journal of Orthopsychiatry* 51:552–59 (July 1981).

> A study of eighteen gay fathers' identities, both as gays and as fathers, as these men participate in both the world of fathers and the world of gays. It is difficult for these men to achieve harmony of both identities and to articulate both, because each of the two worlds tends to reject the other's identity. Explains that by actively functioning in both worlds, these fathers can achieve identity harmony and self-acceptance as gay fathers.

716 Hoeffer, Beverly. "Children's Acquisition of Sex-Role Behavior in Lesbian-Mother Families." *American Journal of Orthopsychiatry* 51:536–44 (July 1981).

> A comparison of children's play and activity interests as indices of sex-role behavior from a sample of twenty lesbian and twenty heterosexual single mothers and their children. More striking than any differences were the similarities between the two groups of children on the acquisition of sex-role behavior and between the two groups of mothers on the encouragement of sex-role behavior. Both these mothers and those from previous studies state that "peers" had the most influence on their childrens' acquisition of sex-role behavior.

717 Kirkpatrick, Martha, Catherine Smith, and Ron Roy. "Lesbian Mothers and Their Children: A Comparative Survey." *American Journal of Orthopsychiatry* 51:545–51 (July 1981).

> An evaluation by a research team of ten boys and ten girls between the ages of five and twelve, living full-time with their

self-identified lesbian mothers. A comparison group of ten boys and ten girls living full-time with their single, heterosexual mothers was similarly evaluated. Gender development of the children was not considered to be significantly different in the two groups.

718   Maddox, Brenda. "Homosexual Parents." *Pschology Today* 16:62–69 (February 1982).

The author conducted forty-seven long interviews with homosexuals and with their present and past wives and husbands in New York City, Boston, London, and Manchester, England. Many married homosexuals are "bi," having equally passionate desires for a homosexual love life and for children of their own. For some homosexuals, children are the overwhelming motive for marriage, and fear of losing the children is the biggest barrier to declaring oneself a homosexual. Presents how and what to tell the children, how gay men and lesbian women relate to their children, and the effects on children of having a homosexual parent. Some unmarried lesbians who want children have turned to artificial insemination, some gay men have turned to adoption.

719   Miller, Judith et al. "Comparison of Family Relationships: Homosexual verus Heterosexual Women." *Psychological Reports* 46:1127–32 (1980).

This study compares nuclear-family characteristics of homosexual and heterosexual women. Data on two samples, thirty-four homosexual and thirty-one heterosexual women, were analyzed for differences and similarities. Gives personal comments by the subjects.

720   Osman, Shelomo. "My Stepfather is a She." *Family Process* 11:209–18 (1972)

This article is about the treatment of a lesbian couple and their two sons.

721   Riddle, Dorothy I. "Relating to Children: Gays as Role Models." *Journal of Social Issues* 34:38–58 (1978).

Traces the developmental aspects of sexual identity. A review of the literature on role modeling leads to the conclusions that children internalize particular traits from a variety of models, and that gays are more likely to serve as nontraditional, sex-role models than as determiners of same-sex sexual preference.

722 Stone, Laurie. "Women Who Live With Gay Men." *Ms.* 10:103–8 (October 1981).

Author read one hundred published testimonies and spoke with thirty straight, gay, and bisexual men and women to write this article. Gives case examples of women who live with gay men, tells what needs they fulfill for each other, and why the relationship is satisfying to them.

723 Van Gelder, Lindsy. "Lesbian Custody: A Tragic Day in Court." *Ms.* 5:72–73 (September 1976).

Covers the custody case of Mary Jo Risher and her children, Jimmy eighteen and Richard nine, who made their home with Mary Jo and her lover, Ann Foreman.

724 Whitmore, George. "Gay Couples: From Closet to Conventionality." *Harper's Bazaar* 118:21 (June 1985).

Tells about homosexual, long-term relationships which face and solve special problems in innovative ways.

13
Miscellaneous Works

A. Books

725 Beer, William R. *Househusbands: Men on Housework in American Families.* South Hadley, MA: J. F. Bergin, 1983. 153 pp.

Inteviews with fifty-six men who, like the author, do a substantial share of the housework in their families, whether or not they also hold a paying job. The author asks about their feelings toward the housework they do, how they came to do it, and how their feelings changed toward themselves, their wives, and their families as a result

726 Burgess-Kohn, Jane, and Willard K. Kohn. *The Widower.* Boston: Beacon Press, 1978. 169 pp.

The authors (a husband-and-wife team) are a widower and his second wife, a sociologist. The husband tells how he became widowed and raised six daughters. His autobiography is followed his second wife's commentary on the broader implications of his experiences. This book shows a widowed father's struggles in learning how to parent.

727 Caine, Lynn. *Widow.* New York: Morrow, 1974. 222 pp.

The experiences of Mrs. Caine, a single-parent widow, who tells of her personal journey through the mourning process.

728 Cameron, Colin. *Displaced Homemaker: A Bibliography.* Monticello, IL: Vance Bibliographies, 1982. 48 pp.

This bibliography emphasizes literature originating in the 1970s through mid–1981. Most of the items are annotated, but not all.

Includes popular and scholarly works, research studies sources, legislation, resources, directories, and films.

729   Cherlin, Andrew J., and Frank F. Furstenberg, Jr. *The New American Grandparent: A Place in the Family, A Life Apart.* New York: Basic Books, 1986. 288 pp.

This is a study by two family sociologists who conducted a nationwide telephone survey of over five hundred grandparents in order to better understand the nature of grandparents today. The survey reveals that the increased divorce rate in the middle generation has changed the role of grandparents, making it more substantial. Also, the increased life expectancy of the average American means that grandparents are now available to interact with their children and grandchildren for a longer period of time.

730   Claire, Bernard E., and Anthony R. Daniele. *Love Pact: A Layman's Complete Guide to Legal Living Together Agreements.* New York: Grove Press, 1980. 222 pp.

Guidebook for married, unmarried, and gay couples which sets forth the legal implications of cohabitation as they relate to property rights of the individuals involved. It shows how the drafting of living together agreements will define, protect, and enforce property rights should the relationship end. Among the areas discussed are ownership of property, income, taxes and estate considerations, and children. Presents sample living together agreements.

731   Corea, Gena. *The Mother Machine: Reproductive Technologies from Artificial Insemination to Artificial Wombs.* New York: Harper & Row 1985. 374 pp.

Combines an in-depth look at historical, social, legal, and medical trends of reproductive medicine with descriptions of the state of the art in eugenics, surrogate motherhood, etc. The author argues that with the advent of new reproductive technologies (e.g., in vitro-fertilization, embryo transfer, sex determination), we face the possible future control by men of female reproductive processes. Raises an awareness of the potential misuse of these reproductive technologies.

732   *Employer-Supported Child Care: Investing in Human Resources.* Sandra L. Burud, Pamela R. Aschbacher, and Jacquelyn McCroskey. Dover, MA: Auburn House, 1984. 362 pp.

Based on the actual experiences of 415 firms with child care programs, the project was designed to help employers explore whether child care might make sense for their companies, and if so, what options might be appropriate. It includes an overview, sections on what companies gain from child care, how the need for child care can be determined, what options companies have, and how these options can be implemented.

733   Fisher, Ida, and Byron Lane. *The Widow's Guide to Life: How to Adjust/How to Grow.* Englewood Cliffs, NJ: Prentice-Hall, 1981. 207 pp.

A resource work to help handle personal affairs, provide support through the transition from married woman to widow, and how to to establish a new identity as a single woman.

734   Goode, Ruth. *A Book for Grandmothers.* New York: McGraw-Hill, 1977. 204 pp.

The author offers advice and shares her experiences as a grandmother in a time when loosening family ties makes old rules out-of-date. Among the topics discussed are: how to stay in touch, how to give advice, and when to keep out of it. Two chapters, "Dissension and Divorce" and "Inlaws and Outlaws" are recommended for all grandmothers before becoming involved in a child's failing marriage.

735   *Grandparenthood.* Edited by Vern L. Bengston and Joan F. Robertson. Beverly Hills: Sage Publications, 1985. 240 pp.

A collection of scholarly articles about grandparents based on papers presented at the National Conference Center in Racine, Wisconsin, October 9–11, 1983. Four themes run through the articles. Grandparenthood is important as a symbolic role and it is important for grandparents to just "be there"; emphasizes the diversity that exists in grandparental experiences; tells of the importance of defining grandparental relationships in divorce; and analyzes social contract that has divested grandparents of strong ties with their families.

736   Harayda, Janice. *The Joy of Being Single: Stop Putting Your Life on Hold and Start Living.* Garden City, NY: Doubleday, 1986. 249 pp.

Written especially for America's sixty million singles, whether they are never-married, divorced, or widowed. Stresses how to live happily without a partner, rather than on how to find one. Gives advice based on the author's experiences and that of other successful singles.

737   Harris, Thomas Anthony. *I'm Okay, You're Okay: A Practical Guide to Transactional Analysis.* Boston: G. K. Hall, 1974. 554 pp.

A classic in the field of self-awareness and personal growth. An excellent introduction to Transactional Analysis.

738   Kornhaber, Arthur, and Kenneth L. Woodward. *Grandparents/ Grandchildren: The Vital Connection.* Garden City, NY: Doubleday, 1981. 279 pp.

Kornhaber, a child psychiatrist, and Woodward, a magazine writer, focus on the emotional attachment between grandparents and grandchildren, and the effect of the loss of this attachment. They quote several known writers about the role of their grandparents, reproduce children's drawings of their grandparents, and conduct a qualitative study of three groups of children paired with their grandparents. Grandparents who want to regain a relationship with their grandchildren are given helpful hints.

739   Lansky, Vicki. *Vicki Lansky's Practical Parenting Tips for School-Age Years.* New York: Bantam Books, 1985. 165 pp.

This book is helpful for "instant mothers and fathers" with no parenting experience. It offers over a thousand "parent tested" tips to help children, ages six through twelve, and their parents through these years. Besides covering the usual topics of setting limits, kids and money, and schoolwork, the author includes a chapter, "The Changing Family," which discusses the working mother, latchkey kids, single parents, joint custody, and stepparenting.

740   Lindsay, Rae. *Alone and Surviving.* New York: Walker, 1977. 235 pp.

Lindsay, a widow with three children, was given two grants for this study of one hundred widows. She offers advice on topics ranging from taxes to social security, children, friends, the new singles scene, and sex.

741   Lopata, Helena Znaniecki. *Women as Widows: Support Systems.* New York: Elsevier, 1979. 483 pp.

Based on a study peformed for the Social Security Administration in the Chicago area. It gives statistics about, and analysis of, the support systems involving widows, such as personal/self, social community, employment, and includes a chapter devoted to "Boyfriends and New Husbands."

742   Nudel, Adele Rice. *Starting Over: Help for Young Widows and Widowers.* New York: Dodd, 1986. 256 pp.

> The author, director of the Widowed Person's Service at Sinai Hospital in Baltimore, tells how the difficulties of widows/ widowers under the age of forty-five differ from their older counterparts. Although many problems are similar, the "under 45s" may also have to raise children alone, feel financially insecure if they are women, and feel helpless to run a household if they are men. While raising a family alone has its problems, remarriage may even offer more challenges, such as dealing with hurt in-laws or dealing with stepfamily relationships. Besides covering these issues and others, the author gives advice on how to cope with depression and loneliness.

743   Porcino, Jane. *Growing Older, Getting Better: A Handbook for Women in the Second Half of Life.* Reading, MA: Addison-Wesley, 1983. 364 pp.

> The author, a gerontologist, has written a guide for older women which covers all aspects of female aging, from changing family roles to fitness and health concerns, from housing to discrimination in employment. Chapters provide sources for further information and assistance such as organizations, publications, and agencies.

744   Procaccini, Joseph, and Mark W. Kiefaber. *Parent Burnout.* Garden City, NY: Doubleday, 1983. 263 pp.

> Two experts discuss the problem of parent burnout and give ways to overcome it with a program of self-assessment and therapy for reversing the burn-out trend. Includes a section on stepparenting.

745   Robertson, John, and Betty Utterback. *Suddenly Single: Learning to Start Over Through the Experience of Others.* New York: Simon & Schuster, 1986. 223 pp.

> Examines the stories of people who have had to make the adjustment of losing a spouse through death or divorce. Provides psychological theory, suggestions, and an annotated reading list.

746   Salk, Lee. *The Complete Dr. Salk: An A-to-Z Guide to Raising Your Child.* New York: New American Library, 1983. 230 pp.

> Well-known child psychologist Salk deals with both general areas and specific problems in bringing up children, covering such topics as acceptance, divorce, hero worship, incest, sex education,

siblings, and terminal illness. All age groups, from infancy to adolescence, are considered. He describes the characteristics of, and the underlying reasons for, problem behavior and suggest methods for solutions.

747 ———. *My Father, My Son: An Intimate Relationship.* New York: Putnam, 1982. 255 pp.

A collection of interviews with men about their fathers and themselves—as sons, and as fathers of sons.

748 Shields, Laurie. *Displaced Homemakers: Organizing for a New Life.* New York: McGraw-Hill, 1981. 272 pp.

Documents the discrimination against older women which prevails in both the public and the private sector and helps to expose the wasteful bias of ageism that prevails in our society today. Encourages older women to take a new lease on life, to work toward building new and satisfying careers, and to do so with firm conviction that all the past years of homemaking can and will provide a valuable foundation for the future. Includes resources and displaced homemakers' programs useful to professionals.

749 Silver, Gerald A., and Myrna Silver. *Second Loves: A Guide for Women Involved With Divorced Men.* New York: Praeger, 1985. 155 pp.

Written especially for women who are involved in second relationships, either as wives or live-in lovers. The authors examine the cultural stereotypes that cast the second wife or lover in the role of a second-class citizen, who is often treated with disdain and not given the support and acceptance the first wife enjoyed. Offers advice on coping with problems presented by stepchildren, in-laws, and old friends. Also addresses the question of sex and love with a new partner, managing money and time, managing a household while working at a job or career, dealing with alimony, child support issues, and facing the legal realities of remarriage and live-in arrangements.

750 *The State-by-State Guide to Women's Legal Rights.* NOW Legal Defense Education Fund and Renie Cherow-O'Leary. New York: McGraw-Hill, 1986. 523 pp.

Part 1 provides an overview of women's legal issues encompassed by these areas: home and family, education, employment, and community. For each state there are brief summaries of the laws relating to these same areas in part 2.

751 Stein, Peter J. *Single Life: Unmarried Adults in Social Context.* New York: St. Martin's Press, 1981. 360 pp.

An investigation of the life-styles and experiences of single adults.

752 Taves, Isabella. *The Widow's Guide: Practical Advice on How to Deal with Grief, Stress, Health, Children, and Family, Money, Work, and Finally Getting Back into the World.* New York: Schocken Books, 1981. 274 pp.

Creates a supportive atmosphere by using the experiences of other widows in similar situations to those being discussed. Advice on how to deal with all the items mentioned in the title is provided. Includes a bibliography and lists programs, groups, and special services for widows.

753 Ullman, Jeffrey. *The Single's Almanac: A Guide to Getting the Most Out of Being Single.* New York: World Almanac, 1986. 208 pp.

The author is founder of the video dating service, "Great Expectations." This book is a result of his observations of all singles, whether never married, newly divorced, or widowed. A self-help for singles which focuses on how to make friends, advice on finding "sleeping partners," veneral diseases, having a relationship with a younger man or woman, breaking up, wills, living-together contracts, and tips for the newly single.

754 Weitzman, Lenore J. *The Marriage Contract: Spouses, Lovers, and the Law.* New York: Free Press, 1981. 536 pp.

Represents ten years of research which analyzes the institution of marriage and its social and psychological implications. Sections examine the legal assumptions about marriage, the need for contracts between husbands and wives as well as for unmarried couples, and the legal consequences of alternatives to marriage.

755 Witkin, Mildred Hope, with Burton Lehrenbaum. *45 – and Single Again.* New York: Dembner Books, 1985. 198 pp.

Witkin, associate director of the Human Sexuality Teaching program at New York Hospital, introduces some of the realities of life to the widowed or divorced man or woman in middle age or older. She reviews the stages of grief, the need to form new relationships, and suggests places to meet people. Sexuality and how to deal with those concerned, including grown children, is also covered.

756 Wydro, Kenneth. *Flying Solo: The New Art of Living Single.* New York: Berkley, 1978. 212 pp.

A self-help book for people who, for one reason or another, are living alone.

757 Yates, Martha. *Coping: A Survival Manual for Women Alone.* Englewood Cliffs, NJ: Prentice-Hall, 1976. 272 pp.

Provides suggestions for helping women live their lives successfully in a couple-oriented society.

B. Articles in Periodicals

758 "After the Baby M Case." *Newsweek* 109:22–23 (13 April 1987).

A New Jersey judge awarded custody of Baby M, now called Melissa Stern, to the natural father, William Stern. Meanwhile the natural mother, Mary Beth Whitehead, who bore the child for a $10,000 fee under contract to Stern and his wife, vowed to continue her fight for the baby's custody. Discusses pending legislation regarding surrogate motherhood in four states: New York, Connecticut, Rhode Island, and Pennsylvania. Also gives attention to the ethical issues and some new reforms in the selection of surrogates.

759 Andrews, Lori B. "Surrogate Motherhood: Should the Adoption Model Apply?" *Childrens' Legal Rights Journal* 7:13–20 (Fall 1986).

This article clarifies the two surrogate roles of surrogate mothers and surrogate carriers and addresses some of the legal and ethical issues. The distinctions between adoption policies and surrogate procedures are covered. Presents other issues such as payment to surrogates, financial motivations, legal parenthood, enforcing the surrogate contract, and the surrogates as legal mothers.

760 Bean, Kathleen S. "Grandparent Visitation: Can the Parent Refuse?" *Journal of Family Law* 24:393–449 (1985/86).

Examines the authority of the state to intervene in the family government for the purpose of ordering grandparent visitation. This examination involves identifying the boundary between the family's authority to make decisions concerning visitation for the child and the state's authority to exercise its power in the best interest of the child.

761 Bell, Cynthia J. "Adoptive Pregnancy: Legal and Social Work Issues." *Child Welfare* 65:421–36 (September/October 1986).

Adoptive pregnancy through embryo transfer is the process which begins when a surrogate or donor mother's ovary is artificially inseminated with the sperm of the husband of the woman who will become the birth mother. Within a week of conception, the embryo is flushed from the body of the genetic mother and implanted in the uterus of the birth-mother-to-be. The sperm donor may be someone other than the husband. Discusses legal, ethical, and policy questions.

762 Cleveland, William P., and Daniel T. Gainturco. "Remarriage Probability After Widowhood: A Retrospective Method." *Journal of Gerontology* 31:99–103 (1976).

Describes a technique for estimating the remarriage probability for newly widowed persons.

763 Crossman, Sharyn M., and Jean E. Edmondson. "Personal and Family Resources Supportive of Displaced Homemakers' Financial Adjustment." *Family Relations* 34:465–74 (October 1985).

This investigation uses Hill's (1958) ABCX model of family-crisis adjustment to examine the coping strategies of women who become displaced homemakers—women whose role as homemaker was disrupted due to death of or divorce from their husbands, and who now assume the provider role.

764 Foster, Henry H., Jr., and Doris Jonas Freed. "Grandparent Visitation: Vagaries and Vicissitudes." *Journal of Divorce* 5:79–100 (Fall/ Winter 1981).

Examines the attitude of the law toward the visitation rights of grandparents in divorce and adoption, and includes state statutes which permit an award of visitation when found to be in the best interest of the child.

765 Gaynor, Charlene. "How Danny Got His Grandma Back." *Better Homes and Gardens Grandparents* (January 1987): 60–61.

After Danny's custody was changed from his father to his mother, his mother refused to let Danny's paternal grandmother, Nancy, see Danny. Nancy thought her ex-daughter-in-law feared that Danny would be snatched by his father, or that Nancy might interfere in the child's upbringing, and perhaps intrude on the new marriage of Danny's mother. Nancy went to court and was awarded visitation rights. Tells how the relationship between the two women improved to such a degree that they appeared on a talk show together. Emphasizes how important the grandparent experience is for children. Divides the fifty states into three categories ranging from the states with the most conservative laws regarding grandparents' rights to the states with the more liberal laws which also award visitation rights to extended family members such as stepparents.

766 Greene, Jill Rothfeld. "They Said We'd Never See Our Grandson Again." *McCalls* 111:36 (September 1984).

Mark's parents were divorced and Mark's father allowed him to be adopted by his stepfather. After the adoption, Mark's mother cut off all relations with his paternal grandparents. This article tells how those paternal grandparents won visitation rights in New York.

767 "I Had to Pay Another Woman to Have My Baby." *Good Housekeeping* 202:32 (April 1986).

A successful story about a couple and a surrogate mother. A young woman tells how she and her husband had a son, but after a miscarriage she learned that her fallopian tubes were blocked and she had only a small chance of getting pregnant again. After discussing adoption and reading everything on the subject of infertility, the couple discussed the posssibility of in vitro fertilization (implanting a fertilized egg in a woman's uterus). Discusses finding the right woman, costs, and the surrogate mother's pregnancy.

768 Kalish, Richard A., and Emily Visher. "Grandparents of Divorce and Remarriage." *Journal of Divorce* 5:127–40 (Fall/Winter 1981).

A dozen grandparent-of-divorce settings are given and their implications discussed. Tells how grandparents react to the divorce and remarriage of their children, which is determined by such variables as which parent has custody, subsequent remarriage and the new grandparental relationships that are established, and the perceptions of the grandchildren of their new family family relationships.

769 Kornhaber, Arthur. "The Vital Connection—1983." *Children Today* 12:31–33 (July/August 1983).

Explains about the relationship between grandparents and grand-children, and why this relationship is so important to both. Includes benefits to grandchildren and how grandparents' roles are unique. Gives information about The Foundation for Grand-parenting and Grandparents' Rights.

770 Kunen, James S. "Childless Couples Seeking Surrogate Mothers Call Michigan Lawyer Noel Keane—He Delivers." *People* 27:93 (30 March 1987).

This article is about Noel Keane, a lawyer and the founder and half-owner of the Infertility Center of New York, who is the undisputed father of surrogate motherhood. Tells how he got into the baby business, explains procedures that are followed in making the arrangements, and stresses the need for legislation in this area.

771 "No Other Hope for Having a Child." *Newsweek* 109:50–51 (19 January 1987).

An account of how Daniel Shapiro and his wife, Lynne, chose a surrogate mother who gave them a child, Abigail Rachael Shapiro, born on 8 August 1985. Gives the details of how the arrangements were made with the lawyer, the search for the right surrogate mother, costs involved, and the surrogate's pregnancy and delivery of Abigail.

772 Wallach, Edward. "Whose Baby Is That? Such Questions Grow in This Era of High-Tech Births, Warns Dr. Edward Wallach." *People* 26:139–40 (3 November 1986).

A question-and-answer format with the questions addressed to the author, chairman of the Department of Gynecology and Obstetrics at the Johns Hopkins University School of Medicine. Correspondent Giovanna Breu interviews him on the subject of the ethical complexities that now accompany the miracle of birth. Some questions asked are: Why do we need fertility guidelines? How has reproductive technology raised new legal problems? What problems concern surrogate mothers? Who is the mother, if the egg comes from one woman, develops in another and a third person rears the baby?

773 Whitehead, Mary Beth. "A Surrogate Mother Describes Her Change of Heart." *People* 26:46–48 (20 October 1986).

The story of Mary Beth Whitehead, a surrogate mother who, upon the birth of her child, turned down her $10,000 fee and refused to surrender the baby to the adoptive parents. Tells about two other surrogate mothers.

774 "Who Keeps 'Baby M'?" *Newsweek* 109:44–49 (19 January 1987). (Cover title: "Mother for Hire: The Battle for Baby M.")

Surrogate mother Mary Beth Whitehead fights for custody of a child who is now nine months old. Mrs. Whitehead, a twenty-nine-year-old homemaker, signed a contract to bear a child for Elizabeth and William Stern by being artifically inseminated by Mr. Stern for the sum of $10,000. Tells how the Whiteheads and Sterns met, follows Mary Beth through the pregnancy and birth of Baby M. After the birth, Mary Beth changed her mind about giving up the baby and fled to Florida with her. The Sterns spent $20,000 to locate Mary Beth and the baby. The Sterns gained temporary custody and, at the time of the article both sides awaited Judge Harvey R. Surkow's custody decision. No matter which way the decision goes, both sides have pledged to appeal. Explains how the case will influence laws in other states and judges hearing similar cases. Gives examples of other surrogate mothers who explain their feelings about being surrogates. (For the outcome see listing 758).

14
Works for Children & Youth

A. Fiction

775 Adler, C. S. (Carole S.). *Footsteps on the Stairs: A Novel*. New York: Delacorte, 1982. 151 pp. Grades 5–9.

> While spending their summer at a haunted beach-house, two rival stepsisters forget their differences as they uncover the story of two other sisters who lived and died there years ago.

776 ———. *In Our House Scott Is My Brother*. New York: Macmillan, 1980. 139 pp.

> A girl's adjustment to her widowed father's remarriage and to a difficult stepbrother.

777 Bach, Alice. *A Father Every Few Years*. New York: Harper & Row, 1977. 130 pp.

> When his stepfather leaves home, Tim must cope with his loneliness by deepening other relationships.

778 Bates, Betty. *Bugs in Your Ears*. New York: Holiday House, 1977. 128 pp. Preteens.

> Disappointed because she dislikes the man her mother marries, Carrie has difficulty adjusting until she realizes that her stepbrothers and stepsister are having difficulties too.

779 Bawden, Nina. *The Finding*. New York: Lothrop, Lee & Shepard, 1985. 153 pp.

> A unexpected inheritance threatens to change the life of an eleven-year-old foundling in his adoptive family, and he runs away from home.

780   Blos. Joan W. *A Gathering of Days: A New England Girl's Journal,*
       1830–32: A Novel. New York: Scribner, 1979. 144 pp.

>   The journal of a fourteen-year-old girl, kept the last year she lived
>   on the family farm. She records daily events in her small New
>   Hampshire town, including her father's remarriage and the death
>   of her best pal.

781   Blume, Judy. *It's Not the End of the World.* Scarsdale, NY:
       Bradbury Press, 1972. 169 pp. Grades 4–7.

>   Karen, a sixth grader, and her sister cope with their feelings after
>   their parents' divorce, and struggle to understand that sometimes
>   people are unable to live together.

782   ———. *Tiger Eyes.* Scarsdale, NY: Bradbury Press 1981. 206 pp.

>   A little girl experiences a single-parent family by death. The story
>   takes you through her reactions to her mom, a new home, death,
>   and the people around her.

783   Boegehold, Betty. *Daddy Doesn't Live Here Anymore: A Book*
       About Divorce. Racine, WI: Western, 1985. 25 pp.

>   Tells how Casey, a little girl, reacts to the separation of her mother
>   and father, and how her parents try to comfort her.

784   Brooks, Jerome. *Uncle Mike's Boy.* New York: Harper & Row,
       1973. 226 pp.

>   A young boy finds in his uncle the friendship and comfort he
>   needs after the divorce of his parents and the death of his younger
>   sister.

785   Byars, Betsy. *The Animal, the Vegetable, and John D. Jones.* New
       York: Delacorte, 1982. 150 pp.

>   Two sisters think of a beach vacation with their father, his girl-
>   friend, and her son, as two weeks with the wrong people.

786   Caines, Jeanette Franklin. *Daddy.* New York: Harper & Row,
       1977. 32 pp. Picture book.

>   Windy, a young black girl whose parents are separated, does
>   special things with her father on Saturdays.

787   Clifton, Lucille. *Everett Anderson's Nine Months Long*. New York: Holt, 1978. 31 pp. Preschool to grade 2.

A small boy and his family anticipate the birth of their newest member. Deals with stepfather relationships.

788   Danziger, Paula. *The Divorce Express*. New York: Delacorte, 1982. 148 pp. Grades 7 and up.

Phoebe's parents are an amateur painter father, with whom she spends the week in Woodstock, and a decorator mother, in whose New York apartment she spends every weekend. Tells of the discovery she makes, while being shuttled back and forth between her parents, on a bus called the "Divorce Express."

789   Eichler, Margrit. *Martin's Father*. Chapel Hill, NC: Lollipop Power, 1977. 30 pp. Preschool and beginning readers.

A matter-of-fact presentation of the daily life of a boy who lives with his father.

790   Emery, Anne. *Stepfamily*. Philadelphia: Westminster Press, 1980. 141 pp.

A year and a half after her mother dies, Liza finds her life complicated when her father remarries and she has a stepbrother she adores and a stepsister she hates.

791   Goff, Beth. *Where Is Daddy? The Story of Divorce*. Boston: Beacon Press. 1969. 25 pp. Picture book.

Describes the fears of a little girl who experiences not only the loss of her father, because of divorce, but also the partial loss of her mother, who must now go to work outside the home. She also must adjust to moving in with grandma.

792   Green, Phyllis. *A New Mother for Martha*. New York: Human Sciences Press, 1978. 32 pp.

Deals with the feelings of a young girl whose mother has died, and whose father remarries. Facing the father's remarriage, she stubbornly insists that her dead mother will return soon.

793   Greene, Constance C. *I and Sproggy*. New York: Viking, 1978. 155 pp.

The meeting between an eleven-year-old boy and Sproggy, his English stepsister who comes to New York, is less than happy, but time and events help to change things.

794   ———. *Your Old Pal, Al.* New York: Viking, 1979. 149 pp.

While Al impatiently awaits word from her father, his new wife, and a boy named Brian, her best friend is in trouble because of the arrival of a house guest.

795   Hamilton, Virginia. *A Little Love.* New York: Philomel Books, 1984. 207 pp.

Through she has been raised lovingly by her grandparents, a black teenager goes in search of her father.

796   ———. *Sweet Whispers, Brother Rush.* New York: Philomel Books, 1982. 215 pp.

Fourteen-year-old Teresa, known as Tree, lives in a fatherless home and is resentful of her working mother who leaves her in charge of her retarded brother. She encounters the ghost of her dead uncle and comes to a deeper understanding of herself, her mother, and their family's problems.

797   Harris, Mark Jonathan. *With a Wave of the Wand.* New York: Lothrop, 1980. 191 pp.

Marlee resorts to magic in her efforts to patch up her family.

798   Helmering, Doris Wild. *I Have Two Families.* Nashville: Abingdon, 1981. 48 pp. Picture book.

Patty, an eight-year-old girl, lives with her divorced father most of the time since her mother's work schedule is irregular. Gradually she learns to cope with her new life-style, which accepting dad's new girlfriend.

799   Hunter, Evan. *Me and Mr. Stenner.* New York: Dell, 1978. 110 pp.

An eleven-year-old girl feels love and loyalty for both her father and stepfather.

800   Kindred, Wendy. *Lucky Wilma.* New York: Dial Press, 1973. 32 pp. Picture book.

A happy story about a girl who enjoys both parents after their divorce.

801   Klein, Norma. *Breaking Up.* New York: Avon, 1981. 174 pp.

While she is visiting her father and stepmother in California, fifteen-year-old Alison learns her mother is a lesbian.

802   ———. *Mom, the Wolfman and Me.* New York: Patheon, 1972. 128 pp.

Brett, an eleven-year-old, describes her life with her mother who has never married.

803   ———. *Taking Sides.* New York: Avon, 1976. 143 pp.

Twelve-year-old Nell adjusts to life with her father and five-year-old brother after her parents' divorce.

804   ———. *What It's All About.* New York: Dial, 1975. 146 pp.

A girl's reformed family grows even more complicated with her stepfather's departure following the adoption of a Vietnamese orphan.

805   Konigsburg, E. L. *George.* New York: Atheneum, 1970. 152 pp.

Ben is a boy who adopts an imaginary character, named George, after his parents get divorced. He only acts out George in front of his brother Howard. George uses dirty words and does disgusting things and makes Ben's brother laugh.

806   Lexau, Joan M. *Emily and the Klunky Baby and the Next-Door Dog.* New York: Dial, 1972. 38 pp. Picture book.

Ever since her father moved out, Emily thinks her mother is too busy for her. Feeling neglected, she runs off with her baby brother.

807   ———. *Me Day.* New York: Dial, 1971. 31 pp. Picture book.

When Rafer's divorced father doesn't visit on his birthday, what should have been a beautiful "me day" is ruined until Rafer is sent on an errand.

808   Lingard, Joan. *Odd Girl Out.* New York: Elsevier, 1979. 187 pp.

Elbie feels cut off when her mother remarries.

809   Lisker, Sonia O., and Dean Leigh. *Two Special Cards.* New York: Harcourt Brace, 1976. 48 pp. Picture book.

Hazel and her baby brother find they have two loving homes after their parents divorce.

810   Madison, Winifred. *Marinka, Katinka, and Me (Susie)*. Scarsdale, NY: Bradbury Press, 1975. 72 pp. Grades 2–4.

Portrays friendship among three fourth-grade girls whose nontraditional families are accepted as they are.

811   Mann, Peggy. *My Dad Lives in a Downtown Hotel*. Garden City, NY: Doubleday, 1973. 92 pp. Grades 3–6.

Convinced that his parents' separation is somewhat his fault, a young boy tries to persuade his father to come home. Gradually he learns to face reality and to cope with life as it is.

812   Martin, Ann M. *Bummer Summer*. New York: Scholastic, 1983. 152 pp. Grades 5 and up.

When twelve-year-old Kammy has difficulty accepting her new family after her father's remarriage, a summer at Camp Arrowhead helps her to put her home life in perspective.

813   Mazer, Harry. *Guy Lenny*. New York: Delacorte, 1971. 117 pp. Grades 6–9.

A twelve-year-old boy begins to feel like a ping-pong ball when his father decides to remarry and plans to send him to live with his mother, whom he has not seen for seven years.

814   Mazer, Norma Fox. *I, Trissy*. New York: Delacorte, 1971. 150 pp. Grades 6 and up.

Trissy, a sixth grader, finds ways to provoke her divorced parents until she manages to face up to her own problem.

815   McCord, Jean. *Turkeylegs Thompson*. New York: Atheneum, 1979. 242 pp.

Betty Ann must bear the burden of care for her brother and sister after her father leaves home and her mother takes a job.

816   McHargue, Georgess. *Stoneflight*. New York: Viking, 1975. 223 pp. Grades 5–8.

Janie suspects that her parents are getting a divorce, but no one will talk to her. Through her uncle, she is finally included in the family discussions of the problem.

817   Mendonca, Susan. *Tough Choices.* New York: Dial, 1980. 136 pp.

A fourteen-year-old girl cannot decide whether to live with her mother or with her father and his new wife and daughter.

818   Miles, Betty. *The Trouble With Thirteen.* New York: Knopf, 1979. 108 pp. Grades 4–7.

Twelve-year-old Annie faces some changes in her life when she learns that her friend's parents have intentions of getting a divorce.

819   Myers, Walter Dean. *Motown and Didi: A Love Story.* New York: Viking Kestrel, 1984. 174 pp.

Motown and Didi, two teenage loners in Harlem, become allies in a fight against Touchy, the drug dealer, whose dope is destroying Didi's brother, and find themselves in love with each other.

820   Naylor, Phyllis. *No Easy Circle.* Chicago: Follett, 1972. 152 pp.

Feeling deserted by her divorced parents and best friend, a fifteen-year-old girl turns to the youth culture of Washington, D.C.'s Dupont Circle in search of meaning to her life.

821   Nelson, Carol. *Dear Angie, Your Family's Getting a Divorce.* Elgin, IL.: David C. Cook, 1980. 119 pp.

Angie tells how she experienced the divorce of her parents.

822   Nelville, Emily Cheney. *Garden of Broken Glass.* New York: Delacorte, 1975. 215 pp.

Brian learns sensitivity while building a life without a father and with an alcoholic mother.

823   Ness, Evaline. *Sam Bangs & Moonshine.* New York: Holt, 1980. 37 pp. Picture book.

Samantha, whose mother is dead, eventually learns to face reality rather than live in make-believe.

824   Neufeld, John. *Sunday Father.* New York: New American Library, 1976. 159 pp.

The story of a young girl who experiences the trauma of divorcing parents. Although her father is planning to remarry, she keeps the dream of her father happily reunited with her mother, brother, and herself. She finally realizes that growing up is not easy.

825   Newfield, Marcia. *A Book for Jodan.* New York: Atheneum, 1975. 48 pp. Grades 3–5.

Jodan, who is nine, doesn't believe her parents' reassurances of their love for her after their separation. She wonders what can be done to keep them together and if she is to blame.

826   Noble, June. *Two Homes for Lynn.* New York: Holt, 1979. 32 pp. Grades K–3.

Lynn's make-believe friend helps her adjust to her two homes after her parents' divorce.

827   Okimoto, Jean Davies. *My Mother Is Not Married to My Father.* New York: Putnam, 1979. 109 pp. Grades 4–8.

Two sisters come to accept their parents' separation and divorce.

828   Perl, Lila. *The Telltale Summer of Tina C.* New York: Seabury, 1975. 160 pp.

Tina learns and grows while figuring out the complications of divorced parents who both intend to remarry.

829   Perry, Patricia, and Marietta Lynch. *Mommy and Daddy Are Divorced.* New York: Dial, 1978. 32 pp. Picture book.

Two young boys try to understand and cope with the confusion and hurt of their parents' divorce.

830   Peterson, Jeanne Whitehouse. *That Is That.* New York: Harper, 1979. 32 pp. Picture book.

When her father leaves home, Emma Rose, an American Indian, refuses to say good-bye. She dances her "magical come home dance" before she is able to accept the situation and wish him well.

831   Pevsner, Stella. *A Smart Kid Like You.* New York: Seabury Press, 1975. 216 pp. Grades 5 and up.

Just as Nina begins to accept her parents' divorce, she discovers her father's new wife is to be her seventh grade math teacher.

832   Pfeffer, Susan Beth. *Marly the Kid*. Garden City, NY: Double-day, 1975. 137 pp.

Marly chooses life with her divorced father and her stepmother.

833   Roy, Ron. *Breakfast With My Father*. New York: Houghton, 1980. 32 pp. Grades 5–8.

After his parents' separation, David looks forward eagerly to Saturday breakfast with his father at Frank's Diner, and is troubled when one Saturday his father doesn't show up.

834   Schuchman, Joan. *Two Places to Sleep*. Minneapolis: Carolrhoda, 1979. 32 pp. Picture book.

A seven-year-old boy describes living with his father and visiting his mother every other weekend after his parents divorce.

835   Schwartz, Sheila. *Like Mother, Like Me: A Novel*. New York: Pantheon, 1978. 166 pp.

When her father abandons his family for one of his students, a sixteen-year-old girl witnesses her mother's painful growth into an independent person.

836   Shreve, Susan. *Family Secrets: Five Very Important Stories*. New York: Knopf, 1979. 56 pp. Grades 3–6.

Eight-year-old Sammy tries to come to terms with several difficult situations, including the death of his dog, the divorce of his aunt and uncle, the suicide of his best friend's brother, coping with his terminally ill grandmother, and cheating on a school test.

837   Shyer, Marlene Fanta. *Stepdog*. New York: Scribner, 1983. 32 pp. Grades 1–3.

When Terry's dad marries Marilyn, Marilyn's dog, Hoover, suffers from jealousy.

838   Simon, Norma. *I Wish I Had My Father*. Niles, IL: Whitman, 1983. 32 pp. Grades 1–3.

Father's Day is tough for a young boy who no longer sees or communicates with his father.

839   Smith, Doris Buchanan. *The First Hard Times*. New York: Viking, 1983. 137 pp. Grades 4–8.

In the sequel to *Last Was Lloyd*, Lloyd's friend Ancil—who is devoted to the memory of her father who has been missing in action in Vietnam for more than ten years—has difficulty accepting her new stepfather.

840 ———. *Kick a Stone Home*. New York: Crowell, 1974. 152 pp.

A shy fifteen-year-old girl, more at ease on the sports field than anywhere else, tries to cope with feelings and a gradual understanding of herself, her divorced parents, and other people around her.

841 Stoltz, Mary. *Leap Before You Look*. New York: Harper & Row, 1972. Grades 7 and up.

The young teenage heroine of this story lives with her mother and has difficulty adjusting to her father's remarriage.

842 Terris, Susan. *The Latchkey Kids*. New York: Farrar, 1986. 167 pp.

Eleven-year-old Callie tries to cope with her new responsibilities when the family's changed circumstances force them to move to a new San Francisco neighborhood, and leave her in charge of her younger brother.

843 Thomas, Lanthe. *Eliza's Daddy*. New York: Harcourt, 1976. 64 pp.

Eliza's feelings about her father's remarriage are erased by visiting his new family.

844 Van Woerkom, Dorothy. *Something to Crow About*. Niles, Il: Whitman, 1982. 32 pp. Picture book.

A bachelor rooster willingly becomes a single parent after finding three orphaned eggs.

845 Vigna, Judith. *Daddy's New Baby*. Niles, IL.: Whitman, 1982. 32 pp. Picture book.

A little girl whose parents are divorced has a difficult time accepting her father's new baby until she assumes the important role of caring for her new half-sister.

846 ———. *Grandma Without Me: Story and Pictures*. Niles, IL: Whitman, 1984. 32 pp.

A young boy finds a way to keep in touch with his grandmother although his parents are divorced.

847   ———. *She's Not My Real Mother*. Chicago: Whitman, 1980. 324 pp. Grades K–3.

When Miles gets lost, his stepmother comes to his rescue, forcing him to reevaluate her. Could she be his friend?

848   Williams, Verna B. *A Chair for My Mother*. New York: Greenwillow, 1982. 32 pp. Picture book.

Rosa, who lives with her loving mother and grandmother, tells of buying a new chair after fire destroys their old apartment.

849   Wolitzer, Hilma. *Out of Love*. New York: Farrar, 1976. 146 pp.

Teddy, a thirteen-year-old girl, schemes to bring her parents back together before finally accepting reality.

850   Wolkoff, Judie. *Happily Every After . . . Almost: A Novel*. Scarsdale, NY: Bradbury Press, 1982. 215 pp. Grades 7 and up.

Eleven-year-old Kitty and her sister look forward to their mother's remarriage, but not to getting a stepbrother.

851   Zindel, Paul. *I Love My Mother*. New York: Harper & Row, 1975. 31 pp. Preschool and beginning readers.

A small boy's story about his single-parent mother, who not only cooks but teaches him to kick a football.

852   Zolotow, Charlotte. *A Father Like That*. New York: Harper & Row, 1971. 32 pp. Picture book.

A little boy whose father "went away before he was born" fantasizes about having a perfect father. His mother encourages him to be that kind of father when he grows up.

B. Nonfiction

853   Adams, Florence. *Mushy Eggs*. New York: Putnam, 1973. 32 pp. For school-age children.

Two little boys describe their life with their single-parent mother.

854 Anderson, Hal W., and Gail S. Anderson. *Mom & Dad are Divorced, But I'm Not: Parenting after Divorce.* Chicago: Nelson-Hall, 1981. 258 pp.

> Focuses on the children's point of view while giving attention to the problems that the marriage partner faces as an individual during the divorce process. Chapter 12 addresses stepparenting.

855 Andrew, Jan. *Divorce and the American Family.* New York: F. Watts, 1978. 138 pp. Grades 7–9.

> Discusses the history and legal statistics of divorce, divorce reform, divorce's effect on adults and children, remarriage, alternative life-styles, and contemporary issues related to divorce and its effects. Concludes by examining the future of family as an institution.

856 Arnold, William V. *When Your Parents Divorce.* Philadelphia: Westminister Press, 1980. 118 pp. Grades 6 and up.

> A Presbyterian minister shares his experiences in dealing with divorce and shows how feelings, thoughts, and actions can be adjusted to when young adults face the separation of their parents.

857 Berger, Terry. *A Friend Can Help.* New ed. Milwaukee: Raintree Editions: Chicago, 1974. 32 pp.

> A young child, whose parents do not live together, acquires strength and self-esteem from her relationsip with a friend.

858 ————. *How Does It Feel When Your Parents Get Divorced?* New York: J. Messner, 1977. 62 pp. Grades 3 and up.

> A girl who is about twelve years old tells this story about her divorcing parents. She tells how she was told about the divorce and her reactions. Discusses the problems and emotions young people experience when parents divorce, the family separates, or life-styles change.

859 ————. *Stepchild.* New York: J. Messner, 1980. 63 pp. Grades 3–5.

> A young boy tries to come to terms with his mother's remarriage and his role as a stepchild.

860   Berman, Claire, G. *What Am I Doing in a Step-Family?* Secaucus, NJ: L. Stuart, 1982. 48 pp. Grades 2–5.

> Offers advice for children of divorced or remarried parents who are adjusting to life with a stepfamily. It is in large print, with colorful illustrations.

861   Bienenfeld, Florence. *My Mom & Dad Are Getting a Divorce.* St. Paul, MN: EMC Corp., 1980. 38 pp. Grades K–4.

> Examines a young girl's feelings about her parents' divorce and how she and her parents cope with these emotions. Includes a counseling guide for parents, teachers, and counselors. It is illustrated with cartoon characters.

862   Boeckman, Charles. *Surviving Your Parents' Divorce.* New York: Watts, 1980. 133 pp. Grades 7–9.

> Gives advice for surviving parents' divorce. Deals with custody, child support, visitation rights, guilt, loneliness, remarriage, step-relatives, organizations to turn to for help, and adjusting to a new life with a single parent.

863   Booher, Dianna Daniels. *Coping—When Your Family Falls Apart.* New York: J. Messner, 1979. 126 pp. Grades 7–9.

> A guide for young people whose parents are divorcing, emphasizing a positive attitude and growth toward a new life. Answers specific questions concerning many puzzling problems facing adolescents whose parents have separated.

864   Bradley, Buff. *Where Do I Belong? A Kids Guide to Stepfamilies.* Reading, MA: Addison-Wesley, 1982. 113 pp. Grades 3–7.

> Discusses the problems children face when a parent remarries.

865   Burt, Mala Schuster, and Roger B. Burt. *What's Special about Our Stepfamily? A Participation Book for Children.* Garden City, NJ: Doubleday, 1983. 148 pp. Grades 3–7.

> Divorced and remarried, the Burts are bringing up offspring from both first marriages, and are also founders of a counseling service for stepfamilies. This is called a "participation book for children," and is based on a fictional stepson who describes sudden, profound changes in his life with a new family, and how he deals with them. There are blanks in the story to be filled in by young readers who are invited to record their own opinions and feelings

on issues involving the make-believe character. A special "advice to parents and stepparents" section is included.

866 Casey, James A. *What's a Divorce Anyway . . . ? A Story About a Tough Problem Written for Kids.* New York: Vantage, 1981. 49 pp.

Guides children through the stages of divorce and suggests a framework that children and their parents can use to help them understand and adjust to the difficult consequences of divorce.

867 Clifton, Lucille. *Everett Anderson's Year.* New York: Holt, 1974. 31 pp. Picture book.

A poem for each month reveals the feelings of a black boy who wishes his divorced father still lived at home.

868 Craven, Linda. *Stepfamilies: New Patterns in Harmony.* New York: J. Messner, 1982. 186 pp. Grades 7 and up.

Each chapter tells the story of a young person who has adjusted to living in a stepfamily. These case histories deal with real problems, their solutions, and the stepparents' point of view.

869 Fayerweather Street School. *The Kids' Book of Divorce: By, For, and About Kids.* Edited by Eric E. Rofes. Lexington, MA: Lewis Pub. Co., 1981. 123 pp.

Twenty school children, fourteen of whose parents are divorced, discuss the various aspects of divorce and give advice on coping with the feelings, fears, and problems caused by divorce.

870 Forrai, Maria S. *A Look at Divorce.* Minneapolis: Lerner, 1977. 36 pp.

Text and photographs describe problems faced by parents and children when a divorce occurs.

871 Gardner, Richard A. *The Boys and Girls Book About Divorce.* New York: J. Aronson, 1970. 159 pp. Grades 4 and up.

This books is about the realities children must face during and after divorce. It discusses and suggests solutions for problems often encountered by children whose parents are divorced, and is meant to be read to children by their parents.

872 ———. *The Boys and Girls Book About One-Parent Families.* New York: Putnam, 1978. 236 pp. Grades 4 and up.

Discusses the various types of one-parent families and examines the problems, including the advantages and disadvantages of being a child in a single-parent family.

873 ———. *The Boys and Girls Book About Stepfamilies.* New York: Bantam, 1982. 180 pp. Grades 4–6 and read to smaller children.

Tells children how to deal with some of the common problems that new stepfamilies encounter. It includes "why" certain things happen and also "what" can be done to avoid and relieve difficulties. Topics included are, "When a Parent Lives with an Unmarried Partner," and "Adoption by a Stepparent."

874 Getzoff, Ann, and Carolyn McClenahan. *Stepkids: A Survival Guide for Teenagers in Stepfamilies.* New York: Walker, 1984. 171 pp.

For annotation see listing 155.

875 Gilbert, Sara D. *Trouble at Home.* New York: Lothrop, 1981. 191 pp. Grades 7 and up.

The author's advice on a variety of family problems and parental behavior. Examines positive responses to common problems, such as death, divorce, or troublesome siblings, that may disrupt family life.

876 Glass, Stuart M. *A Divorce Dictionary: A Book For You and Your Children.* Boston: Little, Brown, 1980. 71 pp. Grades 7 and up.

Alphabetically arranged definitions and discussions of a number of terms relating to divorce, from abandonment to visitation rights.

877 Grollman, Earl A. *Talking About Divorce and Separation: A Dialogue Between Parent and Child.* Boston: Beacon Press, 1975. 87 pp. Picture Book.

A guide to help small children of divorcing parents understand and accept the fact that their parents are no longer able to live together. Includes a parents' guide, sources for additional help, and a bibliography of fiction and nonfiction works about divorce.

878 Hautzig, Esther. *Life With Working Parents: Practical Hints for Everyday Situations.* New York: Macmillan, 1976. 124 pp. Grades 4 and up.

A guide for children who must cope with a variety of daily situations because their parents work. Can be used as a starting point for family discussions. Also useful for single-parent families.

879   Hazen, Barbara Shook. *Two Homes to Live In: A Child's-Eye View of Divorce.* New York: Human Science Press, 1983. 40 pp. Grades K–8.

Deals with guilt about "causing the divorce" and getting it all together again afterwards. A little girl explains how she came to terms with her parents' divorce. This is a book parents can read and discuss with their childlren.

880   Hyde, Margaret Oldroyd, and Lawrence E. Hyde. *Missing Children.* New York: Watts, 1985. 104 pp.

Discusses missing children, including those who run away or are abducted by strangers or parents, and outlines ways to prevent and cope with this increasing problem.

881   Hyde, Maragaret Oldroyd. *My Friend Has Four Parents.* New York: McGraw-Hill, 1981. 120 pp. Grades 3 and up.

Examines various situations that arise from divorce and remarriage, including one-parent families, stepfamilies, and living part-time with both parents. Also includes information on custody, parental kidnapping, and sources of outside help.

882   Ives, Sally Blakeslee, David Fassler, and Michele Lash. *The Divorce Workbook: A Guide for Kids and Families.* Burlington, VT: Waterfront Books, 1985. 147 pp.

Intended for use by parents and children together, it explains separation, divorce, and remarriage. Provides space for drawings and coloring.

883   Jance, Judith A. *Dial Zero for Help.* Edmonds, WA: C. Franklin, 1985. 30 pp. Grades 3–6.

Designed to prevent noncustodial parent abduction. Tells the story of Danny, who is snatched by his father, the noncustodial parent, and how Danny helps in own his recovery. Lists the information children should know, and how parents can help children to know what they can do to help prevent themselves from being snatched. Includes guidelines for parents and lists additional sources.

884 *The Kids' Book About Single-Parent Families.* Edited by Paul Dol-
metsch and Alexa Shih. Garden City, NY: Doubleday, 1985.
193 pp.

> The editors, one a psychiatric social worker and the other a youth
> counselor, both grew up in single-parent families. In this work,
> they hope to give people a better understanding of life for kids in
> single-parent families. This book grew out of an exercise in group
> writing with youth, ages eleven to fifteen, explaining their expe-
> riences and problems. It is an expansion of the work by Eric E.
> Rofes and the kids from the Fayerweather Street School in Cam-
> bridge, Massachusetts, *The Kids' Book of Divorce*, 1981 (see listing
> 869). It includes experiences in single-parent families created by
> death, temporary separation, never-married parents, and divorce.

885 Krementz, Jill. *How It Feels to Be Adopted.* New York: Knopf,
1982. 107 pp.

> Interviews with adopted children and adoptive families about
> their experiences and feelings concerning adoption.

886 ———. *How It Feels When a Parent Dies.* New York: Knopf, 1981.
110 pp.

> Eighteen young people, ranging in age from seven to sixteen,
> discuss the questions, fears, and bereavement they experienced
> when one of their parents died.

887 ———. *How It Feels When Parents Divorce.* New York: Knopf,
1984. 115 pp.

> In this book nineteen young people, ages seven to sixteen, from
> professional family backgrounds, describe the changes, hurt, and
> confusion they had to deal with when their parents divorced.

888 LeShan, Eda J. *What's Going to Happen to Me? When Parents
Separate or Divorce.* New York: Four Winds Press, 1978. 134 pp.

> A book for young readers about the unspoken question which is
> in the minds of most children after divorce. Explores the feelings
> and problems common to the experience of divorce.

889 Lewis, Helen Coale. *All About Families: The Second Time Around.*
Atlanta, GA: Peachtree, 1980. 109 pp.

> This book is for children, parents, and stepparents of second-time
> around families, "stepfamilies," in which one or both parents

have been married previously. It is written simply enough for children and can be read by any family member alone, or by all members together. Offers steps for helping steprelations communicate their feelings.

890   Lindsay, Jeanne Warren. *Do I Have a Daddy? A Story About a Single-Parent Child, With a Special Section for Single Mothers and Fathers.* Buena Park, CA: Morning Glory Press, 1982. 44 pp.

Provides a model for parents who must deal with the difficult situation of telling a child why one parent is absent. Also offers insights that may help young mothers better understand themselves. Includes a section with suggestions for answering the question, "Do I have a daddy?"

891   List, Julie Autumn. *The Day the Loving Stopped: A Daughter's View of Her Parents' Divorce.* New York: Ballantine, 1983. 220 pp. Reprint of original edition: New York: Seaview Books, 1980. 215 pp.

For annotation see listing 549.

892   Livingston, Carole. *"Why Was I Adopted?"* Secaucus, NJ: L. Stuart, 1978. 47 pp.

A simple explanation of adoption.

893   Long, Lynette. *On My Own: The Kids' Self-Care Book.* Washington, DC: Acropolis Books, 1984. 175 pp.

A guide for children of working parents which teaches self-care in such areas as getting ready for school, after school, using the telephone, snacks, outside and inside play, safety, emergencies, and fear.

894   Magid, Ken, and Walt Schreibman. *Divorce Is a Kid's Coloring Book.* Gretna, LA: Pelican, 1980. 52 pp. For very young children.

A coloring book targeting twenty-five top problems of children of divorcing parents. It is illustrated with captions. Introduction is included which instructs parents or counselors in using the book as therapy with children.

895   Mayle, Peter. *Divorce Can Happen to the Nicest People.* New York: Macmillan, 1979. 31 pp.

Offers reassurance and advice on how to cope with a family that is splitting up.

896   Nickman, Steven L. *The Adoption Experience*. New York: J. Messner, 1985. 192 pp.

> Presents various aspects of adoption, including interracial adoption, searching for birth parents, and giving up a child for adoption. Also discusses the feelings of the participants, the provisions of the law, possible problems and their solutions, and ways in which adopted people are different, and similar to those who are not adopted.

897   Phillips, Carolyn E. *Our Family Got a Divorce*. Ventura, CA: Regal Books, 1979. 110 pp.

> A young boy relates how his family coped with divorce with the help of Jesus.

898   ———. *Our Family Got a Stepparent*. Ventura, CA: Regal Books, 1981. 79 pp.

> A young boy tells how, with God's help, he adjusted to his stepfather and the changes in his life caused by his mother's remarriage.

899   Powledge, Fred. *So You're Adopted*. New York: Scribner, 1982. 101 pp.

> A discussion of adoption aimed at adolescents. Discusses the social and legal aspects of adoption.

900   Pursell, Margaret Sanford. *A Look at Divorce*. Minneapolis: Lerner, 1977. 36 pp. Preschool and beginning readers.

> Text and photographs describe changes children and parents may make following divorce. A book to read and discuss with little ones.

901   Richards, Arlene, and Irene Willis. *How to Get It Together When Your Parents are Coming Apart*. New York: David McKay, 1976. 170 pp. For teenagers.

> A guide to help teenagers and persons interested in helping young people deal with parents' separation, divorce, and its aftermath. It deals with situations and feelings teenagers experience before, during, and after divorce. The authors encourage teenagers to voice their preferences concerning with whom they want to live, and to ask to see the part of their parents' separation agreement that deals with custody, child support, and visitation

rights. The last chapter discusses when and where to seek professional help.

902 Robson, Bonnie. *My Parents Are Divorced Too: Teenagers Talk About Their Experiences and How They Cope.* New York: Everest House, 1980. 208 pp. Ages 13 and up.

For annotation see listing 550.

903 Scott, Elaine. *Adoption.* New York: F. Watts, 1980. 58 pp.

Discusses various aspects of adoption, as well as some facts about genes and heredity.

904 Simon, Norma. *All Kinds of Families.* Chicago: Whitman, 1976. 40 pp. Picture book. Grades K–3.

Presents a full spectrum of families, all highlighted by tintype-like watercolors conveying what a family is and how families vary in makeup and life-styles.

905 Sinberg, Janet. *Divorce Is a Grown Up Problem: A Book About Divorce for Young Children and Their Parents.* New York: Avon, 1978. 47 pp.

A story for young children about their emotional reactions in a divorce situation.

906 Sobol, Harriet Langsam. *My Other-Mother, My Other-Father.* New York: Macmillan, 1979. 34 pp. Grades 3–7.

Twelve-year-old Andrea, whose parents have divorced and remarried, discusses the complexities of her new, larger family.

907 Spike, Francine Susan. *What About Me? Understanding Your Parents' Divorce.* New York: Crown, 1979. 80 pp. Grades 7–9.

Helps teenagers understand the reality of, and the need to accept, the termination of their parents' marriage.

908 Stein, Sara Bonnett. *The Adopted One: An Open Family Book for Parents and Children Together.* New York: Walker, 1979. 47 pp.

In this work realistic, black-and-white photographs and simple, direct language reveal family members under the stress of divorce. Includes dual text, one for the adult reader and one for the child, explaining some of the conflicting feelings of an adopted child.

909 Stenson, Janet Sinberg. *Now I Have a Stepparent and It's Kind of Confusing*. New York: Avon, 1979. 47 pp.

A young boy relates his feelings about his stepfather. May be read to younger children and contains a preface for adults.

15
Audiovisuals: Films, Audiocassettes, & Videocassettes

910 *Adoption: A Guide for Parents and Professionals.* Audiocassette, 1 7/8 ips. New York: Cassette Communications, 1978.

> Gives guidelines for reaching the decision to adopt, evaluating and choosing an agency, and preparing for adoptive parenthood.

911 *Adoptive Families Supporting One Another.* Videocassette, 20 min., sound, color, U-matic 3/4 in. or Beta or VHS. Madison, WI: Video Resource Library, School of Social Work, Media Center, University of Wisconsin-Madison, 1981.

> Illustrates the important results derived from adoptive families who have joined together to form support networks and services.

912 *Children of Divorce.* 16mm. film, 37 min., sound, color. Wilmette, IL: Films Inc., 1976.

> Examines the effects of divorce on children. Shows that the real victims of divorce are the children, who are bewildered by events that they do not understand and suffer from feelings of guilt and rejection. Points out that parents should bury their own hostilities, communicate without anger, and provide their children with free access to both parents. Also explores child support, custody, visitation rights, and child stealing.

913 *Children of Divorce.* Videocassette, 37 min., sound, color, U-matic 3/4 in. or Beta or VHS. Wilmette, IL: Films Inc., 1976.

> For annotation see listing 912.

914 *Divorce.* 16 mm. film, 16 min., sound, color. Lawrence, KS: Centron Films, 1981.

> Examines the impact of divorce on both children and adults. Uses the case study of a fictional family to show the problems, adjust-

ments, and critical issues involved when couples decide to get a divorce.

915 *Divorce.* Videocassette, 16 min., sound, color, U-matic 3/4 in. or Beta or VHS. Lawrence, KS: Centron Films, 1981.

For annotation see listing 914.

916 *Divorce.* Videocassette, 29 min., sound, color, U-matic 3/4 in. or VHS. Washington, DC: PBS Video, 1979.

Host Lee Salk explores the real-life situation of divorce from the viewpoint of three children who verbalize their feelings and experiences about the severed marriages of their parents. Interweaves the narrative with real-life vignettes, which portray the problems of money and dating that occur in divorced families.

917 *Divorce . . . and Other Monsters.* 16 mm. film, 22 min., sound, color. Pasadena, CA: Barr Films, 1981.

Shows the emotional turmoil of a young girl whose parents have recently divorced. Tells how she comes to grips with the emotional problems of anger, fear, guilt, and rejection that many children feel when their parents divorce.

918 *Divorce . . . and Other Monsters.* Videocassette, 22 min., sound, color, U-matic 3/4 in. or VHS. Pasadena, CA: Barr Films, 1981.

For annotation see listing 917.

919 *Divorce and Your Family.* 16 mm. film, 20 min., sound, color. Highland Park, IL: Perennial Education, 1981.

Presents many of the problems faced by older children when their parents divorce, such as freedom to choose between parents, and greater household responsibilities.

920 *Divorce and Your Family.* Videocasstte, 20 min., sound, color, U-matic 3/4 in. or Beta or VHS. Highland Park, IL: Perennial Education, 1981.

For annotation see listing 919.

921 *Divorce: For Better or For Worse.* 16 mm. film, 49 min., sound, color. New York: CRM McGraw-Hill Films, 1977.

Examines, through case histories and interviews with judges, lawyers, clergy, and a variety of divorce counselors, some aspects of divorce which add to the problems of divorcing couples, such as lawyers whose interest is in winning a case rather than the welfare of their clients. A conversation with Masters and Johnson, and a section on the displaced homemaker are included.

922 *Divorce: For Better or For Worse.* Videocassette, 49 min., sound, color, U-matic 3/4 in. or Beta or VHS. New York: CRM McGraw-Hill Films, 1977.

For annotation see listing 921.

923 *Divorce Mediation.* Audiocassette, 1 7/8 ips. Indianapolis, IN: ConferenceCorder Productions, 1981?

Presentations recorded at the Association of Family Conciliation Courts Conference in December 1981.

924 *Divorce Mediation.* 4 Audiocassettes, 1 7/8 ips. Bridgeport, CT: University of Bridgeport Law Center, Division of Continuing Legal Education, 1983.

Provides information on combining both counseling and law to provide an alternative to the present adversarial system of divorce.

925 *Divorce Mediation: Dealing with Custody.* Videocassette, 45 min., sound, color, VHS. Stony Brook, NY: School of Social Welfare, SUNY, Stony Brook, 1981.

Demonstrates Dr. John M. Haynes's mediation methods of trying to focus on the future, to negotiate in specific terms, to separate economic from emotional issues, and to plan for the child to have access to both parents.

926 *Families: Will They Survive?* 16 mm. film, 23 min., sound, color. Chicago: Encyclopedia Britannica Educational Corp., 1982.

Examines how different types of family units, including nuclear and extended families, have fared throughout history and how each is faring today. Also describes the effects of the modern, increasingly complex social structure on the family.

927 *Families: Will They Survive?* Videocassette, 23 min., sound, color, U-matic 3/4 in. or Beta or VHS. Chicago: Encyclopedia Britannica Educational Corp., 1982.

For annotation see listing 926.

928 *Family of Strangers.* 16 mm. film, 46 min., sound, color. New York: Learning Corporation of America, 1980. Shorter version, 31 min., also issued. Based on the book, *Bugs in Your Ears,* by Betty Bates.

>   Disappointed because she dislikes the man her mother marries, Carrie has difficulty adjusting until she realizes that her step-brothers and stepsister are also having difficulties.

929 *Family of Strangers* Videocassette, 46 min., sound, color, U-matic 3/4 in. or Beta or VHS. Northbrook, IL: Learning Corporation of America, 1980. Based on the book, *Bugs in Your Ears,* by Betty Bates.

>   For annotation see listing 928.

930 *A Family Portrait: The Marinos.* 16 mm. film, 9 min., sound, color. Wilmette, IL: Films, Inc., 1979.

>   Mr. and Mrs. Marino, in separate interviews, discuss the custody battle over their three children.

931 *A Family Portrait: The Marinos.* Videocassette, 9 min., sound, color. U-matic 3/4 in. Wilmette, IL: Films Inc., 1979.

>   For annotation see listing 930.

932 *A Father Like That.* 16 mm. film, 18 min., sound, color. New Brunswick, NJ: Phoenix/BFA Films & Video, 1982. Based on the book by Charlotte Zolotow. For primary through elementary grades.

>   A ten-year-old boy is given a homework assignment to write an essay about his father. Since he has never met his father, his teacher suggests that he write about the kind of father he would like to have.

933 *A Father Like That.* Videocassette, 18 min., sound, color, U-matic 3/4 in. or Beta or VHS. New York: Phoenix/BFA Films & Video, 1982.

>   For annotation see listing 932.

934 *Four Foster Parents: Their Own Stories in Their Own Words.* Video-cassette, 42 min., sound, color, U-matic 3/4 in. St. Louis, MO:

Learning Resource Video Center, George W. Brown School of Social Work, Washington University, 1982.

Four adults share their expriences in dealing with the foster care program.

935   *Issues of Working Parents.* Videocassette, 20 min., sound, color, U-matic 3/4 in. or Beta or VHS. Brooklyn, NY: Human Services Development, 1981.

Presents problems and concerns of working parents such as children alone at home, conflicting demands for time, marital stress, and others.

936   *Joint Custody: A New Kind of Family.* 16 mm. film, 85 min., sound, color. Wayne, NJ: New Day Films, 1983.

Presents the pros and cons of coparenting while investigating the emotional entanglements, financial arrangements, and logistics coparents must resolve for the success of a joint custody arrangement.

937   *Joint Custody: A New Kind of Family.* Videocassette, 85 min., sound, color, U-matic 3/4 or Beta or VHS. Franklin Lakes, NJ: New Day Films, 1983.

For annotation see listing 936.

938   *Kramer vs. Kramer.* Videocassette, 105 min., sound, color, Beta or VHS, Burbank, CA: RCA/Columbia Pictures Home Video, 1984. Videocassette release of the 1979 motion picture. Based on the novel by Avery Corman.

A woman abandons her husband and young son, leaving them to struggle and make a new life for themselves. Eventually she returns to fight for her son's custody. Although she wins the court case, she realizes that her son should remain with his father.

939   *Marriage.* Videocassette, 30 min., sound, color, U-matic 3/4 in. Ann Arbor, MI: Michigan Media, University of Michigan, 1980.

Examines some of the marital problems common at mid-life, such as a trapped wife, a May/December affair, and a stale marriage.

940   *Mother May I?* 16 mm. film, 28 min., sound, color. Los Angeles: Churchill Films, 1982. Also available in school edition.

Deals with the sexuality and teenage pregnancy as seen through the eyes of an eleven-year-old girl and her sixteen-year-old sister, who thinks she is pregnant. They learn how to communicate about sexuality and how to act responsibly on sexual issues.

941   *Mother May I?* Videocassette, 28 min., sound, color, U-matic 3/4 in. or Beta or VHS. Los Angeles: Churchill Films, 1982. Also available in school edition.

For annotation see listing 940.

942   *Mothers After Divorce.* 16 mm. film, 20 min., sound, color. Boston: Polymorph Films, 1976.

Several divorced women, with children in high school, discuss their lives before and afer divorce, and their concerns as parents.

943   *Not for Women Only: Children of Divorce.* Videocassette, 33 min., sound, color, 3/4 in. New York: WNBC-TV Community Affairs, 1979? Distributed by New York State Education Dept., Bureau of Mass Communications.

For annotation see listing 912.

944   *Single-Parent Families.* 2 Audiocassettes, 116 min., 1 7/8 ips. Washington, DC: National Public Radio Education Services, 1981.

A four-part review of the problems experienced in a single-parent household. Interviews parents and children in broken homes to gain a better understanding of their feelings and prejudices. Also interviews family experts and examines how schools deal with children from single-parent families.

945   *Single Parent Families.* Videocassette, 29 min., sound, color, Beta. Cleveland, OH: Cuyahoga County Cooperative Extension Service, 1984.

Discusses common problems of the single-parent family. Points out that 90 percent of single-parent households are maintained by women who need better day care opportunities in the face of poverty and isolation.

946   *The Single Parent Family.* 16 mm. film, 15 min., sound, color. Lawrence, KS: Centron Films, 1981.

Examines the adjustment that children and parents must make after a divorce. Follows the lives of Helene and Alan, a fictional couple, whose divorce results in Helene having to face the problems and issues of single parenthood.

947 *The Single Parent Family.* Videocassette, 15 min., sound, color, U-matic 3/4 in. or Beta or VHS. Lawrence, KS: Centron Films, 1981.

For annotation see listing 944.

948 *Step Family.* 16 mm. film, 13 min., sound, color. Lawrence, KS: Centron Films, 1981.

Examines the impact of remarriage on both children and adults. Uses the case study of a fictional family to show the problems that children face in accepting new parents and siblings. This is the continued story of Helene and her children (see listing 946) after divorce.

949 *Step Family.* Videocassette, 13 min., sound, color, U-matic 3/4 in. or Beta or VHS. Lawrence, KS: Centron Films, 1981.

For annotation see listing 948.

950 *Stepparenting.* Videocasstte, 30 min., sound, color, U-matic 3/4 in. or VHS. Released by Wisconsin Educational Communications Board, 1980.

Discusses the difficult job of stepparenting and how to handle it with grace and a sense of humor. Interviews with stepparents explore the solutions and problems concerning these stepparent challenges.

951 *Stepparenting.* Videocassette, 28 min., sound, color, VHS. Tucson, AZ: Medical Electronic Educational Services, 1985.

Professional counselor interviews stepparents for discussing stimulus in parenting workshops or undergraduate courses in sociology, psychology, or nursing departments.

952 *Stepparenting Issues.* 16 mm. film, 20 min., sound, color. Boston: Human Services Development, 1981.

Fourteen vignettes depict common problem situations in stepfamilies, such as no time alone for the new couple, conflict over childbearing, testing of authority, and sibling rivalry.

953 *Stepparenting Issues.* Videocassette, 20 min., sound, color, U-matic 3/4 in. or Beta or VHS. Boston: Human Services Development, 1981.

For annotation see listing 952.

954 *Stepparenting: New Families, Old Ties.* 16 mm. film, 25 min., sound, color. Boston: Polymorph Films, 1977.

Focuses on the problems of being a stepparent and ways in which families deal with them. Documentary scenes of life in stepfamilies illustrate what is involved in weekend visitation when "his" and "hers" combine and become "theirs."

955 *Stepparenting: New Families, Old Ties.* Videocassette, 25 min., sound, color, U-matic 3/4 in. or Beta or VHS. Boston: Polymorph Films, 1977.

For annotation see listing 954.

956 *Strengthening Stepfamilies.* 3 Audiocassettes, 76 min., 1 7/8 ips. Circle Pines, MN: American Guidance Association, 1986.

A group-study program for people living in stepfamilies, designed to increase their knowledge, skills, and effectiveness.

957 *Teen Mother: A Story of Coping.* 16mm. film, 24 min., sound, color. Franklin Lakes, NJ: Mobius International, 1981.

A young woman, on her own with her son since age seventeen, shares the reality of a teen mother's life. Shows the love, motivation, and energy that is required of anyone who tries to cope with parenthood at such a young age.

958 *Teen Mother: A Story of Coping.* Videocassette, 24 min., sound, color. U-matic 3/4 in. or Beta or VHS. Los Angeles: Churchill Film, 1985.

For annotation see listing 957.

959 *Teenage Mother: A Broken Dream.* 16 mm film, 15 min., sound, color. New York: Carousel Films, 1977.

Explores the teenage-pregnancy problem. Shows a young girl who attended a state school for unwed mothers and how she must face problems of handling her dream home, family, and the responsibility of caring for a baby.

960   *Teenage Mother: A Broken Dream.* Videocassette, 15 min., sound, color, U-matic 3/4 in. or Beta or VHS. New York: Carousel Films, 1977.

For annotation see listing 959.

961   *Teenage Motherhood.* Audiocassette, 29 min., 1 7/8 ips. Racine, WI: Johnson Foundation, 1979.

Explores the problem of teenage motherhood in the United States, including the number of teenage mothers, consequences for the child, need for training in parenting, need for community support programs, and other issues.

962   *Teenage Father.* 16 mm. film, 30 min., sound, color. Los Angeles: Children's Home Society of California. Made by New Visions, Inc., 1978.

A look at teenage parenthood from the viewpoints of the unmarried father, his peers, the mother, and both sets of parents.

963   *Teenage Father.* Videocassette, 30 min., sound, color, U-matic 3/4 in. or Beta or VHS. Los Angeles: Children's Home Society of California. Made by New Visions, Inc., 1978.

For annotation see listing 962.

964   *Teenage Parents.* 16 mm. film,20 min., sound, color. Del Mar, CA: CRM/McGraw-Hill Films, 1981.

Discusses the life-styles of two married teenagers who are discovering what it is like to have the responsibilities of both marriage and parenthood while still teenagers.

965   *Teenage Parents.* Videocassette, 20 min., sound, color, U-matic 3/4 in. or Beta or VHS. Del Mar, CA: CRM/McGraw-Hill Films, 1981.

For annotation see listing 964.

966   *The Teenage Pregnancy Experience.* 16 mm. film, 26 min., sound, color. Crystal River, FL: Parenting Pictures, 1981.

Traces two school-age mothers through pregnancy, labor, and birth. Shows them caring for their young infants. Discusses birth control, teenage fathers, child rearing, relinquishing for adoption, and other problems faced by these young mothers.

967   *The Teenage Pregnancy Experience.* Videocassette, 26 min., sound, color, U-matic 3/4 in. or Beta or VHS. Crystal River, FL: Parenting Pictures, 1981.

For annotation see listing 966.

968   *Teenage Sexuality: You Don't Have To Be in Love To Make Love.* Audiocassette, 30 min., 1 7/8 ips. Ithaca, NY: Media Services, Cornell University, 1983?

A documentary dealing with the issue of teenage sexuality. Notes that marriage rates among teens have declined while divorce rates and abortions have increased. Asks where the responsibility lies, and what teenagers and parents can do. Hopes to open up communication between teenagers and adults.

969   *We Were Just Too Young.* 16 mm. film, 30 min., sound, color. Schiller Park, IL: MTI Teleprograms, 1979.

A case study on teenage parents whose lives have been burdened by bad decisions and unrealistic expectations. Presents the problems of employment, lack of education, child care demands, and lack of freedom.

970   *We Were Just Too Young.* Videocassette, 30 min., sound, color, U-matic 3/4 in. or Beta or VHS. Schiller Park, IL: MTI Teleprograms, 1979.

For annotation see listing 969.

16
Late Additions

Brusko, Marlene. *Living With Your Teenager*. New York: McGraw-Hill, 1986. 193 pp.

Clark, Don. *Loving Someone Gay*. New York: New American Library, 1977. 274 pp.

Dynes, Wayne. *Homosexuality: A Research Guide*. New York: Garland, 1987. 880 pp.

Gay and Lesbian Parents. Edited by Frederik W. Bozett. New York: Praeger Publishers, 1987.

Hechinger, Grace. *How to Raise a Street Smart Child: The Complete Parents' Guide to Safety on the Street and at Home*. New York: Facts on File Publications, 1984. 160 pp.

Lees, Dennis. *Successful Parenting for Stressful Times*. Saratoga, CA: R & E Publishers, 1985.

Marafiote, Richard A. *The Custody of Children: A Behavior Assessment Model*. New York: Plenum Press, 1985. 277 pp.

Morrison, Kati, and Airdrie Thompson-Guppy, with Patricia Bell. *Stepmothers: Exploring the Myth*. Ottawa: Canadian Council on Social Development, 1986. 126 pp.

Norris, Gloria, and JoAnn Miller. *The Working Mother's Complete Handbook*. Rev. ed. New York: New American Library, 1984. 336 pp.

Pennetti, Michael. *Coping With School Age Fatherhood*. New York: Rosen Publishing Group, 1987. 148 pp.

Rosin, Mark Bruce. *Stepfathering: Stepfathers' Advice on Creating a New Family*. New York: Simon & Schuster, 1987. 285 pp.

Sanger, Sirgay, and John Kelly. *The Woman Who Works, the Parent Who Cares: A Revoluntionary Program for Raising Your Child*. Boston: Little, Brown, 1987. 288 pp.

Shreve, Anita. *Remaking Motherhood: How Working Mothers are Shaping Our Children's Future.* New York: Viking, 1987. 227 pp.

Spouse, Parent, Worker: On Gender and Mutiple Roles. Edited by Faye J. Crosby. New Haven: Yale University Press, 1987. 256 pp.

Steven, Kirsty, with Emma Dally. *Surrogate Mother: One Woman's Story.* London: Century, 1985. 181 pp.

Appendix:
Associations & Organizations

Academy of Family Mediators
P.O. Box 4686
Greenwich, CT 06830

Adam and Eve
1008 White Oak
Arlington Heights, IL 60005

Aid to Incarcerated Mothers
St. Pauls Cathedral
138 Vermont St., 4th floor
Boston, MA 02111

American Association of
    Marriage and Family Therapy
1717 K Street, NW #407
Washington, DC 20036

American Psychological
    Association
1200 17th Street, NW
Washington, DC 20036

American Society for Adolescent
    Psychiatry
24 Green Valley Road
Wallingford, PA 19086

American Society of Separated
    and Divorced Men
575 Keep Street
Elgin, IL 60120

Association of Family and
    Conciliation Courts
Oregon Health Sciences
    University
Dept. of Psychiatry
3181 SW San Jackson Park Road
Portland, OR 97201

Big Brothers/Big Sisters
117 South 17th St., Suite 1200
Philadelphia, PA 19103

Committee for Mother and Child
    Rights
Box 481
Chappaqua, NY 10514

Committee for Single Adoptive
    Parents
P.O. Box 15084
Chevy Chase, MD 20815

Commuter Couples Association
    of America
1109 South Plaza Way, #242
Flagstaff, AZ 86001

Concerned Parents for Adoption
P.O. Box 179
Whippany, NJ 07981

Concerned United Birthparents
184 N. Main St.
Rochester, NH 03867

Displaced Homemakers Network
1010 Vermont Ave., NE, Suite
   817
Washington, DC 20005

Division of Family Psychology
Dept. of Specialized Services
Herbert Lehman College
CUNY
Bronx, NY 10468

Divorce After 60
c/o Truner Geriatric Clinic
1010 Wall St.
University of Michigan
Ann Arbor, MI 48109

Divorce Anonymous
P.O. Box 5313
Chicago, IL 60680

Ex-Partners of Servicemen for
   Equality
P.O. Box 11191
Alexandria, VA 22312

Families Adopting Children
   Everywhere
P.O. Box 28058, Northwood
   Station
Baltimore, MD 21239

The Family Education Center of
   Florida
P.O. Box 260421
Tampa, FL 33685

Fathers are Forever
P.O. Box 4804
Panorama City, CA 91412

Fathers for Equal Rights
P.O. Box 010847, Flagler Station
Miami, FL 33101

Fathers' Rights of America
P.O. Box 7596
Van Nuys, CA 91409

Federation of Parents and
   Friends of Lesbians and Gays
P.O. Box 24565
Los Angeles, CA 90024

Foster Grandparents Program
806 Connecticut Ave., NW
Room M-1006
Washington, DC 20525

Foundation for Grandparenting
Route 86
Joy, NY 12941

Gay Fathers Coalition
P.O. Box 50360
Washington, DC 20004

Grandparents'/Children's Rights
5728 Bayonne Ave.
Hasbelt, MI 48840

Infertility Associates
   International
5530 Wisconsin Ave., Suite 940
Chevy Chase, MD 20815

International Association for
   Widowed People
P.O. Box 3564
Springfield, IL 62708

Joint Custody Association
10606 Wilkins Ave.
Los Angeles, CA 90024

LADIES
P.O. Box 2974
Beverly Hills, CA 90213

Men's Rights Association
17854 Lyons
Forest Lake, MN 55025

Michigan Association of Single
  Adoptive Parents
P.O. Box 601
Southfield, MI 48037

Mothers Without Custody
P.O. Box 5672
Houston, TX 77256

National Academy of Counselors
  Family Therapists
225 Jerichs Turnpike, Suite 4
Floral Park, NY 11001

National Action for Former
  Military Wives
1700 Legion Dr.
Winter Park, FL 32789

National Adoption Center
1218 Chestnut St.
Philadelphia, PA 19107

National Association of Social
  Workers
7981 Eastern Ave.
Silver Spring, MD 20910

National Center for Missing and
  Exploited Children
Missing Children's Division
1835 K St., Suite 700
Washington, DC 20006

National Center for Special
  Needs Adoption
P.O. Box 337
Chelsea, MI 48118

National Center on Women and
  Family Law
799 Broadway, Room 402
New York, NY 10003

National Child Support
  Enforcement Association
P.O. Box 6068
Des Moines, IA 50309

National Committee for Fair
  Divorce and Alimony Laws
217 Broadway, Room 404
New York, NY 10007

National Council for Children's
  Rights
2001 O Street, NW
Washington, DC 20036

National Council on Family
  Relations
1910 W. County Road B, Suite
  147
St. Paul, MN 55113

National Foster Parent
  Association
226 Kilts Dr.
Houston, TX 77024

National Gay Task Force
80 Fifth Ave.
New York, NY 10011

National Institute for Latchkey
  Children
P.O. Box 682
Glen Echo, MD 20812

National Organization for Men
381 Port Ave., S
New York, NY 10016

National Organization of
   Adolescent Pregnancy and
   Parenting
P.O. Box 2365
Reston, VA 22090

National Single Parent Coalition
1165 Broadway, Room 504
New York, NY 10001

North American Center on
   Adoption
67 Irving Plaza
New York, NY 10003

North American Conference of
   Separates, Divorced, and/or
   Remarried Catholics
1100 South Goodman St.
Rochester, NY 14620

North American Council on
   Adoptive Children
P.O. Box 14808
Minneapolis, MN 55414

The Organization for the
   Enforcement of Child Support
110 Nicodemus Road
Reisterstown, MD 21126

PACE (Parents & Children's
   Equality)
2054 Loma Linda Way
Clearwater, FL 33575

Parents Sharing Custody
P.O. Box 9286
Marina Del Rey, CA 90295

Parents Without Partners
7910 Woodmont Ave., Suite 1000
Bethesda, MD 20814

Remarried Parents, Inc.
102-20 67th Dr.
Forest Hills, NY 11375

REUNITE, Inc.
P.O. Box 694
Reynoldsbury, OH 43068

Second Wives Association of
   North America
720 Spadina Ave., Suite 509
Toronto, ON, Canada M5S 2T9

Single Mothers by Choice
Box 7788, FDR Station
New York, NY 10150

Single Parent Resource Center
1165 Broadway, Room 504
New York, NY 10001

Stepfamily Association of
   America
60 E. Joppa Road
Baltimore, MD 21204

The Step Family Foundation,
   Inc.
333 West End Ave.
New York, NY 10023

Surrogate Parent Foundation
8447 Wilshire Blvd., Suite 306
Beverly Hills, CA 90211

THEOS Foundation (Widowed
   Persons)
410 Penn Hills Mall
Pittsburgh, PA 15235

WAIF (adoption)
67 Irving Place
New York, NY 10003

Women Helping Women
c/o Ruth Kvalheim
525 N. Van Buren Ave.
Stoughton, WI 53589

Index of Subjects

Note: All numbers refer to item numbers, not page numbers. Subjects representing fiction works for children and youth will have the item numbers 775–882; subjects representing nonfiction works for children and youth will have the item numbers 853–909; and audiovisuals will have item numbers 918–70.

Custody—history, 467, 483
Custody, joint, 87, 106, 121, 159, 174, 339, 377, 409, 412, 418, 419, 423, 427, 429, 433, 434, 435, 437, 440, 441, 444, 445, 446, 449, 451, 452, 453, 456, 457, 460, 461, 462, 463, 466, 467, 468, 470, 471, 472, 474, 475, 476, 478, 479, 482, 483, 485, 489, 490, 534, 582, 593, 714, 739, 758, 936
Custody—laws and legislation, 20, 32, 401, 406, 407, 417, 418, 421, 424, 437, 443, 444, 465, 466, 467, 476, 489, 491, 587, 680
Custody—legal aspects, 420, 424, 447, 448
Custody mediation, 402, 406, 435, 441, 447, 458, 469, 491
Custody—mothers. See Mothers, custodial; Mothers, noncustodial; Parents—custody
Custody—professionals, 401, 406, 411, 413, 414, 438, 443, 475, 479, 491

Dating, 93, 119, 124, 330, 531, 552, 574
Day care, 82, 87, 138, 615
Discipline, 152, 223, 345, 555
Displaced homemaker, 748, 763
Displaced homemaker—bibliography, 728
Divided custody. See Custody, joint
Divorce, 6, 11, 19, 23, 27, 29, 30, 49, 55, 59, 73, 83, 89, 97, 105, 106, 170, 191, 315–400, 408, 411, 414, 423, 427, 433, 434, 444, 445, 477, 478, 479, 489, 541, 546, 548, 550, 551, 555, 556, 557, 558, 559, 560, 562, 566, 574, 603, 604, 746, 753, 755, 768, 781, 783, 784, 786, 788, 791, 798, 800, 803, 805, 806, 807, 811, 814, 815, 816, 817, 818, 821, 824–29, 831, 833, 834, 835, 836, 845, 846, 849, 854–58, 861, 862, 863, 869, 870, 871, 875, 877, 879, 881,

882, 887, 888, 891, 894, 895, 897, 900, 901, 902, 905, 907, 912–14, 916–22, 938, 942, 943
Divorce—bibliography, 38, 319, 343, 347, 358, 359
Divorce—bibliography for young people, 343
Divorce—Catholic Church, 346
Divorce counseling. See Divorce mediation
Divorce—dictionaries, 876
Divorce—laws and legislation, 13, 20, 32, 369
Divorce—legal aspects, 8, 317, 318, 324, 327, 344, 350, 364, 372, 377, 379, 394, 538
Divorce mediation, 10, 320, 324, 333, 339, 342, 354, 388, 923, 925
Divorce—men, 112, 321, 374
Divorce—statistics, 8, 42, 44, 316, 381, 482
Divorce—women, 76, 86, 129, 316, 331, 332, 336, 366, 367, 439
Divorced fathers, 78, 89, 97, 101, 115, 437, 490, 582, 584, 588, 589, 591, 594, 595, 596, 597, 599, 600, 601, 602, 606, 611
Divorced mothers, 58, 59, 76, 103, 106, 126, 127, 129, 135, 316, 332, 426

Fairy tales, stepfamily in, 205
Families of the hospitalized, 70
Families of the incarcerated, 40, 47, 54, 70
Family and Medical Leave Act, 633
Family Impact Analysis, 458
Family—laws and legislation, 11, 13, 17
Family life-styles, 24, 28, 372, 719. See also Life-styles
Family, military. See Military family
Family relationships, 29, 30, 328, 583, 586, 589
Family—statistics, 25, 44
Family—textbooks. See Marriage and the family—textbooks

74, 75, 76, 77, 79, 80, 85, 87, 89, 91,
97, 99, 100, 101, 103, 104, 106, 107,
108, 109, 110, 117, 125, 127, 128,
130, 132, 134, 135, 137, 138, 139,
140, 141, 556, 565, 580, 782, 796,
844, 851, 853, 863, 872, 878, 881,
884, 890, 944, 945, 946, 949
Single-parent family—bibliography,
84, 131
Single-parent family—statistics, 42,
69, 95, 98, 107
Single parents, 11, 23, 55, 57, 58, 59,
60, 62, 63, 64, 65, 66, 67, 68, 69, 70,
71, 73, 74, 75, 76, 77, 78, 82, 83, 85,
87, 88, 91, 92, 93, 94, 97, 105, 108,
110, 112, 119, 124, 128, 129, 134,
136, 137, 139, 140, 141, 147, 439,
584, 620, 655, 727, 739, 740. *See also*
Single fathers; Single mothers
Single parents and the schools, 67,
74, 107, 599
Single parents, black, 77, 102, 125
Single parents—education, 111, 120
Single parents—housing, 95, 109
Single parents—men. *See* Single fathers
Single parents—organizations, 61
Single parents—sex, 72, 87, 88, 100,
119, 127
Single parents—Women. *See* Single
mothers
Single women, 64, 86, 99, 102, 355,
733
Singles, 64, 86, 99, 102, 355, 733, 736,
740, 745, 751, 753, 755, 756, 757
Singles—bibliography, 357
Stepchildren, 39, 145, 146, 147, 149,
150, 151, 153, 154, 155, 157, 162,
164, 165, 172, 174, 175, 176, 178,
182, 183, 184, 185, 186, 189, 200,
203, 204, 206, 208, 209, 217, 221,
223, 250, 575, 749
Stepchildren—bibliography, 171
Stepchildren in folklore. *See* Folklore,
stepchildren in
Stepfamilies and the schools, 205

Stepfamily, 3, 6, 9, 33, 45, 55, 56,
142–254, 345, 348, 353, 372, 385,
433, 543, 548, 556, 565, 775, 777,
779, 780, 790, 793, 794, 801, 804,
808, 812, 832, 837, 841, 843, 845,
850, 859, 860, 864, 865, 868, 872,
873, 874, 881, 889, 898, 906, 909,
928, 929, 948, 949, 950, 951, 952
954, 955, 956
Stepfamily—bibliography, 38, 144,
156, 241, 357
Stepfamily—case histories, 33, 155,
159, 165, 175, 180, 251
Stepfamily counseling. *See* Marriage
counseling
Stepfamily in fairy tales. *See* Fairy
tales, stepfamily in
Stepfamily, myths about, 211, 216,
244, 248, 251
Stepfamily—textbooks. *See* Marriage
and the family—textbooks
Stepfamily—weddings, 201, 360
Stepfather/stepchildren relations,
158, 237, 240, 254. *See also* Steppar-
ent/stepchildren relations
Stepfathers, 179, 186, 189, 198, 202,
229, 236, 238, 247, 570, 584, 585,
589, 596, 587, 787, 799, 839
Stepfathers—bibliography, 171, 592
Stepgrandparents, 188, 195, 208
Stepmother/stepchildren relations,
199, 201, 221, 231, 243, 548. *See also*
Stepparent/stepchildren relations
Stepmothers, 145, 168, 169, 179, 180,
181, 189, 197, 200, 201, 202, 203,
206, 209, 213, 216, 221, 226, 239,
243, 686, 847
Stepparent/stepchildren relations,
161, 202, 227. *See also* Stepfather/
stepchildren relations; Step-
mother/stepchildren relations
Stepparenting. *See* Parenting
Stepparents, 142, 143, 146, 147, 149,
150, 151, 157, 159, 160, 161, 162,
165, 166, 169, 172, 173, 174, 175,
179, 183, 184, 185, 187, 189, 194,

Index of Authors

Index of Titles: Books

Index of Titles: Articles